The Essential Guide for Buying from China's Manufacturers

Visit www.booksurge.com to order additional copies.

The Essential Guide for Buying from China's Manufacturers

The 10 Steps to Success

James Vincent Lord

2007

The Essential Guide for Buying from China's Manufacturers

Contents

Dedicated to Rosel Edit Villavicencio Inocente who, while choices and opportunities are becoming greater and the world around us more complicated, reminds me that the simplicity of real love and happiness is in uncomplicated things ..

—-

To the man who shares my initials, my sincerest thanks for taking me under your wing and enrolling me in the Chinese school of hard knocks so that I may learn the real China it is not possible to learn in any institute of higher education ..

—-

And to my dear mother and father for whom China is still largely a mystery and are happy for it to remain that way..!

STEPS TO
SUCCESS

INTRODUCTION

What is Success in China?

When I arrived in China, I was taken directly to the office of the owner and President of the Chinese company in which I was to start work. After a brief, perfunctory discussion I was shown to an empty desk in an obscure corner of the office and told, "here's your desk, welcome to the company" then left alone. Except for a brief introduction to the other staff, all of which were Chinese, there was no further ceremony or instruction. Looking back, this was probably because they didn't quite know what to do with the first white-faced employee ever to work in their company. They had a few foreign customers, yes, but never a white face *inside* the company!

That was 1995, while Hong Kong was still a British colony and a mere decade into China's present economic boom that effectively started in the mid 1980's. What followed can only be described as a journey of discovery—the discovery of a dynamic people and a unique culture. It was a journey of adventures, from being a guest at 10-course banquets at luxury hotels, to being offered snake's blood or plates of fried insects in rural restaurants; slowly sailing for hours and hours up China's muddy rivers to reach remote factories and lighting firecrackers to commence the celebrations of the Chinese New Year in dark towns without streetlights; from lunches with workers at the factory canteen to dinner meetings with Chinese CEOs. It was an odyssey of faces and experiences, while getting to know and understand a country in the middle of a great transition.

It was also a time of great frustration and sometimes despair as I learned through mistakes to do business the hard way with the Chinese in their own backyard. I had been thrown in at the deep end and, over many years, under the wise guidance of a fabulously successful and entrepreneurial Chinese company president, I became familiar with Chinese business practices and learned how things get done in China. It was the real-life apprenticeship in Chinese business that proved to be the hardest and most challenging, yet ultimately, the most rewarding experience.

It was also an opportunity to watch numerous foreign CEOs, business managers, project managers, and buyers as they came to China to conduct business. Some were seasoned and experienced "China hands;" others were taking their first stumbling steps and trying to do business in China's unfamiliar environment. It was an ideal vantage point to learn from the Chinese and from the best practice and methods employed by the most successful foreign executives. It was a unique vantage point to see first-hand the meeting of East and West, to watch the way they interacted and to learn from them both; an opportunity to appreciate both ways of thinking and see both sides of the story. As I regularly found myself perched in the middle of negotiations, it provided the opportunity to see which approaches worked and produced the best results and which approaches commonly led to failure.

As I say, I learned the hard way, through my own mistakes, by observing the mistakes and best practice of other business people, and under the guidance of the Chinese. It was a long, painful, and frustrating process. China is like a giant jigsaw puzzle but without the benefit of a picture on the front of the box. I often wished there had been a book that contained all the important information, advice, and tips that I needed to work successfully in China; a book that outlined and explained many of the difficulties in advance, all of which could have saved years of growing pains and frustration, or at least helped to avoid the worst. What I had needed was a framework to put in order the apparent chaos that surrounded me, explaining why things were as they were and what action to take to properly deal with it. As I watched wave after wave of new visitors to China suffering the same frustration and making the same predictable mistakes I had made, I decided to write the book myself. This is that book.

While China is becoming the focal point for foreign companies within their global business strategy as a manufacturing base for export, as a location for outsourcing of call centers and professional expertise, or as a destination market itself, this book is primarily concerned with the former: China as a manufacturing base. This is a book that will better prepare someone for doing business in China *and in particular to prepare buyers, purchasing managers, and executives to better perform their purchasing roles in relation to the thousands of small and medium sized Chinese factories and businesses.* It is a book that encapsulates and condenses more than ten years of experience that will provide foreign business people with a head start and a short cut up the China learning curve.

Some business people go to China and through a combination of luck, intuition, and persistence are successful in their endeavors from the outset. The majority suffer a combination of poor results, no results, or spend a disproportionate amount of time solving endless problems that pop up with frustrating regularity. The recent opening of China's economy to foreign business, improvements in travel, and the ease with which willing Chinese partners can be found can give the first time visitor an impression that China is easy; that it is open for business, has all the fundamental institutions in place, and that it is operating more or less along the same lines as the market economies we are familiar with. This is a misleading fallacy that can easily blind business people to the complications and risks. *The fact that things often don't go as smoothly as we would like or expect should lead to the conclusion that there are other factors at work, factors which are elusive and that the visitor typically doesn't get the chance to see.* It is true that while interest in China is high, most business people's practical understanding is low.

China is like a theatre: we go there to see and engage in the play, yet there are numerous fleeting silhouettes behind the scenes, of which we are unaware, influencing the actors. While China is open for commerce and keen to attract foreigners for business, business is still done the Chinese way—a way influenced by a combination of its unique culture and history, and particularly by its recent communist past. If we could only get a peek behind the scenes and see what is going on, our chances of understanding China would increase exponentially and with it our chances of business success. This is the intention of this book—to provide a look behind the "silk curtain."

China is culturally, linguistically, and ideologically different. The ways of doing business are also different. As soon as foreigners arrive in one of China's bustling, crowded, noisy cities, they are operating in an environment where people are playing by different rules, on a playing field with different customs, and communicating in different languages, both literally and metaphorically. Working in China can feel like being on a different planet, where the rules and conditions that one grew up with and has taken for granted no longer seem to apply. It is a country where "no problem" can mean things are just about to go horribly wrong; where "meeting specifications or standards" is sometimes translated as using the cheapest quality materials available and hoping buyers don't notice; where "exclusive design" could mean one copied from the previous customer who just left the office. The consequences of not being fully informed or prepared for China are mistakes: mistakes in perceiving the situation, failures in communication, small misunderstandings that grow into bigger problems. These mistakes lead to loss of money, reputation, jobs, and in some cases the loss of entire businesses.

Sometimes the problem is that while foreign business people understand that the culture, the rules, and practices are completely different, they are still completely unprepared to deal with them; China is not a place where knowledge is intuitive or obvious.

The uninitiated visitor doesn't know which companies to work with, doesn't know how to get things done, and is unable to recognize signs that would tell the seasoned China hand that things are not as they should be. As these are not familiar or apparent to the business visitor, he or she proceeds to act and make decisions based on the framework and value systems of his or her own culture—a culture they are familiar with. This decision-making framework and value system are at best inappropriate, at worst completely detrimental to business objectives. *To operate successfully in China means learning a whole new set of skills.* It can sometimes mean forgetting all one has learned, going back to the drawing board and starting all over again.

I have witnessed numerous ambitious managers and executives arriving in the Far East to work full time in China on contracts for foreign subsidiaries or for Chinese companies. Many are completely ineffective for the first year. I term this the year of "cultural dissonance"—a year when newcomers are so bewildered by cultural differences and the seeming chaos that they are unable to function properly in the workplace or contribute in any meaningful sense. This year of "cultural dissonance" is the time to realize all the concepts, ethics, values, work styles, and negotiating methods one is familiar with don't apply here and indeed can be counter-productive. It appears that at least a year is needed to "re-boot" the internal operating and value systems where a whole new batch of cultural software is installed that will enable one to carry out his or her work.

If it takes this long for foreigners to adjust when working full time in the midst of the culture, imagine the time needed for the average business traveler, who visits for one or two weeks at a time, several times a year, to become familiar enough with China to operate effectively. The requisite "re-boot" is a much longer and more gradual process; normally the cumulative effect of numerous problems, mistakes, financial losses, delays, and misunderstandings. These problems are often via email communication when thousands of kilometers away—too far to be able to exert proper control over the situation. With infrequent visits to China, it takes the business visitor several years to become familiar with how Chinese companies work, to avoid the common mistakes, and begin to understand how to effectively work with the Chinese. And things still go wrong!

What is needed is not *more information*; with China's economic rise and the fact that China has become a hot topic in business, there is an abundance of information available on economic statistics and predictions, Chinese communism and Chinese culture. What is needed is the *right* information—practical, relevant, straightforward information that can be put to use right away. Unfortunately, preparation for most purchasing managers consists of reading a travel book with a section on Chinese culture, a few books on China's history or economy, or even just the odd article from *Time Magazine*—clearly not enough to operate successfully in China. The aim of this book therefore is not just to give practical guidance that will allow visitors to operate successfully; the additional aim is to provide a framework which in turn will give the reader the confidence and certainty to operate in such a dynamic environment.

No one can be a China expert on the first visit. Or second. Or third. It takes time. In China, there is always something new to learn, always a new challenge with the potential to ruin the best laid plans. *However, with the correct framework, principles, and approach it is possible to avoid ninety percent of the most commonly encountered problems.* There is certain information that will guarantee avoidance of many of the most common mistakes and spare the business person much of the frustration of inexperience. There is information that can compress the learning curve and significantly enhance the chances of getting what one wants from cooperation with Chinese companies. What visitors need is a look behind the scenes and *practical* information: practical tips, insights, hints, and real life examples that explain what things are really like in China; knowledge of how things really work from someone who has lived in China and has years of experience working inside Chinese companies. In other words, information that Chinese manufacturers would rather you didn't know!

Practical, straight-to-the-point advice and information can circumvent years of costly mistakes. The correct approach based on a single insight can level the playing field so new visitors to China are no longer at a significant disadvantage. Reading the right tip and remembering it at the right time can make or break deals or working relationships in China. The information in this book is offered to readers with this end in mind. The purpose is to provide readers with the information that those with China experience already know, so that they don't need to go through the same learning curve, suffering the same mistakes and losses that experienced "China hands" invariably suffered in gaining that experience. The book presents a bounty of incisive, informative and, most importantly, *practical* inside information organized in 10 Success Steps. Most problems that occur in China are usually due to the violation or failure to follow the advice, principles, and rules presented in this book.

As with most information, this book will only benefit the reader who incorporates this information into his or her way of thinking and way of working. It may be necessary to let go of preconceived ideas and old methods of working that may form the basis for success at home, yet may not serve objectives in China. One must come to terms with an entirely new set of business practices and norms.

As you read this book, I hope readers with a basic familiarity with China will experience some "ah-ha" moments. For the reader completely unfamiliar with China, I hope that he or she will begin to understand why dealing with China is considered difficult by so many. The more that is understood, the more quickly the mystery disappears—to be replaced with the requisite mindset for success in China. *A single idea, insight, or distinction from this book could save readers thousands, tens of thousands, or millions of dollars.* All the information together should provide the reader with a systematic approach to handle business in China with confidence, instead of uncertainty and trepidation. In addition, at the end, the reader should have a framework with which to order the massive amount of cultural information and new experiences once the first steps are taken into this new world.

The generally accepted definition of power is the ability to do or act; the capacity to accomplish something. This is especially true in China. There are instances where Harvard and Wharton Business School graduates have applied for jobs with multinationals in Beijing and other Chinese cities and who have been turned down in favor of reasonably educated locals who have experience and understand the arena. People are useful in China in so far as they can get things done. In China what matters is results, or borrowing a phrase from China's former leader Deng Xiaoping, "it doesn't matter whether a cat is black or white so long as it catches mice." In China, you can either get things done, or you can't. *The foreigner in China must learn that it is our responsibility to get results, more than the responsibility of the Chinese to give them to us.* The information contained in this book will provide the framework for results, significantly enhance the reader's ability to get things done and clear the path to success in China.

10
STEPS TO
SUCCESS

SUCCESS
STEP 1

Behind China's Silk Curtain

An Economic and Cultural Backdrop

With the huge upheavals China has experienced in recent history, it is useful to put present economic developments into perspective. This chapter is not intended to be an exhaustive account of Chinese history, politics, economics, or culture; indeed, it would be impossible to do justice to China's complex and fascinating past. The principal interest is where China is now in its current phase of economic development and the impact this has on the collective Chinese psyche, Chinese companies, and workers. This knowledge is beneficial in that it should influence our approach to business in China and shape the decisions we make.

From Communism to "Entrepreneurism"

When arriving in China, the first thing the visitor will notice is that general behavior is decidedly un-communist; the Chinese are certainly no longer running around in pajamas shouting communist slogans! To the contrary, the recent visitor will find the Chinese to be the most hard-working, ambitious, entrepreneurial and capitalist-minded people on the planet. China may be a socialist country, yet it is one of the most competitive societies that can be found anywhere. As Andronova said, "it's still supposed to be communist, but all everyone talks about is money, money, money".[1]

While the founding fathers of the United States were engaged in their struggle for independence in 1776, China was the most populous and among the most technologically advanced and wealthiest nation on Earth, wielding great cultural, political, and economic influence. Then followed two hundred years of upheaval with wars, revolutions, famine, and ideological changes that reduced China to a backward economic state and into international isolation.

The Chinese communists came to power in 1949, starting a new cycle of economic upheaval and social chaos that started with the collectivization of agriculture and nationalization of industry. This reorganization was followed by three tumultuous movements. The "Great Leap Forward" that began in 1958 was an attempt to industrialize China through the mass production of steel in backyard furnaces, which, by the redeployment of farmers to steel production, is reported to have indirectly caused one of the greatest famines in human history with a death toll of 30 million people. This movement was followed by the "Cultural Revolution" that started in 1966 when Mao Zedong hijacked the communist party and encouraged teenage Red Guards to go on the rampage in the destruction of "old" Chinese culture and to purge the country of anyone resisting the socialist revolution, which resulted in the denunciation, torture, and killing of "enemies of the state." Finally, the "Down to the Countryside Movement" in 1968 gutted the country of intellectuals, scientists, teachers, and educated professionals who were sent to the countryside for "re-education" at the hands of peasants.

The Cultural Revolution lasted more than a decade, ending only with Mao's death in 1976. During this period, China suffered economic and social destruction that left few families untouched. When Deng Xiaoping became *de facto* leader of the People's Republic of China in 1977[2] he inherited, in the words of Hugo de Burgh:

> "...a mess so monstrous as to daunt Solomon: the largest population and a ruined economy; a subverted culture, millions of victims, no legal system, unkempt communities with decaying housing; a ravaged environment and feral youths, no education for ten years .. and all at a time when the world around them was advancing into a high-technology and materially prosperous future".[3]

Deng Xiaoping reversed the nation's course by deciding that China must focus on economic development to raise the standard of living[4] and started the shift from a centrally planned economy to a more market oriented system. The result was a "socialist market economy" in which the Communist Party retained political power while encouraging a free market economy. As part of the reforms, three special economic zones were created in Guangdong province (Shenzhen, Zhuhai and Shaotou) and one in Fujian province. The first of these was opened to foreign investment in 1979, which marked the first influx of FDI,[5] the beginning of China's re-opening to the global economy, and its recent economic prosperity. Further reforms in the 1990's included the privatization of state-owned enterprises and collectives together with the decision to enter the World Trade Organization (WTO). Where before business was despised, it is now viewed as the focal point of national development. These reforms have led directly to the present where China has become a foreign investment magnet[6] and undisputed "workshop of the world." Foreign participation in Chinese companies has been encouraged through joint ventures and Wholly Foreign Owned Enterprises (WFOEs) and, since its re-integration into the global economy, China has enjoyed consistent annual economic growth rates of 8% or above. China is apparently achieving the remarkable: it is *evolving* from a totalitarian regime to a market economy without war[7].

The Chinese economy is now open for business and enterprise. After what has been technically fifty years of communist rule, during which personal ambition had been effectively bottled, we are witnessing an explosion of pent-up entrepreneurial activity in the most populous nation on the planet. During the tumultuous communist years, wearing the uniform of an official was one of the few ways to gain some sense of certainty in a highly uncertain environment. That certainty has been effectively replaced by money (with officialdom now in many cases providing the means and access to money) and while complacency seems to have gripped the West, the Chinese are embracing these new opportunities for wealth creation with zeal as if they don't trust the opportunities created by China's experiment with capitalism to last. In the absence of a public welfare system, the ingrained industriousness of the Chinese worker is being unleashed in a torrent of capitalist enterprise; the Chinese are willing to work long, hard hours and don't mind cutting a few corners to make their lives better.

A nation of 1.3 billion people is again in the process of reinventing itself. It is an economic awakening on a truly unprecedented scale and a watershed in history that is affecting the global balance of power. China is again taking its place among nations as an economic giant and beginning to flex its political muscle, which is a natural consequence. With economic prowess comes geopolitical power. What we are witnessing is a new era of entrepreneurial activity under the auspices of communism and within the confines of a huge state bureaucracy run by a centralized, non-representative government.

It is easy for the business visitor to China to be misled into simplifying these momentous changes. Many assume that because China is no longer strictly communist and is open for business, it is now a capitalist country, functioning along the lines of capitalist principles. However, just because one can freely enter China to conduct business, it is important not to be complacent and to recognize that this is not entirely the case. It is more a case of communism with capitalist characteristics, or "Chinese-style" capitalism.[8] *What we must bear in mind is that China is still in transition, with all the attendant complications, changes, and uncertainties this entails,* run by a government that is only beginning to get used to the idea of free markets and what this implies.

On the micro-economic level, that means that while Chinese companies are aggressively marketing their products and Chinese businessmen are opening their doors to welcome foreign customers, they are still not completely familiar or at ease with market fundamentals such as being customer-oriented and demand driven, operating at peak efficiency, and being familiar with the functions of marketing and public relations. But Chinese companies are learning fast.

On the macro-economic level, China may be open for business and intent on delivering economic growth, yet government regulations, market mechanisms, and institutions are still in the *process* of forming and lagging behind the fast pace of economic development. China is becoming a success story by trial and error, and government institutions are "groping for stones as they try to cross the river:" intellectual property law and general commercial law are not to a standard that allows either effective support for truly open markets or protection to market participants to the extent they would hope. The central government still tightly controls and censors the media, mobile phone companies, the Internet[9], and religious freedom. In addition, there is ubiquitous corruption and suppression of dissent. China is in an "in-between" stage between a planned economy and a market economy. It pays to remember that China is perhaps more a communist state with capitalist characteristics, rather than a capitalist country with remnants of communism. In a *Newsweek* article Ramo questioned this apparent contradiction:

> *"At the same time, the government and the Communist Party have oscillated between moments of cutting-edge ambition and innovation, and old-style ideological control and corruption .. how do you explain a political system that holds onto deeply socialist values even as it relies on market forces to reshape the economic landscape of the country?"*[10]

The Chinese government is gradually coming to grips with how to handle the new-found political and economic power resulting from increased economic integration, while at the same time striving to balance its needs for security, holding the country together (Taiwan, Xinjiang, Tibet), and trying to curb growing social unrest between the rural poor and the rich urban population. It is said in jest that economists don't see how China can fail, while political scientists don't see how it can succeed! All of this means that while China is open, we should bear in mind that business may not always be as smooth as we hope and a degree of volatility should be expected.

An Inferiority or Supremacy Complex?

When collaborating with factory employees and corporate staff, the foreign business person that is willing and able to teach will find the Chinese have a thirst for knowledge and will be intent listeners. Often heard phrases are "thank you for your help and support," "we are learning from you," and "thank you for teaching us." This is part politeness, part appreciation for the opportunity of financial reward, and part gratefulness for bringing new ideas, new technology, and improved processes to China. As Simon Elegant explains,

> "The modern history of China is a still-unfolding tale of a proud, millennia-old civilization coming to terms with a new, shocking world in which other nations are more powerful and technologically advanced."[11]

Coming from a low base, the Chinese are playing catch up; even obsolete machinery, technology, and processes that are familiar to foreign companies can be new to a factory in China. This lack of modern technology can lead some visitors to feel superior and perceive China as economically inferior. Don't be fooled. True, at the individual level the Chinese are grateful for the new ideas that are pouring in, yet on a macro-economic level it is important to note that this is only a learning stage, a transition period in the long march of Chinese economic growth. For China as a whole, it is a time of contradictions and an identity crisis where feelings of inferiority lie side-by-side with feelings of impending superiority. The Chinese want to lead the world, yet at the same time they know they are behind. Minxin Pei describes this general feeling of the Chinese toward the West:

> *"They mix resentment with admiration, fear with respect, jealousy with the desire to emulate."[12]*

Meanwhile, French refers to China as:

> *."..a country that actually longs for leadership and respect but is deeply conflicted about how to emerge from its shell."[13]*

China has been denied its leading role in the world for two centuries by internal political disintegration and outsiders that have attempted, and in some cases succeeded, to dismember the country.[14] While foreign visitors and business people receive the red carpet treatment and are genuinely appreciated for their assistance, behind the facade is a growing feeling of superiority that has lain dormant for decades and is fast emerging with China's economic resurgence. Increasing economic success and political recognition come hand-in-hand. US Deputy Secretary of State Robert Zoellick used the phrase "responsible stakeholder" referring to China's position in the present global power structure. From being an economic backwater just two decades ago, the Chinese are now watching their leader on the lawn of the White House, greeted by the US President with pomp and pageantry, followed by dinner at Bill Gates' mansion with State officials and the elite of US industry. The Chinese have a strong sense of identity and nationalism. As economic influence and political confidence grow, it heralds a corresponding rise in the confidence and pride of the Chinese worker.

Thus far, the Chinese economic success model has depended on exports for growth. In 2005, the U.S. trade deficit with China was US$200 billion and exports by multinationals accounted for an estimated 58.5% of China's total exports. However, China's dependence on export-led growth is unlikely to be a close prediction of the future. The main theme of China's 11th Five-Year Plan is to rotate economic growth away from exports and towards domestic consumption. Encouraged by the government, per capita annual consumer spending has dramatically increased over the past decade and, within five years, 200 million Chinese will be considered "middle class" with income sufficient to be of interest to sales departments.[15] I recall a Chinese CEO was asked seriously during a formal lunch which market he saw growing the most over the next ten years: Europe or America? After a slight pause to think, he simply replied, "China is the future!" Aside from macro-economics and competitive advantage, one consequence of the rising value of the Chinese currency will be to diminish exporters' profit margins and increase their incentive to supply the local market. As general wealth and living standards increase in China, so too will domestic consumption, which will lead to a corresponding decrease in dependency on export markets. Stabilization of the domestic economy and growth based on domestic consumption will make the Chinese economy stronger and less dependent on western economies.

Another trend that is making China economically more powerful is its steady drive up both the technology ladder and the value chain. China peered out from behind the silk curtain after Deng's economic reforms and quickly established a reputation as being a low-cost manufacturing base of low-end products. As Van der Kamp explains:

> "The character of China's industrial revolution is different from that of the US and Japan. It is one of producing everyday appliances and gadgets at prices no one else can match. China's achievement lies not so much in technological advances as in making conventional consumer goods affordable to almost everyone in the world. Unfortunately, China has made itself hostage to others in order to achieve this. When Wal-Mart is the customer Wal-Mart calls the shots. It is hard for a country to break out of a mould like this and establish its own brand names, much harder than it was for the US and Japan."[16]

Since the economic reforms of the eighties, China is making steady improvements in quality and swiftly moving up the value chain, sometimes with the help of foreign partners, to produce a wider range of products of increasingly higher quality and value. China is competing against established Western manufacturers in ever more sophisticated fields, cutting a swathe through markets with the double-edged sword of quality improvements that are fast approaching international standards, while maintaining low price levels. We are also witnessing more effort and investment directed at research and development, design, logistics, and distribution. China is investing massively in science and technology education and its conversion into commercial application. While China is infrequently referred to as a center for innovation, once the Chinese come to grips with the strategic use of design, understand global market trends, and are able to commercialize the results of investments in research, with or without the help of foreign partners, it will prove unstoppable when combined with low labor costs, increases in efficiency, and a financial system that encourages domestic innovation and ownership.

While there is the predictable rise of joint ventures between foreign and Chinese companies to serve the export market or position themselves to supply the mainland market, as well as an invasion of western brands into the Chinese market, the most interesting trend is the forays of Chinese companies and brands into global markets. The Chinese government has begun to implement policies designed to spur the growth of Chinese brands; a "going abroad" policy has started to remove some of the bureaucratic roadblocks and is providing subsidies for mainland companies that want to be global players. A number of these have experienced enormous success in the mainland domestic market and are seeking to leverage this success abroad. Foreign companies should beware the "hybrid" or mixed ownership Chinese companies that are technically privately owned and driven by the profit motive yet still receive support from various arms of the Chinese government where industrial policy is fashioned to assist them, particularly in industries that are open to foreign competition. On the back of low labor costs and their ability to adapt technologies and products to meet the price points for cost conscious mainland Chinese consumers, a number of Chinese companies are using economies of scale to build global brands. Firms such as Haier (refrigerators), Galanz (microwave ovens), Lenovo (personal computers) and Pearl River Piano (pianos) have already proven themselves to be powerful rivals to the world's incumbent and leading brands.

Riding on China's rising economic tide, Chinese companies are also getting richer and using this wealth to make acquisitions of Western companies and brands, encouraged by the appreciation of the Yuan. As Chinese companies become increasingly ready and willing to take their products and brands to a global market we are witnessing acquisitions of foreign companies and brands to facilitate this strategy. It will be interesting to watch the reaction of Western governments as the first Chinese MNCs emerge and more Chinese companies purchase traditionally European and American companies. The China National Offshore Oil Corporation (CNOOC) bid for Unocal (at the time the ninth biggest oil firm in the US) was one of the first shots across the bough. Chinese personal computer manufacturer Lenovo Group's[17] acquisition of IBM's personal computer unit for US$1.75 billion in late 2004 was another example of China flexing its muscle in the global marketplace; under the terms of this acquisition, Lenovo can use the IBM brand until 2010 by which time it hopes to have established its own brand. In the banking industry, there is the example of China Construction Bank's acquisition of Bank of America (Asia) Ltd.

Western multinationals have moved their production to the low-cost manufacturing base of China through commercial self-interest, concentrating on China as a consequence of efficient market theory. Tighter quality control procedures have been imposed on Chinese factories to meet western quality expectations. Improved processes have been introduced to more efficiently utilize the large pool of low-cost labor. Each time manufacturing and services are out-sourced to China, so too are knowledge, technology, and skills. With a bit of help from the outside and the sheer hard work and resolve of the Chinese worker, an economic giant is being re-made.

However, lets not be mistaken. The Chinese don't wish to be the production engine of the world. The Chinese don't want to improve economically and merely compete with the United States. The Chinese want to *replace* the United States as world economic leader; the general expectation is nothing short of global economic supremacy. While certainly not representative of all Chinese thinkers, it is interesting to refer to the content of an article published by a foreign policy expert from Shanghai, Wang Yiwei, provocatively entitled "Preventing the U.S. from Declining Too Rapidly." In the article it says that the United State's role in the world is due for decline and that China must abandon its traditionally passive role and act to shape an international system in its own interest. Some analysts predict that China's economy could overtake the United States by 2045.[18] If China's provinces were treated as separate economies, China would already account for twenty of the thirty fastest growing economies in the world between 1978 and 1995, according to World Bank estimates.[19]

Therefore, don't go to China with feelings of superiority or act like some sort of benefactor; recognize that a subtle shift in power is happening that may not be immediately apparent. China is not growing into an economic powerhouse by expansion or by challenging the existing system. It is becoming powerful through *integration*[20] into the existing global economic order and, by moving production to China, we are a part of that process.

The Reality of Cheap Labor

The first thing that springs to mind about China is that of a low-cost manufacturing country; wages are relatively lower in China than many other developing nations, and significantly lower than wages in the developed world. China has been particularly adept at leveraging an inexpensive workforce for international competitive advantage.

Now, one may think that this is stating the obvious. Indeed, the very reason manufacturing is moving to China is to capitalize on these low labor costs. However, it is surprising the number of business people, mainly those from first world developed nations, who recognize this *intellectually* yet at the same time fail to properly comprehend what this entails on a practical level or fail to act in a manner befitting the situation.

If a company is paying $20, $30, $50 or $75 per hour for labor at home, there is a good probability that it can delegate a task to a reliable person and walk away comfortable in the knowledge that the person will take responsibility and do a good job. *If a company is paying US$1 per hour, regardless of the country, it can and should expect surprises.*

Low labor costs are normally found in countries with an abundant supply of workers often without the benefit of a good standard of education; in China, many workers will not possess the fundamentals of reading and writing. *The consequence is that while labor is cheap, a higher level of training and supervision is required and more foresight and planning are needed in relation to tasks that are moved to China.* Workers cannot instinctively be expected to understand what one wants, coming from a low economic base and an environment that has been closed and communist for decades. Workers as a whole will be unfamiliar with strategic thinking and may struggle to understand the demands of a foreign market and the role of detail to operational and strategic success. In addition, the average worker is not predisposed to thinking outside the box. In communist China (and in the Asian education system generally) creativity wasn't exactly encouraged. Mao's little red book was more intended for memorization and indoctrination rather than to stimulate creative thinking, while Confucianism emphasized restraint on the part of the ruler and obedience on the part of the ruled. Therefore, unless one is working with artistically inclined Chinese, those who have received design training or studied outside of China, one shouldn't expect creative solutions or creative input into projects or product design; often such requests can be met with blank stares.

With low labor costs, a lower standard of living and poorer living conditions are typically to be found. Again, this is obvious, yet the consequences are not so obvious to visiting buyers. It is unlikely the Chinese worker will be acquainted with the international marketplace or the latest western design trends. Unlike the visiting product designer, the average worker is unlikely to be jetting around to visit the capital cities of the fashion world. The average factory worker is likely to be living in basic, cramped conditions, more often shared with fellow workers or family members. Wages earned typically don't allow the worker to regularly go shopping to buy the latest luxury goods or technological innovations. The lifestyle of the Chinese worker is totally different from the comparatively rich consumer lifestyle that we are familiar with. As a result, they are often not intimately familiar with the high quality of products we have come to expect, or the products themselves that we take for granted. *Therefore, when the visiting buyer takes designs to China for a new product to be manufactured, what is obvious and familiar to the buyer may not be obvious or familiar at all to their Chinese counterparts.* Bear this in mind at all times.

The main point to remember is while a company is attracted to China where labor rates are much lower, it is not a case of *Ceterus Paribus;* all other things *do not* remain the same. Cheap labor is cheap for a reason; a consequence of a multitude of associated issues related to the particular environment. Companies should expect, therefore, to make corresponding adjustments in their approach, actions, and manner of communication.

The foreign executive should not just consider China to be one cheap pool of labor that is uniform throughout China. Regional labor is in a state of flux, labor rates differ by area, and there are certain wage trends that we should be aware of. In general, if the central Chinese government wishes to stimulate the economy in certain areas of China, for reasons of stimulating efficiency in previously state-run industry sectors or preventing social unrest as a result of high unemployment, it often does so through tax incentives or other terms that are then comparatively more favorable than in other areas. In the past decade, the Chinese government has attempted to share with China's northern cities the phenomenal success of the industrialized South-Eastern coastal area in order to address the imbalance. This decade sees the focus on addressing the imbalance between the east and west of China. Income disparity between industrialized Eastern China and the backward interior prompted Beijing to launch the "Develop the West" campaign in 1999 in order to direct the economic surge into China's western interior.

Throughout much of the 1990's, much of China's industrial development centered on the Pearl River Delta region, just north of Hong Kong, which includes Shenzhen, Dongguan, and Guangzhou. The Guangdong area accounted for more than 30% of China's exports in 2005. Rising rural incomes keeping many would-be migrant workers back on the farm have caused increasing labor shortages in this area. To address these shortages, the provincial government has been phasing in successive minimum wage increases, the latest of which saw an average increase of 17.8 per cent across the province.[21]

Bearing in mind that labor typically accounts for 30 — 60% of production costs in many labor-intensive industries, the effect will be to make this region less competitive and drive both manufacturers and buyers to other regions of China, increasingly to China's north and inland west. Factories in the Guangdong area have accumulated twenty years of experience manufacturing and exporting to foreign markets. Generally speaking, the further the buyer travels outside this area, the less experience and familiarity with global markets the factories will have. As with most investment decisions, the higher the potential return, generally the higher the risk. This holds true in China when seeking to work with inland factories so one should expect to commit a higher level of supervision to this region.

Foreign executives should also be aware of a trend toward the wholesale unionization of Chinese labor. This follows Wal-Mart's collaboration with the All China Federation of Trade Unions (ACFTU). With more than 75% of its products made in Chinese factories, equating to an estimated $US18bn in business, Wal-Mart is considered one of China's top ten trading partners, taking its place alongside the European Union, the US, Japan, and a handful of other big nations. As reported by Jonathan Watts in Beijing:

> "Wal-Mart, the world's biggest retail company, conceded defeat yesterday in a two-year battle against the world's largest labor federation, by offering to support the formation of labor unions at its 60 stores in China. The American supermarket giant— which is notoriously reluctant to support workers' organizations throughout its global empire—said it would cooperate with the government-controlled labor federation to establish unions for its 28,000 Chinese employees."[22]

It is predicted that acquiescence of such a high profile company to unionization will create a domino effect throughout China. However, while the standard aim of unions is to help and protect the rights of workers, it is debatable whether this will be the case in China. Due to the abundance of cheap labor and the fact that unions are organized from the top down, unions have often been manipulated by government and management alike and have been seen more as a way of controlling workers so they are less likely to strike than offering workers any material benefits. This situation could change with the anticipated new labor contract law that hopes to see a higher degree of union participation in management discussion on personnel issues and in turn may have a general impact on labor costs.

Chinese Culture: Family, Food & Festivals

It is useful to bear in mind that when buying, selling, or negotiating with the Chinese, all actions are taking place within a broader cultural context dominated by deep rooted Chinese values and traditions. Things are done in a certain way in China and it is highly relevant to understand why. It is important for the business person in China to modify his or her conduct accordingly. Those who ignore Chinese cultural norms do so at their peril.

The following is not intended to be an exhaustive or in-depth study of Chinese culture. The intention is merely to provide a general cultural background that will enable the business visitor to better understand the Chinese people and avoid making the more obvious blunders that could be embarrassing both to visitors and their hosts. This orientation should also help to put some of the behavior that will be encountered in China into a cultural perspective, explaining behavior that might otherwise be considered strange or confusing. It is admitted that by providing generalized information, it is unavoidable that sweeping statements are made that might appear simplistic and unfairly stereotype the Chinese.

Chinese Culture

Chinese society is relationship-based and can be considered to be organized in concentric circles. In the center circle is the closest family, in the adjacent outer circle are the extended family, friends, associates, and colleagues, and in the outer circle is anyone else. Treatment accorded to others is strongly influenced by the circle in which they fall.

Accordingly, the family will be helped, taken care of, and protected at all costs. If a person's relationship with a Chinese person is ever referred to as "family" it is a special relationship indeed. The visitor should be aware that the practical Chinese nature extends also into the realm of personal relationships. It has been a long established practice for wealthy men to have "official" wives and one or more "concubines." The practice still exists today, more in the form of having a wife and one or more secret girlfriends. Therefore, if business people have developed sufficiently close relationships, they should not be too surprised to find themselves having dinner with their Chinese counterpart and his wife on one occasion, and with his girlfriend the next.

Friends and associates constitute a complex network of contacts or connections (*guanxi*) that are the first port of call when any assistance is needed. This is discussed more fully in Success Step 2. It is common practice when Chinese people need to know something to call on their friends to solve problems, rather than seek professional advice. Due to strong agrarian roots, survival for the Chinese has long depended on group cooperation. This bias toward personal relations permeates all areas of life. With business in particular, due to issues of trust, it is common for friends to be given positions even when they might not be the ideal or most qualified candidate, which often results in inefficiencies. Relationships are particularly strong between companies if strong personal relations exist at the highest level and *within* companies where the existence of personal fiefdoms is common.

In China, it is beneficial to make connections, form friendships, and generally get on the inside circle, rather than being on the periphery. Complete strangers may be treated with indifference or, at worst, with treatment that visitors might consider inhumane. For example, it is not uncommon to see hoards of bystanders watching and doing absolutely nothing to help the hapless victims of the numerous accidents on Chinese highways.[23] There is a distinct "nothing to do with me, better not get involved" attitude. In public places, where no one recognizes you, it is common to see people pushing and shoving, throwing trash, and spitting.

Chinese society is also hierarchical where social harmony according to Confucian values dictates a strong bias toward obedience in relationships, for example between father and son, husband and wife, older brothers and younger brothers, rulers and the ruled. This means that we must take note of a person's rank within Chinese organizations and ensure that respect is given to seniority.

The Chinese are neither particularly spiritual nor gentle, being more practically inclined.[24] It might save a degree of unease by recognizing and being prepared in advance for the fact that the Chinese have almost no concept of privacy. Chinese tourists move around in large noisy crowds, with jostling and pushing considered normal. Roads and pavements are crowded and dinners at average restaurants can be noisy affairs. After business meetings or a long day, in China it is common for the foreign visitors to just want to return to their hotel room to get some peace and quiet. However, one must remember that the desire to be left alone rather than to accept an invitation to dinner may be interpreted by the Chinese as unusual, eccentric, or even rude. To avoid offending hosts, therefore, it is better to express disappointment and return under the pretext of a conference call, replying to important emails or working on budgets.

A final note on gifts: If you bring gifts for your hosts, it is common that they will not be opened in front of you, nor will profuse gratitude be shown. The Chinese tend to express gratitude through reciprocal actions rather than words.

Food and drinking

The importance of food should not be underestimated in Chinese culture.[25] Each regional cuisine has its own special dishes—Canton, Sichuan, Peking, Shanghai, etc., and provides some of the most exotic and delicious food in the world. Chinese cuisine also has some of the most *unusual* dishes (including endangered species)—snake, dog, cockroaches, wild animals, shark's fin. In general, "anything with its back to the sky" (which is pretty much everything!) can be found on the table, in contrast to the food that is typically served in Chinatowns from New York to Sydney. Even though the thought of eating such things might horrify you, try to put your squeamishness aside and try something that you consider palatable; anything is preferable and less insulting to the Chinese than ordering a plate of French fries.

For the Chinese, getting together to eat is more than just eating. It is an opportunity for sharing the company of friends, to socialize with colleagues, to discuss business, to impress guests, and even to gain face by bringing along distinguished foreign guests and sitting next to them! The choice of restaurant is even an opportunity to demonstrate the importance of the issue to be discussed and to give "face" to those who are invited; for this reason expensive restaurants can serve interests of a more strategic nature. In the west, an invitation to lunch or dinner can be easily brushed off with "I haven't time." In China, it is often worth considering the strategic value of relationships and accepting the offer. It can be a great opportunity to build relationships and give *face* to your Chinese counterparts, the company owner, or a factory manager. Eating is also more of a ritual in China. Knowledge of food and the ability to order well are signs of both education and culture. It is therefore not uncommon for the host to engage the restaurant manager or head waiter in a twenty-minute discussion just in deciding what to order.

In addition, and something which is generally not appreciated, it is an opportunity to show your face and get to know on a personal basis the people who are taking care of the day-to-day activities relating to your business; to "put a face to an order." When lower level employees or factory workers receive an order, it is ordinarily on paper or in the computer system; in other words, to them it is just a company name and order details. *If a business person takes time to get to know the people involved, from production manager to office staff, his or her order is no longer just anonymous paperwork but a person they know and remember. This will get different results.* The personal impression could prove invaluable in a business relationship with the Chinese, especially in times of emergency or should a business person ever need a favor where personal leverage can make the difference. The business visitor shouldn't be afraid to take the initiative and invite staff to dine; it can act as a reward (typically the lunch or dinner would be taken in a better restaurant than the one that the staff would use on a daily basis), in addition to giving them face. Remember that visiting business people tend to spend time developing good relationships with the company President, yet it is the merchandiser or clerk who will be processing their orders.

At Chinese lunches and dinners, it is common to eat in private rooms, which reflects the importance of the host and the guests. Typically, guests will be escorted from the entrance to the room. Particularly at banquets, it is important for the host to arrive before his or her guests and depart after them. Similarly, guests should take care to arrive after, and leave before, the host. Seating arrangements are stricter than in the West and guests should never assume they can sit where they please. Regardless of your status, it is better to wait for your host to guide you to your seat. Important guests are normally seated to the right of the host, as the right side is regarded as superior. Chinese hosts generally go out of their way to please and to impress guests and it is common to order more food than can reasonably be expected to be finished. Be prepared to expect abundant amounts of food that seems to be in endless supply. It is recommended to start slowly and pace yourself; otherwise, you could be full by the second course and it would be considered rude to stop eating in the middle of a lunch or dinner. The host might incorrectly think he has done something to offend you! If you are vegetarian or have special meal requirements, it always pays to give your host advanced warning so he will not consider you difficult once you are already at the table.

While the Chinese are generally forgiving toward foreign visitors, it is still necessary to be aware of Chinese table etiquette. The most important thing to remember is that if you are a guest, you should not start eating until your host has served you. As a host, it is necessary to serve the most important guest first, preferably with the serving chopsticks. At most restaurants, particularly following the scare of SARS, there are two sets of chopsticks: serving chopsticks for taking food from the common dishes and those for personal use. These are often different colors; for example, black for serving chopsticks and white for personal use. It is advisable to always lay chopsticks down together and horizontally on the plate, bowl, or on the small stand provided. If you leave them sticking out of a bowl up in the air, they resemble incense sticks at a funeral and are considered unlucky. It is considered rude to dig around in a dish with chopsticks in search of the choicest morsels. It is also considered bad manners to put your fingers in your mouth to extract bones, and chopsticks or toothpicks should be used for such purposes. It is certainly worthwhile to practice using chopsticks before arriving to avoid awkwardness at the table and having to rely on others to serve you for the duration of the meal. In main cities, there is usually cutlery available for "tourists" although, when you are in less cosmopolitan areas, chopsticks are the only option. With regard to thanking your host, comments on the quality of food such as "thank you, the food was delicious" are generally preferable to more general comments such as "thank you for dinner" (even if you are not sure what it was you just ate!)

There are also rules of etiquette concerning drinking. The Chinese rarely expect a guest to serve. If your glass becomes empty, it is likely it will be filled for you immediately if your host is observant. If you are serving, make sure to serve others before filling your own cup or glass and fill it as full as you can without spilling the contents over the rim. This symbolizes full respect and friendship. At more formal functions and banquets, no one should drink until the host has proposed a welcome toast and the chief guest has replied; after that, people can drink and propose toasts at will. The host will typically hold out his glass with both hands and say a few words. If the host uses the words "gan bei," which means bottoms up (literally dry glass) it is expected that all present should drain their glasses. After the initial toast, drinking and toasting are open to all and while it is respectful to drain your glass this is not necessary. The Chinese consider that hard liquor should not be drunk alone and it appears to be a matter of courtesy for a host to attempt to get their guests drunk, especially the men. If you are at a business function in New York or London, at the very least it would be mildly embarrassing to get so outrageously drunk that you fall off your chair and have to be carried back to your room; the same behavior in China, however, demonstrates that you are willing to let your defenses down among "friends," builds trust, and might even help to seal a deal! Here is a story described by Graham and Lam:

> "On the eve of negotiations between the chief executive of a U.S. firm and one from a major Chinese company, the Chinese hosted a lavish dinner at the best banquet hall in the city. The Chinese CEO proposed a toast: Let's drink to our friendship! We will have long cooperation! But if you aren't drunk tonight, there will be no contract tomorrow." The executive from the American firm matched him drink for drink—and couldn't remember how he got back to his hotel. The next morning he was greeted with a hangover, a big smile, and a fat contract."[26]

If one is teetotaler by habit or religion, it is best to make this known beforehand; it is exponentially harder to refuse a drink once at the table, and peer pressure should never be underestimated in China. Drinking toasts together is a way to give face to Chinese counterparts; refusing to drink is tantamount to an insult. However, at large scale Chinese New Year dinners in particular, beware of groups of three or four Chinese workers that come toward your table to drink a personal toast with you; in an effort to get you more drunk, rather than all raising glasses and drinking together, a common tactic is to attempt to get you to drink a separate toast with each person in turn.

There is not much ceremony to signify the conclusion of a lunch, dinner, or banquet; the end is generally announced by the arrival of fruit. Remember never to offer to share the bill with your host, as this would indicate a state of poverty and cause embarrassment. Restaurant bills are not shared; instead, people go to great lengths to claim the honor of paying, which normally falls on the person perceived as most senior or successful.

Chinese Festivals

While China uses the Gregorian calendar for civil purposes, the lunar calendar is used for determining holidays and festivals. As the start of the lunar year is based on the cycles of the moon, the beginning of the year can fall anywhere between late January and the middle of February. For those who are conducting business with Chinese companies, the most significant holidays to be aware of are the three "Golden Weeks"—Spring Festival (Chinese Lunar New Year), which begins in January or February; Labor Day, which begins on May 1st; and National Day, which begins on October 1st. While three days paid holiday is normally given, these holidays are normally arranged so that Chinese workers have seven continuous days of holiday. In relation to production, these holidays need to be planned for accordingly.

Chinese New Year is the biggest holiday in the Chinese calendar. It is a time to celebrate with family members and, for migrant factory workers, this means traveling great distances to be with families. The resulting mass exodus of factory workers on the same dates causes the greatest congestion for public transport throughout the whole of China. The problem in recent years has become so acute that the Chinese government has enacted rules to allow workers to travel at different times to ease the burden on infrastructure. Unless the purpose is a cultural visit, it is advisable to avoid traveling to China during this time. While companies and offices in Hong Kong normally close for a few days or some for a full week, factories in China can be closed for production for anything up to a month or more. Particularly significant for companies dealing with Chinese factories, this is typically the busiest time of year for production and when most importers are trying to get their orders shipped before the holiday. There are often container lorries waiting in line for several kilometers outside the main Chinese ports. If your orders are not produced and shipped before Chinese New Year, shipments can be delayed for four, six, or eight weeks later.

It is necessary to plan ship dates well in advance if you must have orders shipped before Chinese New Year. Ideally, shipments should be arranged for December or mid-January to avoid problems. If you leave things to the last minute, it can require a great relationship with the company owner or factory manager to ensure that your shipment is among those produced before the holiday. With limited production capacity, combined with sometimes poor planning of their own, Chinese factories often have to decide which orders for which customers are going to be produced, and which are going to be left pending until after the holiday. While the effects of the other two Golden Weeks around Labor Day and National day are typically not as disruptive to business as Chinese New Year, each raises important issues concerning production, planning, and order shipment.

It is important to be aware of these and other numerous one-day holidays in China and Hong Kong, which will avoid demonstrating inexperience (or disrespect) by sending emails and expecting replies during or just before a holiday. For Chinese New Year in particular, it would be the equivalent of receiving correspondence just before the Christmas holiday and expecting action on Christmas day. In addition, bear in mind that while a company's Hong Kong office may be open, a proper response may still depend on communication with factories in China that are closed. It is a good idea to obtain a Chinese calendar and keep it on your desk for easy reference. For visitors to China during holidays and festivals, it is also wise to be familiar with cultural celebrations and customs associated with each holiday so as to avoid behavior that potentially could be seen as incongruent with etiquette and tradition.

STEPS TO
SUCCESS

SUCCESS
STEP 2

Do You Have
Good Guangxi
(Connections)?

In China, relationships and connections are key. They are the invisible hands that get things done and keep things running smoothly. *While in the West we often think in terms of doing business between companies; in China we must think of doing business with people.* With the enormous changes happening in China at the moment, the underlying business culture of *guanxi* is still the same.

"*Guanxi*" is "Chinese-style networking," which involves building long-term relationships and connections based on mutual trust and reciprocity. Connections are one of the most important aspects of doing business; to have good connections in China is to have power. A person with good connections is therefore a person with social capital; such people are referred to in China as having "good *guanxi*." It is important to understand that *guanxi* transcends personal connections or the casual making of friends and to recognize the intangible existence of the fundamental system of *guanxi,* how it operates, how to build and develop it.

The Chinese have an almost inherent suspicion of strangers[27]. As a consequence, wariness and distrust tend to characterize all meetings with foreign business people where there is not the pre-existence of interpersonal relationships. While in the West there is a tendency to trust people until there is a good reason not to, the Chinese distrust all strangers until given ample assurance or evidence that they are worthy of trust. Western executives must be aware of this contradictory point of view and must therefore approach business in China in a different way.

Western business people, with their characteristic "task-orientation," often attempt to get straight down to business with the Chinese, without first taking time to build a network of interpersonal relationships, or placing the necessary emphasis on developing relationships on the "non-task" level. This is perfectly understandable given a Western cultural background where there is a presumption of trust. However, with an inherent level of distrust in China, the Chinese require time for the transference or development of trust before getting down to the specifics of business.

Additionally, China is traditionally a relationship-based culture. Confucianism emphasized the role of the family and, in the absence of a properly functioning social welfare system, it is natural that there is more reliance on family and friends. A general mistrust of strangers and a reliance on informal relationships were almost natural consequences of the years of communism; in a system where the monetary incentive became generally obsolete and people lived in a constant atmosphere of fear, the only way to get things done was through trusted contacts, connections, and people in the right places. *Guanxi* runs very deep in Chinese culture. It pervades businesses that are built on a web of connections—networks of invisible loyalties and alliances that the visitor is often not aware of, or the importance of which are underestimated.

Anthony Russo, a friend and Engineering and Aircraft Maintenance Advisor in China once related a light hearted example concerning the delivery of some spare parts that were due into a factory that day. The conversation is related as closely as possible:

Russo:	"Do you know where are the spare parts that are due in today?"
Worker:	"Not coming today."
Russo:	"Why aren't they coming today?"
Worker:	"My cousin's car broke down."
Russo:	"Your cousin! Your cousin was delivering the parts?"
Worker:	"No. My cousin had the box of lychees in his car." (A Lychee is a red fragrant spiky fruit the size of a golf ball)
Russo:	"What do you mean lychees?"
Worker:	"The lychees for the customs officer."
Russo:	"What customs officer?"
Worker:	"The customs officer who will help us with the processing of documentation to ensure the lorry with the spare parts arrives on time!"

While this is a light hearted example, it is indicative of a phenomenon that is all-pervasive in China. Getting things done often relies on an intricate web of personal friendships, connections, gifts, and inducements. It also helps us to understand why business does not always function in a straightforward, transparent manner, or according to efficient market principles. However, Western business people should not make the mistake that *guanxi* is automatically associated with corruption; it is not inherently unethical. From a Western moral vantage point, the idea of corruption is inevitably invoked with the existence of any non-transparent or "gray" area.

However, the quasi-official system of *guanxi* is traditional Chinese culture and should not be condemned through a Western lens. Guanxi simply means that business partners often develop much deeper and more personal relationships than are usual in the West.

Due to a mistrust of strangers, Chinese business people do business with those within their network of family, social, or business connections; those with whom they have *guanxi*. What is the origin or basis of these connections? The basis of *guanxi* is most commonly through family relatives, school friends, previous business relations, relationships developed between former work colleagues, or even the fact of sharing the same hometown. The common thread is the existence of some personal link or some form of common ground by which the transmission of trust is facilitated.

Social capital is afforded to those with the best connections. If the Chinese want to do business yet lack the requisite relationships, it then becomes a question of knowing friends or connections that are in turn able to make an introduction to the right contacts. Business in China might therefore be thought of as conducted through a system of intermediaries. It is necessary to have a contact with the right ties who is able to set up a meeting where parties can be personally introduced, and one that allows trust to be personally transmitted. The fundamental premise is that the contact will do his best to help the newly introduced member not only because of honor but also because there is a risk of losing face should assistance be deemed inadequate and word makes it back to the intermediary who recommended or introduced the parties; similarly, an intermediary will only introduce a connection that is proven to be reliable; otherwise, the intermediary risks loss of face. In this way the system of *guanxi* is both self-reinforcing and self-policing.

It is important to recognize the reciprocal nature of connections in China. If someone is doing you a favor, it is expected that the favor will be returned. In business, relationships are typically mutually profitable. Relationships in China are therefore not about driving the hardest bargain to the point where it is hardly worth the other party to perform. It is about ensuring both parties benefit from the relationship. For instance, where prices are concerned, both parties need to make a profit; if the relationship is with a customs officer who helps to ensure shipments are "smoothly" expedited there will usually be some "gifts" in return. Gifts are also a means of giving face to demonstrate appreciation of their help.

With connections in China, the reciprocal nature of guanxi is based more on the notion of long term reciprocity, rather than the short term reciprocity characteristic in the West. In the West, the expectation of reciprocity tends to be more immediate, expressed in the manner of "if I do something for you, you now need to do something for me in return." In the context of negotiations, western negotiators tend to expect a concession to be granted immediately in return for a concession on the other side. Chinese reciprocity is more about what goes around comes around; favors are expected to be remembered and repaid at some unspecified time in the future, not right away. That a favor is expected in return is an unspoken rule, breach of which is a serious social misdemeanor. The long term nature of reciprocity is enduring and forms the cornerstone of *guanxi* in Chinese relations.

It should also be appreciated that the system of connections can be a complex global web; if a well-positioned government official awards a company a contract, it may be appreciated by way of a new sports car for his cousin living in Canada, paid for and delivered by another connection called upon to repay a previous favor. *Guanxi* can sometimes operate through elaborate, convoluted and clandestine means.

Being a successful businessman in China means that one has built a network of connections that are synonymous with trust, loyalty, and reciprocity. Employees are sometimes strategically chosen for their connections with people in government departments. Business partners are, wherever possible, friends or those referred by friends. In the absence of such deep rooted cultural values or a comparable network of connections in the West, it is common to formally research and analyze competing companies or offers in the marketplace, or consult the yellow pages. When the Chinese need something done, the first step is to ask among their friends, relatives, and associates to see if they know someone who is able to help them, or know of someone who may know someone who can help.

Since business in China is so firmly based on trust, to do business successfully, foreign executives need to have either pre-existing personal connections or access to an intermediary with the right connections to make the necessary referrals or introductions, at a suitable level. Good connections or introductions, by surmounting the issue of suspicion, circumvent the many years that would normally be required to painstakingly develop trust to the point where things run smoothly.

Since the Chinese operate on the basis of *guanxi*—the transmission of trust—and have an inherent distrust of anyone who does not come personally recommended, it poses a particular problem for foreign companies without the right *guanxi*. In addition, it may turn out that the scope of an intermediary's *guanxi* is less than promised and limited in its strategic usefulness.

In this case, and for many foreign business people desiring to do business with Chinese companies, it is necessary to start without relationships and build them from scratch. We are faced with a conundrum: without trust, business relations cannot even be formed, yet it is necessary to have some form of history in order for trust to exist. Without existing relationships and without the facilitation of an intermediary able to imbue the relationship with the required level of trust from the outset, *the only alternative is to develop your own guanxi*.

This development often means being initially less task-oriented and taking time and effort to slowly develop relationships on a more personal level. There is no shortcut. Trust can only be developed gradually and diligently over time. A good place to start is simply taking a relationship to a social level outside the workplace; at the very minimum, we should accept the occasional lunch, dinner, or other social invitation. Certainly, it involves making the effort to visit factories rather than conducting all business at the head office; this participation shows a deeper interest in developing a partnership, instead of taking a hands-off approach. Inviting Chinese management or counterparts for a tour of your operations also sends the right signals. In my experience, European businessmen tend to take more time and effort to cultivate personal relationships with Chinese counterparts, while American business people tend to have a more strict focus on business and results, *perhaps not fully realizing that one way to get better results is through building better relationships!* We must understand the need to be more personal in our business dealings in China and balance this with the need for maintaining codes of ethics and conduct required by our own companies. Chinese business people feel the need to spend time together on a personal and informal basis to evaluate the person, judge the level of sincerity, and to see if they are people (and by extrapolation the company) of the type they want to do business with. Consider this time spent together as a form of interview during which they are "sounding you out." This sounding out period is just as important, if not more important, than subsequent cooperation. *It lays the foundations for cooperation.* If this informal interview phase is not handled well, future cooperation may not be smooth; if on the other hand, the Chinese get to know you and like what they see, things thereafter can happen quite quickly and proceed in an almost effortless fashion.

Due to the importance of personal relationships in China, decisions as to which staff are put in charge of China projects and sent to work with Chinese suppliers take on added significance. In the West, there is a tendency to keep personal and professional lives separate, while in China the lines between family, friends, and the workplace are more blurred. It is common that business partners in China will expect to develop closer personal relationships than are standard in the West, and business people working with the Chinese should therefore expect to do so on a more friendly and personal basis than in a strictly professional capacity. If your company is having trouble dealing with China, the trouble can often be traced to personal relationships or interpersonal communication.

It is therefore important that those chosen for China assignments have the right personal qualities to be able to function properly in such a different and demanding environment. No amount of training can compensate for selecting people with unsuitable personalities. *Western executives must sometimes recognize that personnel with an excellent track record at home may simply not be suitable for assignments in China.* To operate properly in China requires the *strength* of character to handle the many contradictions, the *patience* and *calm* to deal with problems and the *tenacity* to see projects through to their conclusion. China hands must also possess the *flexibility* to adapt to different ways of working and be *open-minded* and *respectful* of other cultures. The nature of working with China also requires a level of *independence* because those responsible for China purchasing often need to solve problems on their own rather than relying on help from colleagues who are less familiar with the way things are done in China; it is often a matter of synchronizing the familiar operations of home with the unpredictable nature of working with Chinese companies. A *friendly* and *personable* character is also a great advantage to facilitate the advancement of personal relationships. Finally, two other attributes should be requisites: prior international experience with exposure to different cultures, and that those representing the company have a broad and deep knowledge of their own company. Executives who believe they can send inexperienced team members to cut their teeth in China without the supervision of more experienced managers are mistaken; the inexperience of staff members reflects on the whole company and sends a clear message to Chinese companies. Suppliers with whom a company has a long standing business relationship might take the time to teach company staff, although they will be prejudiced in the interests of the Chinese company; those suppliers without a long standing history will often think they are wasting their time. In addition, be aware of changing staff that are handling China relations. Since personal relations are important, continuity in staff also has a premium and any changes need to be carefully managed, preferably involving the personal transfer of *guanxi* to the new person. For best results in China, send the best people.

The seniority or position of representatives from a company also has an important bearing on the development of *guanxi*. If the most senior members at the top of the corporate structure are involved with Chinese suppliers it raises the importance with which the Chinese company is perceived. Meetings of "equals" at the highest levels also gives "face" to participants and will assist the fast tracking of company relationships: The direct involvement of company presidents and vice-presidents bridges the trust divide. Involvement from the very top signals that intentions are genuine and the Chinese are unlikely to be wasting their time with inferiors that may not have the full backing of the real decision makers.

It is important to emphasize to Chinese executives that you intend to build something of lasting mutual value together, rather than just a standard business affiliation. When placing orders for example, it should be stressed that while you have received several offers from other companies you prefer to work with the Chinese partner due to personal cohesion and because you *trust* them. During meetings with the Chinese, one way to more effectively convey the message that you are interested in a mutually beneficial venture is to hold onto their hands longer as you shake hands as you are finishing the meeting and to look your Chinese counterpart in the eye while continuing to speak. This was a suggestion from Anthony Russo that can profoundly affect the building of relationships and getting things done. It communicates on an almost primitive level that you are both "in this together"—that if you jump they are coming with you, and visa versa. It helps to establish a stronger bond and emphasizes mutual cooperation on a subconscious level.

There are significant advantages to consciously taking the time and effort to cultivate personal relationships in China, particularly with your most strategic partners or suppliers. Working in China without *guanxi* can be a constant uphill struggle. *If you find the going tough, it is often that sufficient time and effort have not been invested to cultivate relationships*[28]. Conducting business on a strictly formal level keeps the business relationship on a strictly formal level. Results might be successful and trust can be gradually developed by consistently doing what you say you are going to do; however, be aware that by taking the opportunity to develop deeper personal relationships it is correspondingly possible to take the relationship between companies to an entirely different level.

Personal connections and trusted relationships can be worth their weight in gold, especially in times of crisis, or should you need to override standard operating procedures to get things done, or get things done quickly. I have witnessed instances when customers have been up against almost insurmountable production and shipping deadlines when just one personal phone call to a key person resulted in materials being ordered and production started without any contractual documents. I have seen orders manufactured and shipped to some of the world's largest retailers without any signed paperwork at all, or even an agreement on price![29] Good personal relationships can result in more favorable payment terms, provide access to privy information or new designs reserved only for loyal and trusted customers. During times when production capacity is limited, lead times for those with good relations may be shorter than for those without relations. Service levels also tend to be higher because there is potential loss of face involved when relationships exist, either directly or through an intermediary. At the very least, good personal relations can, if desired, make the difference between arriving in a strange Chinese city and an anonymous hotel, to being treated like a special guest.

There are several facets of *guanxi* that should be recognized:

Loyalty: The Chinese value loyalty. For instance, a factory likes to consider itself as the main supplier or most valued supplier. If you are shopping around China looking for the cheapest price (as opposed to just comparing prices from two or three favored strategic partners), it sends the message that you are not interested in building a long-term relationship. A little healthy competition is acceptable, yet loyalty should be emphasized. Once loyalty has been demonstrated the resulting level of service can often be disproportionately better than the monetary level of your business.

Language: When you discuss business in China you will frequently hear Chinese speak in terms of "working together," "supporting each other," "cooperation," "relationships," "loyalty," rather than simply buying and selling. There is an almost innate tendency to believe you need not only to work with others but to establish a bond to get things done. It may be worthwhile to adopt this style of vocabulary to enhance the feeling of loyalty and level of *cooperation.*

Reciprocity: Both parties need to gain through being in a relationship and if the Chinese help you they expect something in return—"you scratch my back and I'll scratch yours!" The Chinese express appreciation through reciprocal action rather than with words. The reciprocal nature of business favors is like a silent understanding—favors are expected to be remembered and repaid. Once you enter into the system of *guanxi* it is entering a system where your support should be counted upon. In China business, if you become "one who forgets favors" then all future business relations will be soured.

Time horizon: The Chinese concept of reciprocity is long term, rather than the short term expectation of return characteristic of the West. While there are some that are in business for an immediate profit, most serious Chinese businessmen think long-term and expect to develop relationships that will be enduring and reap long-term benefits. While the West is in a hurry, China is patient.

Trust: It is vital to develop trust. The essence of *guanxi* is the transference of the currency of trust. With uncertainty and upheaval characterizing China's history, trust has greater weight than words printed on a document. Many things carried out in China are not all black and white and a great deal of trust is required to manage the gray areas. Trust is the most valued attribute in the Chinese community and if you lose trust, you lose everything. In China, key positions are often filled with employees who can be trusted over employees who may be better qualified.

Integrity: In China, it is important to keep promises; it is important to demonstrate that your word is cast in stone, for both small details and big issues, by consistently doing what you say you are going to do. It is necessary to show the Chinese that they can depend on you, and there is scarce tolerance in China for those who just talk. If you say you are going to place an order after you receive samples, make sure you place an order. If you promise a million dollars of business, make sure you do a million dollars worth of business.

Sincerity: Part of the reason the Chinese like to spend time together with potential foreign partners in a personal capacity before business commences is to gauge sincerity. There may be a cultural divide and a language problem but this does not prevent the Chinese from being able to spot insincerity.

Giving Face: Apart from the business, it is also important to maintain face in the relationship. Always treat your counterpart with respect, don't take him for granted, and make sure you don't cause the other party to lose face, or lose face yourself (more about this in the next section). Face provides cohesion for the network of *guanxi, just* as failing to act honorably results in mutual loss of face to participants and intermediaries alike. It is also necessary to appreciate that giving gifts and creating money through cooperation reflect the importance of the relationship and are also forms of giving face.

Introductions: Cold calling or starting a relationship without a history can be difficult. If you would like to meet someone, it is better to call upon your network of intermediaries to arrange a personal introduction or to recognize those within your organization who has social capital or might share attributes or a common background with a person in the company you wish to work with. An introduction or referral carries far more weight in China than a self-introduction; the Chinese are then honor bound from the outset to assist you.

Results: At the end of the day, the perceived value of a relationship is intricately tied to results, usually of a financial nature or another perceived benefit. The determinant of whether a person has good *guanxi* is the quality of his connections or "social capital" and his ability to get results.

It is certainly necessary to have good *guanxi* in China and to invest the time and effort required to build connections and relationships. It is often these mysterious connections behind the scenes that make the difference between success and failure. We have commonly heard that it is not what you know but who you know that counts; in China this is especially the case.

It is also the case that with relationships between foreigners and Chinese the bond is typically not as strong as that which exists between the Chinese. This is due in part to the cultural divide—the Chinese perceive it as something more consequential as opposed to something their Western counterparts might perceive as more frivolous; in part because the cultural value system and peer incentive for honoring commitments does not exist to the same extent. Additionally, while relationships have been, and will continue to be, an important social force in China, deeper integration of Chinese companies into efficient global markets, the Westernization of business practices and increased population mobility will lead to a gradual decline in the emphasis on relationships. As Chinese companies find themselves increasingly integrated within global supply chains where buying becomes more systematized, procedures more compatible, organizations more interdependent, price competition greater and with a faster turnover of staff at large companies, the emphasis on loyalty and relationships will decline naturally.

Of particular relevance to those who are inexperienced with China, once good relationships have been developed, don't believe they can achieve miracles or that the partnership formed is unassailable come hell or high-water. Notwithstanding a minority of cases, fundamentally it is a combination of financially motivated business prudence and friendly business tactics. If you are a relatively small customer and your Chinese partner is presented with a more lucrative deal, your project will soon find itself on a backburner! Should business together decline, you will become relatively less important and the relationship may correspondingly lose its shine. If loss of money is involved, you will soon find out how deep the friendship is!

In addition, there are times when having a good relationship can work against you. For example, suppose you have a personal relationship with a company owner, the factory is at full capacity and the owner must decide which orders to delay. It is generally the case that those orders with the severest financial or other penalties, or a case of "he who shouts loudest" will get their orders shipped, regardless of the relationship. Due to your personal relationship, the owner might consider the consequences less adverse and could therefore leave your orders until last.

It is therefore advantageous to view the personal relationship as something that takes place within the business relationship, rather than something that is overriding under all circumstances. For a foreigner, the optimal approach is to proceed with a high level of professionalism, yet still taking the time and effort to build personal relationships and *guanxi*. The objective should be to leave your Chinese counterparts with the impression that they have a personal connection within a professional organization, rather than a personal relationship *per se*. The bottom line is that building personal relationships in China is about creating the right atmosphere so that business relationships can proceed harmoniously. Developing good

Guanxi is a way to get things done *and should therefore be considered one of the critical success factors for doing business in China.* There is an old adage that says if you try to cultivate a flower in salty land, it does not grow; cultivating good connections in China is quite simply about "preparing the soil for business to flower."

SUCCESS
STEP 3

Understanding the Concept of "Face"

We are all familiar with the terms "saving face" and "keeping face." While these terms are familiar expressions in the West in relation to public image and self esteem, these same terms embody more profound implications in China. All visitors to China are aware of "face" yet few immediately recognize its full significance in Chinese culture and the pivotal role that face can play in business relations and the achievement of objectives.

Causing your Chinese counterpart to lose face can sometimes be obviously noticeable. At other times, in relation to its more subtle aspects, it can be harder to perceive, although the consequences can be equally profound. In general, it is to the visitor's detriment if face is not properly understood, or the unwritten rules concerning face not properly adhered to. For anyone working with the Chinese it is of great advantage to understand the various facets of face and to be able go about one's business conscious of the potential effects of one's actions, decisions and words (including correspondence).

The Three Levels of Face

So what exactly is face?

Face is closely related to Western concepts of pride, self-respect, dignity, and prestige. However, in China it is a concept that carries more weighty import. Face is an important measure of social standing that acts as an external reference point for peers, subordinates, and superiors. There are many sources of face, such as having good *guanxi,* a senior corporate position or official title, attractiveness, wealth or talent. The most noteworthy feature of face is that unlike in the West where a person is either prestigious or not, in China face is similar to money in that it is something that can be earned, given or lost. *It is therefore something fluid that must be taken note of and carefully managed.*

Although it is useful to regard face as being multi-leveled and multi-faceted, it may be considered generally as having three levels: basic respect, extreme loss of face, and what we might refer to as "the middle ground."

Basic respect, the primary level, is simply being friendly, polite, affable, and treating others with respect and common courtesy. It is much the same as having good manners, observing etiquette according to the particular situation, and not offending others. In a business setting, it means such things as being suitably dressed, arriving to meetings on time, and advising in advance if you will be arriving later than scheduled. More specific to Asia, it includes giving and receiving business cards with both hands,[30] or if invited for dinner, complimenting the quality of food served. In Asia, it also means respecting the other's stature by behaving toward him in accordance with the position he has in the organization. This means that if you are meeting the Chinese boss, you shake hands but don't slap him on the back as though he is a familiar acquaintance. When speaking to a group you predominantly address the most senior Chinese participant, and when the most senior Chinese participant speaks, you listen, and don't interrupt, as though his words carry more import (even if they don't!).

At the other end of the spectrum is extreme loss of face. It is the taboo end of a relationship where you have intentionally or unintentionally violated the "rules" and, as a consequence, the relationship is gravely or irreparably damaged. Depending on severity, these encompass the things you can't do with any hope of continuing a normal relationship afterwards; for instance, venting anger or losing your temper, composure or emotional control, or arguing vociferously with your Chinese business partner. When there are differences of opinion, it helps to bear in mind that we are predisposed in the West to think in terms of right and wrong. In the West, this implies that there is a "right" interpretation of a situation, while the Chinese way of thinking allows two sides to hold equally valid yet opposing positions.[31] This means that with a Western mindset we often fail to accept the other side's point of view and attempt to bring the other side around to our way of thinking, while the Chinese can agree to disagree. The Chinese might even agree with our rational suggestion but it still may not match their priorities.

It should be noted that the result of any display of anger or aggression is usually *mutual* loss of face and we should therefore consider making a greater effort at humility. Sun Tze spoke of using humbleness to mislead the enemy and prevent them from gaining a true understanding of the strength of your position. It is not only a characteristic of many Chinese managers but also conducive to maintaining face. Humbleness need not necessarily mean weakness; when resolving issues it is quite possible, in fact *desirable,* to be both strong and humble at the same time. It is often necessary in China to be firm and say exactly what you mean, but say it with a smile on your face!

Alternatively, severe loss of face can result if you deliberately or unintentionally cause your Chinese counterpart to look stupid in front of his peers or subordinates. Relations might continue with the outward appearance of normality, yet underneath lack personal respect for the perpetrator. As an example, a foreign executive for an import company was visiting the factory of his main Chinese suppliers accompanied by one of his assistants who was responsible for quality control. During the visit, the executive and his assistant were walking through the production floor to inspect an order together with the Chinese company president and his entourage. The assistant, an inexperienced man in Chinese affairs, picked up some of the work-in-progress and noticed the materials were not to the specified standard. He pointed this out to the group in a rather tactless, undignified manner, partly with the intention of impressing his superior. To emphasize the apparent mistake, not only did he point this out once, he repeated it several times in a similar manner, directing the comments in particular to the president of the Chinese company. As he happened to be fluent in spoken Chinese, he not only repeated it several times, he also repeated it in Chinese so that the president's assistants and subordinates could all understand. To all appearances, it appeared much like the president was being dressed down in front of his subordinates by a young and inexperienced foreign customer—a formula guaranteed to cause loss of face for the president! In short, the Chinese company president turned a shade of Pantone red, and only some diplomatic and very carefully chosen words from the Western boss, who was more experienced in Chinese affairs, diffused the situation and restored harmony. I don't believe the quality control assistant ever returned to the factory again!

It is generally accepted in Western behavioral psychology that the average person will do more to avoid pain than to gain pleasure. Similarly, *the average Chinese person will do practically anything to avoid the pain and embarrassment caused by loss of face.* In a political context, this partly explains why the Chinese often conduct themselves with such an outwardly serious demeanor. It is this demeanor which led England's Prince Charles to controversially refer to the Chinese leaders in his Hong Kong diaries during the handover of Hong Kong as "appalling old waxworks." It is implied that by allowing themselves to be funny or emotional there is a greater risk of losing face than by remaining serious and proud.

While it may be possible in Western cultures to apologize for causing loss of face and be consequently forgiven for transgressions (with some degree of awkwardness afterwards), *once you have caused the Chinese serious loss of face there is usually no going back*. If business dealings continue after an event that precipitates an extreme loss of face, these will often be delegated to a person lower in the hierarchy—and don't expect favors! It would be as well to expect never to have a normal relationship afterwards, or one based on scarcely concealed lack of respect or perhaps no further relationship at all with the person or company. If a transgression has occurred by fax or email, you can expect stonewall treatment and receive no further correspondence. If you are in a meeting, don't be surprised if the offended person turns a shade of red and never looks you in the eye again. I recall an instance when a senior manager who had made a blunder, causing significant loss of money, had a meeting with the company owner that lasted almost half an hour during which the owner failed to look the manager in the eye even once. *The most important thing to bear in mind is that if relationships are well managed in Chinese business, business can proceed smoothly and on a friendly basis; if loss of face is caused, the atmosphere can turn a steely cold and it can be difficult to get anything done at all*—as though the lights have been turned out on a relationship and everyone has gone home!

The problem for foreign business people in China is that the line between what is acceptable, and what is not acceptable, is difficult to precisely define. On the surface, the business person might feel that matters were agreeably handled. However, under the surface, an imperceptible loss of face could have caused the tectonic plates to have shifted under the relationship. Business might continue with the outward appearance of normality, but loss of face might have caused the Chinese to lose respect for the transgressor, which in turn might result in a lowering in priority of current projects, and a general lack of attention to his company's requirements. In China, it is therefore common sense to be keenly aware of the issue of losing face, until sufficient experience has been gained that would allow one to better gauge where the line between what is, and what is not, acceptable. No matter how angry or frustrated you may feel, it is necessary to avoid causing loss of face at all costs, I have never seen an instance where a situation or outcome has ever been improved or served by causing a person to lose face. The key in Asia is to remain in control at all times, even when you may be furious; be friendly, business-like, calm and professional, firm when necessary, yet always in control emotionally.

When we consider the "middle ground" that exists between basic respect and extreme loss of face we find ourselves in a complex area where Chinese behavior, responses, and decisions can be "face-based" rather than the consequence of logic, which can cause the Chinese to act unpredictably at times. Sometimes, avoiding potential loss of face can prove to be a better motivator than money and, therefore, we need to weigh the impact of our actions, decisions, and words to make sure they are appropriate for achieving our objectives without causing any harmful consequences.

We must ensure that we do not cause our Chinese counterpart to feel he has made a mistake, or that he is not making a useful contribution, which could also cause loss of face. Loss of face inevitably results in defensive behavior rather than behavior or action designed to overcome or solve a problem.

Here is an example to illustrate the point, in the form of a fax communication written by the purchasing director of a large UK company, referring to the receipt of a shipment of inferior quality goods:

> "Dear Mr. Lee (name changed),
> We have just received delivery of our recent order of X products and must say we are totally disappointed. The quality of the products is terrible. It is so bad that it is completely impossible to sell to our customer. Therefore we demand our money back and also any and all expenses incurred in shipping and transporting the goods to our warehouse. In addition, we expect to be reimbursed for the costs of inspection that we were forced to pay in order to determine just how bad the quality was. As a result of such poor standards and obvious lack of attention to quality, we have no intention of doing business with you in future.

> *Please deal with this matter without delay, let me know precisely*
> *what you intend to do about this and what you would like us to*
> *do with the goods.*
> *Regards,*
> *Purchasing Director*

The response to this communication was...no response at all. And furthermore, there was no solution forthcoming. It was clearly a communication written under stress and more a means to let off steam after a disappointment than designed to get any meaningful result. While the Chinese partner may have been at fault, a Chinese recipient will not see the letter in this way. Apart from the fact that the writer *terminated the relationship* mid-way through the letter *and then* proceeded to ask what the company was going to do about solving the problem; and apart from the obvious assumption that because the Chinese side was at fault they must take it upon themselves to rectify the situation (based on a false assumption that the "customer is king" in China), the letter is more likely to cause Mr. Lee to feel useless, to lose face, and become defensive, rather than disposed toward finding a solution. In such instances, it is important to recognize that the Chinese have an almost innate cultural *inability* to admit responsibility. In such cases, due to the absence of effective and efficient legal recourse in China, even if the Chinese company is obviously at fault, you have little choice but to adopt a more conciliatory manner at the outset. If angry, it is better to count to one thousand and ten before composing a letter to a Chinese company! There are few second chances.

The key in such circumstances is not to seek the perfect solution at the first attempt, but instead to set the tone for a subsequent discourse that is conducive to reaching an equitable solution. State both the facts and a suggested solution in an objective, rather than an emotional tone, and treat it as bait to see how the supplier will respond. Give the supplier an opportunity to put the situation right in the absence of negative coercion. Then, as a dialogue is established, the issues involved can be pushed further until an acceptable solution is achieved. To start out by creating a bad "atmosphere" will leave a bad taste in the mouth even if the issue is resolved.

The Chinese perceive themselves as put on the Earth to be useful, to contribute. For the Chinese, to help others is a means to feel whole;

therefore, if you criticize their actions or tell them they have made a mistake it makes them feel that they are serving no useful purpose and are thus "un-whole." For this reason, criticism is rarely perceived as constructive and rarely has beneficial results. This is similar in all cultures, but especially in China where there is no forgiveness and any challenge or criticism is viewed as a loss of face. Differences of opinion must be handled in a different way.

If a mistake is made, it is better to use it as an opportunity to problem-solve or educate rather than criticize. Don't show anger; instead, learn to communicate disappointment in a way that is not critical. In face to face meetings, use your expression and demeanor to show dissatisfaction instead of negative words. Problem solving in China should be approached with the aim of working out an amicable solution that allows the other party to save face, and should not be fault based.

Giving and Keeping Face

We should also bear in mind that it is oftentimes necessary to "give face." This is equally relevant to the small details of interpersonal communication and important operational issues. Recognizing the status of your Chinese counterpart within their company hierarchy is important and to treat them in a manner befitting their position. In the West, while status is obviously important, we tend to treat each participant, regardless of status, with similar respect. *In China we must be aware of the pecking order.*

If the Chinese company is of strategic importance to your organization, make the effort to personally visit the factory with the owner. Remember that when Chinese staff are waiting at the factory for your arrival they are nervous and there is face at stake; therefore, upon arrival break the ice and make the effort to create a positive personal impression. Take time to eat with people, instead of trying to maximize time-efficiency by having a whistle-stop meeting before dashing off to the next appointment without lunch, and make sure all the relevant people are invited (failing to invite a person for lunch can cause a great deal of resentment in China). Giving face can be as simple as complimenting a person for a job well done, particularly if it is done in front of their peers and subordinates. If done sincerely you will likely be rewarded with more effort and better results. Give the impression that you are working together on a more mutually supportive basis rather than just the standard contractual buyer-supplier relationship.

To give face we need to make the Chinese feel that they are important and valued, that you value the relationship and value their company as a supplier. Complement the factory manager on the efficiency of the operation, the quality of their products or the size of the factory. As you walk around Chinese trade fairs, you will notice that many brochures feature the factory on the front cover, rather than the products that are produced. This is more due to pride and face than any attention to marketing strategy. In addition, job titles tend to be more important in China than in the West and define a person's role, status, and rank (not ability!). Therefore, when preparing business cards for a trip to China, it is important to portray a good social position; for instance, instead of "Buyer" consider using "Senior Purchasing Manager" or "Buying Director." It is such details that "give face" to the people you will work with. This is not a matter of being superficial; it is simply a matter of adapting to cultural expectations, choosing words more carefully, and paying more attention to detail in China than you would at home.

It is important that our Chinese business partners maintain respect for us; therefore, we must also ensure that we don't lose face ourselves. This can entail keeping our promises, making sure we are properly briefed and prepared for meetings, remaining professional and in control. Appearances are also important: when you are booking your hotel in China, remember that staying in a five-star hotel will can grant you more prestige, more respect, and more *face* than a cheaper alternative. Impressions are sometimes more important than budgets in China!

Finally, during strategic discussions or negotiations, aim to get what you want while making sure the Chinese side also goes away with something. Try to resist playing hardball. Even if you have a stronger negotiating position, it may at times pay to leave something on the table to allow the other party to "save face." If you use your power or position to push the Chinese into a corner, they will rarely do what you wish through coercion. Leaving a face saving way out, or letting it appear the Chinese are taking action by their own volition usually gets better results.

A prime example was the Chinese decision to allow the Chinese currency to break through the psychological barrier of 8 Yuan to the US dollar in May 2006. The U.S. has long been petitioning the Chinese government over the Yuan-Dollar exchange rate, which the U.S. considers gives China an unfair trade advantage, and this has become a politically contentious issue. A stronger Yuan is in US interests as it makes imports more expensive, helping the China-US trade deficit. It is also in China's interests to have a stronger Yuan that lowers the local currency costs of imported goods, such as oil. Allowing the Yuan to appreciate also allows China to tighten financial conditions without taking recourse to higher interest-rate increases. However, if the US Treasury Department had pushed Beijing into a corner and attempted to *force* this change on the Chinese currency, it is unlikely to have been met with a positive response.[32] China would appear to be kowtowing to international pressure, which means loss of face on the international political stage. Whether by informed design or accident, the US Treasury Department decided not to force change on the Chinese by branding Beijing a "currency manipulator,"[33] which has the potential to lead to trade sanctions against China.[34] Just days after this announcement, Beijing allowed the People's Bank of China to strengthen the Chinese currency, setting the dollar-Yuan central parity at 7.9982, the first time it has been below 8. With room to move, the Chinese perceived the timing as an opportunity to move the pegged exchange rate without giving the impression of yielding to outside pressure; therefore, the Chinese were able to give the U.S. what they wanted, while also saving face.[35]

When working with China, "face" is an added dimension that needs to be borne in mind at all times. It is important to understand the concept, recognize when you are in a situation where saving face could be an issue, and remain continually alert so that your actions are not likely to be the potential cause of someone losing face. An understanding of all the various nuances of "face" needs to be blended into all your words, actions, and endeavors. If you are unsure, it is better to tread carefully rather than burn bridges. China is a less forgiving environment.

SUCCESS
STEP 4

Behind the Scenes at the Average **Chinese** Organization

It is generally acknowledged that working with Chinese companies or manufacturers is not always easy. We have heard the horror stories from those who have received perfect samples followed by a container of sub standard products. We have read the reports of investors who buy into a Chinese operation only for the Chinese partner to make money, while the foreigner loses his shirt. The question is *why* is it difficult? What can be done to protect ourselves and the companies we work for from such risks? The *why it is difficult* part is addressed to some extent in this section; *what can be done to better protect ourselves* is addressed in more detail in successive Success Steps.

The process of taking control must begin with a look behind the scenes. If visitors could catch a glimpse of what it is like to experience working alongside factory managers and factory staff on a day-to-day basis, seeing firsthand how decisions affecting their orders are really made, it would shed light on the process. We must have an understanding of how Chinese organizations function, the environment in which they operate, how managers think, how decisions are made, and what motivates workers. In particular, we need to be familiar with the problems managers face when running a company. *The key point to remember is that the problems they face are problems that we face, indirectly.* Therefore, taking a look under the hood of the Chinese operation will allow us to better understand the problems that invariably arise, anticipate them, and then deal with them in a proactive manner.

The fourth step to being successful in China is to take a look behind the scenes at an average Chinese factory. It is only with an understanding of what is going on behind the scenes that one can hope to deal with them with any degree of success. The main problem for most business people is they start projects and place orders with Chinese companies and have little idea what happens afterwards. It is no surprise that things don't go as planned. It is like passing the supply chain baton to China and the Chinese partner promptly disappears behind the curtain with it until it is time to deliver, or *not* deliver as the case may be!

The average foreign executive normally only gets a cursory glimpse of things once or twice a year during the relationship-building exercise of paying a visit to their supplier's company or factory, which has been swept and tidied the day before the visit; and that is all it is—a glimpse—a superficial impression of one of the Chinese companies that collectively constitute the engine of the world. What surely would help buyers and investors is to receive an insight of what it is like working *inside* a Chinese factory.

First and foremost, *the most common cause of mistakes and loss of money in China is that foreign business people go to China with a fundamentally incorrect perception of Chinese organizations.* Many proceed to do business the way they do business in their home countries; uninitiated purchasing managers still behave as if they are buying from German, British, American companies, or for some unknown reason they expect German quality, British organization, American efficiency and innovation. Time and again I have witnessed inexperienced buyers from Europe and America arrive in China and hand over their carefully prepared project, just as they would to a department of a European or American company, then walk away with a smile on their face. Two months later, they are often facing a disaster, or it has become the product of "creative misinterpretation" (more on this later), or nothing has happened at all. The first thing the China rookie needs to undergo, therefore, is a shift of his universal thought paradigm.

Most of us are familiar with dealing with top companies in the world, either professionally or as consumers. The company is contacted, an order is placed, and after the specified time period the order is delivered as promised, often with periodic updates in between. This is because the best run companies have highly qualified, carefully chosen professional staff, working in efficient, well organized departments, receiving expert training and guidance, with well planned, implemented and tested systems and procedures, assisted by the latest information technology, under management on performance-based packages that expects results, answerable to shareholders who understand the importance of investing in research and are able to look ahead to re-position the organization for the market requirements of the future.

The average Chinese company is not like this! Don't misunderstand—there are Chinese companies that are as well managed and operated as any of the world's best companies. However, many simply do not have the familiarity of operating in efficient, highly-competitive, performance-based markets. For the purposes of this section we are interested in looking under the hood of the *average* Chinese operation, or the "less good performers" to understand why problems occur so that the information can be used to guide our own approach in dealing proactively with them. In addition, while China in general has a highly motivated and hard working labor force, not all workers are the same. For our purposes we are interested in familiarizing ourselves with those least desirable traits and practices; traits and practices that affect the ability of managers to operate their factories in an efficient manner.

Everyone appreciates that China is different. The key is to understand *why* it is different and crucially, if we want to *anticipate* problems, we need to know where they are coming from. Following is a selection of topics to give the reader a flavor of what it is like inside the average Chinese organization that will help us understand the complex issues faced by management.

Corruption

Corruption is deep rooted and endemic in China. It is sometimes hard to recognize the fine line between *guanxi* and corruption, or to distinguish where one finishes and the other starts. Gift-giving, nepotism, and the entertainment of clients are long running business practices in China. Where is the point where wining and dining an alumni friend, who is willing to introduce an important professional contact, becomes illicit entertainment?[36] Where does bringing a family member into the company to manage a department stop as a rational decision based on the necessity of trust in China and become nepotism because that family member may not be as *professionally* qualified as other applicants? Bearing in mind not only the issue of trust but also the wide variances in experience and expertise among Chinese companies, when does the award of a contract to a trusted and reliable business associate of thirty years become cronyism?

The issue of corruption is a gray area in the world of Chinese business relations. Nepotism, bribery, kickbacks, and illicit exchanges of business favors for personal gain are almost a way of life. Corruption finds its way into business operations through a multitude of different ways—workers augmenting their salaries by accepting money on the side, contracts awarded to companies that would not receive them in more transparent markets, loans awarded on the basis of personal connections rather than commercial analysis, payments to officials in strategic positions to ensure operations continue to run smoothly. Chinese company owners and managers must be continually vigilant and have the ability to subtly manage these additional demands, both financially and in terms of personal relationships.

There is systemic corruption throughout China's bureaucracies. Government officials appear to use their positions as an opportunity to make as much money as possible during the time they hold the position and get out before any wrongdoing is discovered. Long-term thinking seems to be sacrificed in modern China where those who are able to make short term riches are idolized. Who wants to work his whole life when corruption offers a shortcut?

Chinese companies must cooperate with the numerous government officials at various government departments—such as building departments, fire departments, labor departments, and export departments—to obtain permits and licenses to operate, manufacture, and export. If relations with the relevant government officials are not properly "cultivated," the smooth flow of official documentation required for unhindered operations can soon become a laborious, time consuming "bottleneck." With the complexity of running an operation in China and the various government departments that companies must deal with, it would be an extraordinary feat to operate a company smoothly *without* some form of *extra-curricular* payments or *"entertainment expenses."*

For manufacturers, there are innumerable ways that corrupt practices creep into operations. I was informed of a case where a factory manager and his export department manager colluded to export shipments on behalf of a friend's factory, which did not have the appropriate license to export. This is a serious offense in relation to taxes and customs where goods are declared to be manufactured in one factory but are actually produced in another. This discrepancy was brought to the attention of the local authorities then passed to national authorities and the case was destined to go to court proceedings...until the relevant people were sufficiently compensated.

I have seen foreign business people invest jointly with a Chinese partner to take over the fixed assets of a printing company with a view to running a profitable business together. After three years, during which the business had "not turned a profit" and all the money had been lost (by the foreign partners), it was later learned the Chinese partner had been fulfilling orders on his own without the knowledge of the foreign partners. Unless one is physically present, such incidences are difficult to control.

I recall an instance where sub-standard materials were used for orders, with the consequence that orders failed quality inspections, orders were cancelled and large sums of money lost on both sides. Subsequent investigations revealed that one of the workers in the warehouse, responsible for testing and inspecting raw materials as they were delivered to the factory, had taken bribes from various material suppliers to accept deliveries that would otherwise have been turned away. A delivery driver related another example to me. The delivery driver's job was to make routine deliveries of materials to a factory and upon delivery would receive future new orders. After a period of time, he noticed that he was receiving orders that he was not subsequently delivering. It turned out that one of the staff at his office was secretly sub-contracting the orders to his friend at a third company, in return for commission.

Corrupt practices pervade product quality inspections. Quality inspectors are routinely paid a month's wages or sufficiently "entertained" to pass an inspection that might otherwise fail, particularly on borderline cases. Indeed, dishonest quality inspectors are only too pleased to come across or *create* borderline quality issues. These problems are not so bad that passing them would later put themselves at high-risk, yet ambiguous enough to use as leverage to extort a *"red pocket"*[37] from a manufacturer facing penalties for late shipment.

Factories are required to pass a Factory Audit to manufacture and export to many of the major retailers. The auditors that conduct these factory audits can make it more difficult than necessary to pass the audit; that is, until adequate "encouragement" is provided. I am certainly not saying that all inspectors and auditors are dishonest, only that such practice regularly occurs. Inspection and auditing companies are in a constant battle to update their procedures and rotate staff to remain credible and continue to provide a quality service.

For our purposes, it is necessary to be aware that corruption is all-pervasive in China—from large sums of money changing hands on huge projects, to small-scale illicit endeavors at the lowest levels and smallest recesses within companies. It is often hard to detect and, for larger companies, harder to control. It is a constant preoccupation for both lower level and senior management who must remain constantly vigilant to winkle out corruption at all levels inside the organization. On one side they are tasked with running operations; on the other, they must know the right people, cultivate strategic relationships, and entertain officials to ensure operations run smoothly. The practice of making courtesy calls to officials to show respect, give face, and build relationships is a time consuming burden for management and constitutes a set of skills in its own right.

Economic Temptation

When I first arrived in China, one of earliest projects I worked on was to help design the layout for a new 3-storey 6,500 square meter factory in Guangdong province. After several weeks of study and numerous meetings with the various production managers, I presented what I thought was the most efficient factory and work-flow layout. The Chinese company president studied it carefully for a few minutes, looked up and remarked, "it looks very good, but there are two main doors." I raised my eyebrows and thought his was a strange observation, and replied: "Yes, this one is the entrance for raw materials, and that one is for the loading of finished goods into containers"—quite obvious I confidently thought to myself. However, what I hadn't considered and what the president was quick to point out, was that two entrances effectively doubled the liability for theft and made the disappearance of materials twice as hard to control.

This was one of my earliest lessons; indeed, the first paradigm shift. I thought the objective was to design the most efficient layout for workflow. However, the overriding principle for the Chinese, practical as ever, was security. Efficiency was a secondary consideration.

Theft is a constant pre-occupation for Chinese management. Having materials, components, and finished products stolen from the warehouse or production floor is only part of the problem. There is also the issue of disloyal staff taking ideas, designs, and products out of the factory and giving them to friends at other factories to copy. As you might imagine, this impacts the ability of Chinese companies to manage and control their customers' intellectual property rights, regardless of the good intentions of those who sign agreements at the corporate level. It is particularly easy to smuggle small products that fit easily into a pocket. I remember an instance, certainly not an isolated one in China, where a company known for its famous brand of pocketknife discovered its patented designs in the market before the company had even received their first shipment.

Job Hopping

With more than 1.3 billion people and more than twenty percent of the world's population living in China, it is easy to look at China as an almost endless source of cheap labor for production (or as one huge end market for consumers). However, such a simplistic view obscures the reality of the Chinese workforce and the difficulties companies face in recruiting and retaining suitable staff. Such large numbers obscure the fact that much of China's labor pool is mismatched with the requirements of the labor market. While sixty percent of China's 4.13 million university graduates were facing unemployment by the end of 2006, due to a mismatch between education and market demand for professionals,[38] there is a shortage of low-skilled workers in the southern industrialized areas, notably Guangdong. While in the early days of China's economic opening, industrial development was focused on China's southern coastal provinces, the recent boom has been China's northern cities, which means there is no longer much advantage or incentive for workers to travel south for wages. Subsequent labor shortages in Guangdong province have forced wages to be increased and conditions improved to attract and retain sufficient numbers of workers. While raising standards at factories in order to attract staff is clearly a benefit for workers on one hand, it creates continuous difficulties on the other for management whose goal is to maintain consistent and smooth operations. The problem has become especially acute in Guangdong in recent years just after Chinese New Year as significant numbers of migrant workers from China's North fail to return to work in the South after the holiday. It is not uncommon for a factory to lose 20% or more of its workforce during this period. For a factory with 1,000 workers, this means having to find, employ, and train 200 new workers each year, which is a significant operational upheaval.

There is also a severe shortage of management talent in China, particularly in the 45-65 year old age group—those whose education was interrupted during the Cultural Revolution. The educational experience of this age group typically comprised of communist indoctrination, work at an inefficient state-owned enterprise with no exposure to capitalist market principles, or working in the remote countryside alongside the peasants. In contrast, managers in their thirties have experience in the new market oriented economy and are in high demand for management positions. Due to the scarcity of senior management talent in China and competition between both Chinese companies and multinationals for such talent, many employers are utilizing younger staff and having to spend more time in guiding, training, and grooming them for positions of responsibility. The professionalism and supply of qualified managers is improving year by year with China's growth and developing a record of exposure to competitive markets, but demand still outstrips supply.

In the fast growing Chinese economy there is also a paradox emerging in relation to loyalty: due to the traditional Chinese propensity for developing relationships, loyalty within Chinese companies tends to be personal, and to direct supervisors rather than to the overall company, while workers tend to treat their colleagues almost as a second family. On the other hand, with the emerging opportunities in China, workers are beginning to take an opportunistic view of employment, and job-hopping is becoming more routine. Chinese workers are constantly screening the market for opportunities and are acutely aware of the going rates of comparative pay rates. If a factory down the road is offering slightly better pay, benefits, or conditions, workers will quickly change jobs. In order to attract good quality staff, companies must offer good opportunities for training, education, and professional development; yet the best and brightest are often the quickest to leave, lured by competitors and jumps in pay scale. Professional staff training has almost become a disadvantage, making capable employees bigger targets for competitors! The owner of one large Guangdong chemical factory made a significant investment in new machinery, then hand-picked a management team to be sent for special instruction to learn how to operate the specialized machinery. Two months after completing the training course the whole management team migrated to a competitor, leaving the factory without any skilled operators.

In the atmosphere of entrepreneurial zeal, workers are grabbing the new economic opportunities with both hands and causing a dilemma for Chinese employers. It is common for ambitious workers to learn as much as possible from their employer then, at the earliest opportunity, take the know-how, secrets, designs, price, and customer information to other companies, or launch their own enterprise nearby to compete directly with the former employer. With intimate knowledge of the former employer's business, the employee then sends email solicitations to their former employer's customers offering to undercut prices. It is an ever-present preoccupation of factory owners, verging at times on paranoia; when owners sense that an ambitious worker *might* be planning something of this nature, key information is withheld, responsibilities arbitrarily shared, or the person can simply find themselves re-assigned.

Human resource issues such as the hiring and retention of well trained staff have become one of the greatest challenges faced by fast growing Chinese companies, and non-compete agreements commonly used by Western corporations are tougher to enforce in China's legal environment. It certainly makes it harder to run an efficient organization under such conditions.

"Putting Out Fires"

The Chinese approach to everything is very practical. Instead of contingency planning and *proactively* teaching workers so they are prepared to deal with problems that may arise, the general approach is to deal with problems *as they arise*. A pragmatic deal-with-it-as-it-comes way of thinking pervades Chinese companies, reinforced by practically oriented managers that belonged to the "lost generation" who saw their education interrupted or aborted during the Cultural Revolution.

Instead of anticipation and prevention, problems are studied and solved as they emerge—a distinct "putting out fires" mentality. The Chinese way places an overriding emphasis on doing rather than thinking, planning, or organizing. Partly as a consequence of cheap labor, the general approach is to throw people at a job, instead of planning in advance the optimal way of performing it. With China's fast economic growth, another organizational problem emerges as the ad-hoc processes that worked well during the entrepreneurial start up phase of a company are no longer effectual when scaled in response to rapid growth. While truly efficient organizations think like big companies even when they are small by standardizing procedures even when not justified by volume, Chinese companies tend to expend no energy in standardizing any processes until the point where the present system is breaking down under the strain, and change is absolutely forced upon them.

In relation to projects, *potential* problems will rarely be examined when a project is initially received. Instead of sitting together with people from the relevant disciplines to brainstorm, study feasibility, consider potential scenarios, and pro-actively plan for contingencies, the Chinese will generally get straight on with the job and attempt to overcome problems when and if they occur. While the ideal may be to think twice, work once, there is more the tendency to work three times and hardly think at all!

It is useful to recognize this approach to work because it means you have to do more thinking yourself at the outset of a project, in conjunction with as much technical advice as is possible to obtain at this point. It is often necessary to ask the pertinent and fundamental questions yourself and become involved with guiding the project planning rather than handing the project over to the Chinese and expecting this will habitually be done. When a project has already traveled a significant way along the development process, it can often be too late to alter assumptions or re-evaluate critical elements. Even if fundamental changes are possible, time has inevitably been wasted.

A natural consequence of the "putting out fires" mentality is that problems get solved, yet their solutions do not get systematized. In highly efficient organizations, each time a new problem is encountered, a new training procedure is set up to share that information with others and incorporate the learning experience into new organization-wide procedures. Formalization of the learning curve in this way tends to prevent similar problems from occurring in future because either the new procedure stops the problem from occurring again or a solution is readily at hand the next time similar problems are encountered.

In the average small Chinese company, however, it is not uncommon to see the same problems occurring again and again. Indeed, if you ask the average Chinese worker to set up a system for which the benefits are not immediately apparent or quantifiable, it is rare that anything will be done because the worker just can't see the point of doing it. This helps explain why there are hundreds, if not thousands, of companies in each industry sector, yet only a very few go to the next level to become large, efficiently run operations with a thousand or more employees.

The average Chinese company either does not see the value in investing money in education and training, or is not willing to do so. When a new employee starts work, it is rare that he or she will be handed a company manual from which the new employee can understand the organizational structure, become familiar with the nature of the job and its responsibilities and learn about the company's customers and products. There usually isn't a manual! This is because everyone is too involved in doing the day-to-day work to think about streamlining the organization and putting all the useful information into a formalized training system. Each time a new person enters a company, he or she is given a desk or position, starts completely from scratch each time and generally has to teach himself! The philosophy seems to be that employees are paid money and are simply expected to work, not learn something about the company that would make their work more effective! As discussed previously, this is also partly due to the fear that once an employee has learned something, he becomes more valuable in the marketplace, which makes him more likely to leave to gain a better position elsewhere. The result is self-fulfilling inefficiency.

Management and cultural attitudes to work are also partly at fault. Whereas talent is valued in the West, hard work and long hours are valued in China. However, longer working hours do not necessarily translate into higher productivity. When employees are busily running around and have piles of work-in-progress on their desks, they look busy and managers are happy. If an employee is sitting around thinking how to plan and make operations more efficient in the future, the person doesn't *look* busy. In China, workers must be *seen* to be busy, fully-utilized assets; not engaged in inspirational strategic thinking whose results are not immediately quantifiable even though the result is increased efficiency in the long run. In Chinese companies, short term appearances are often valued more than long term contributions. This leads to the conclusion that while many Chinese operations give the appearance of a busy beehive, a more accurate analogy would be a busy warren of firefighters. It is certainly questionable whether all the activity is being directed in an organized and efficient manner!

Machinery and Technology

Due to lower labor costs, it often makes more economic sense to throw more people at a job, instead of upgrading machinery, equipment, and information technology systems. Many Chinese companies are therefore relatively low tech and unsophisticated when compared to equivalent companies in developed economies: materials are cut by hand instead of by automatic machinery, warehouse shelves are stocked by people climbing up ladders not by robots with the aid of bar-codes, stocktaking is performed manually by note-taking and ledger rather than software programs, and heavy items and cartons are carried fifty yards by hand instead of using conveyor belts or fork-lift trucks.

However, with rising labor costs and increasing competition, Chinese factories are increasingly being forced to focus on efficiency. Factories are seeking competitive advantage through new processes and it is beginning to make more economic sense to upgrade assets, modernize outdated equipment, and invest in higher end production technology. This change has been facilitated by joint ventures with foreign companies; China is increasingly importing machinery and equipment from US and European factories that are scaling back or ceasing production because they are no longer competitive with cheaper Chinese imports. The machinery and equipment is shipped to China and the training and expertise provided to the Chinese partner to operate the "new" equipment. Chinese factories then commence production on products that were previously made in the US or Europe, leaving the foreign partner to focus on marketing and sales, sometimes with limited residual production capacity to fulfill orders with a short lead time.

The same products are now made with the same machines but are now imported from China, causing low and semi-skilled redundancies in the West and facilitating China's march up the value chain. A recent and large scale example is the purchase of British company MG Rover by Chinese Nanjing Automobile (Group) Corporation.[39] The car production plant from Longbridge in England was shipped to China container by container. Machinery and equipment were loaded into no less than 4,500 containers and then re-assembled at the Chinese factory, overseen by British production technicians. This means that production engineers previously working in factories in Europe and the United States now find themselves jetted off to remote factories in the Chinese countryside to teach former competitors how to perform their jobs; the "jet-set" lifestyle is no longer the exclusive preserve of white-collar workers!

It is useful to bear in mind that while investment in computer technology and systems is growing rapidly, there are still some factories, companies and departments of companies that operate without computers, or with only limited computer support. Thus, processing orders and inter-departmental communication are still predominantly paper-based.

To do business successfully in China, we must appreciate that China is relatively lower tech. When operations in China appear inefficient at first glance, before condemning them, we must recognize there are often social, political, practical, or financial reasons for the apparent inefficiency. We need to appreciate that while a factory may have new machinery, the learning curve, skill, and expertise to use them at peak performance may not exist and is an ongoing process. While an office may have new computers and Internet access, due to unfamiliarity with the software or a lack of training and discipline in its use, it may sometimes be more effective to send a fax.

In conclusion, we would be wise to modify our conduct accordingly. If we are moving production from our own facility to China, we need to be aware that parts previously made by semi- and fully-automatic machinery may now be handmade in China. This may require design modifications and new quality control processes. For western companies, the latest generation of computer technology is taken for granted; however, if the Chinese company we are working with is not at the same level, we would do well to modify the manner of our communication so that it is compatible with the Chinese company's systems and operations. Consider the level of sophistication at the other end and build it into your procedures. We may have created beautifully complicated spreadsheets with specialized software, which (if able to be opened at all) may need to be broken down into basic drawings when they are received at the other end. If you know the factory is paper based and relies on sketches, why not start with faxed drawings instead of computer graphics files until such time as they are ready to upgrade?

It is advisable to be aware of the level of sophistication of the Chinese partner and modify communication so that it is in a compatible format. *The better we adjust our operations to complement the operations of our Chinese partner the fewer mistakes will occur and the fewer communication problems we will have.*

Power Shortages

Nearly all provinces in China are subject to power shortages. The unprecedented increase in economic activity demands more electricity than China's power infrastructure is able to supply. The result is power shortages, blackouts, and power rationing. There are two consequences for business people, particularly for buyers of manufactured goods.

First, power shortages result in higher unit costs. If a six-day week becomes a five or four-day week, the factory's fixed costs are absorbed by a lower number of units produced. Second, we must ascertain during the factory selection process the back-up power generating facilities and the number of hours these can keep production running when there is no power. Some provinces are affected more than others and this should also influence the location of our chosen production partner.

Operating in China's Dynamic Environment

With China's rapid integration into global markets, continuous technological innovation, the fast pace of economic growth, and with Chinese laws and administrative institutions racing to keep up with all these changes, China has become a difficult and uncertain regulatory environment for both foreign and Chinese companies to operate within. In China's fast moving economy, new laws and regulations can be released and go into effect within a month, which makes planning exceptionally difficult and stands in stark contrast with practice in the United States and Europe.[40] New business-related laws and regulations that are required for compliance with China's entry into the WTO have also placed a great strain on China's immature regulatory and legal system. In turn, China's legal system is responding to the requirements by creating a plethora of new laws, some of which are incomplete, contradictory, or vague and therefore lead to problems in their interpretation and implementation. In addition, new regulations can be interpreted differently by different government bodies in different provinces and between the national and local government level. Sometimes central and local level governments disagree on regulatory issues and it cannot be assumed that the central government can always override local government officials when regulations are vague or local government officials disagree.

In China, a flexible approach is often taken toward regulations and legislation. With new laws where consequences cannot be accurately predicted, it is commonplace for local government institutions to grant approval for operations and take a wait and see approach, judging the impact on business before deciding whether the new laws should be implemented or not. Sometimes laws are applied and tested at the local level before their adoption at the national level. It is not uncommon for laws to be implemented to give legitimacy to something that has already taken place, or for laws to be enacted retrospectively.

In summary, what this means for companies operating within this environment is a great deal of uncertainty as they try to adapt and respond to the changes and struggle through legal gray areas in their dealings with central, provincial, and local government agencies with contradictory interests. It also means that to comply with the rules or to get approvals to get things done can be a laborious process. When government regulations are vague and subject to discretion, good personal relations or *guanxi* with officials can speed up or ease the process, although this cannot be guaranteed. What could be relied upon six months ago might not be valid today. This uncertainty makes it difficult for Chinese companies to plan ahead with any degree of certainty and leads to a reactive and practical management style.

In addition to these bureaucratic challenges, Chinese companies are facing severe domestic competition together with unpredictable access to financing. If an industry sector or product line is successful, twenty other companies jump into the fray lured by actual or perceived success. China may be a "socialist" country but it is also one of the most competitive environments for companies in the world. In relation to financing, China's financial systems are not the transparent and efficiently operating systems that European and American companies are familiar with. Funding for private companies has been traditionally sporadic while funds allocated to state owned enterprises are often tied to compliance with changing policy initiatives. Stock markets have not proved an entirely reliable alternative to raise funds because of large scale government involvement and perceived price manipulation. The central government from time to time issues edicts for banks to reduce lending or changes the criteria for lending. It can be frustrating for companies that access to financing often does not coincide with the periods and timing of a company's need for capital. Some Chinese companies can gain access to global capital markets although this depends on whether this is "in favor" with Chinese government policy at the time. The situation is gradually changing with China's increased willingness to open the banking system to foreign involvement; however, there is a long way to go until banking and financing is in alignment with the needs of companies.

Responsibility and "Bu Zuo Bu Cuo"

While the Chinese generally are hard working, either through opportunity or ambition, constant supervision is a necessity. It is generally accepted wisdom that while the cat is away, the mice will relax. Especially Chinese mice. It is a familiar occurrence on a factory tour to walk into a room or production area and find a whole group of workers sleeping or lolling around pretending to be doing something, who all suddenly jump to action and appear busy for the duration of the visit. It is like a throwback to the days of the communist centrally planned economy where inefficient state-owned enterprises with lifetime employment and guaranteed benefit systems created workers with a sense of complacency and entitlement; workers who had jobs but nothing to do, viewed work with indifference, lacked motivation, and toiled under uninspiring managers.

In China, particularly at the unskilled and semi-skilled level, it is often difficult to find workers who are willing to accept real responsibility. There is an axiom in Chinese—*zuo duo chou duo, bu zuo mei chou*—which roughly translates as: "the more you do, the more mistakes you are likely to make and therefore if you don't do anything you can't make mistakes." The inherent logic is that you can't get in trouble for something you don't do, so it is best just not to do it at all! In a society where there is little kudos for success, and severe reprimand is inevitable for failure, the Chinese will hesitate with real fear of taking a wrong action or making a bad decision and being harshly (and publicly) punished for it. In group meetings, this translates into silence, which is considered safer: if you don't say anything you can't get chastised for it, so it is best to remain quiet. Further, speaking out at meetings, making suggestions, or voicing your own opinion is perceived as rude and disrespectful to superiors, and being the person to broach the subject of a problem is seen almost as an admission that the person addressed is partly to blame for it. Saying nothing, even though problems remain unaddressed and unsolved, preserves face and harmony.

This presents challenges for managers, raises questions about operational efficiency and, for a large organization, it can often be difficult to find a sufficient number of employees who are both willing and able to accept true responsibility for their functions, which makes the necessary delegation for a company to expand and evolve more difficult. Delegation for the MBA student of business management is detailing what needs to be done, explaining the project very carefully, making sure everything is understood, setting targets for completion, reviewing progress, and checking completion. Delegation in China is dumping the relevant paperwork onto someone else's desk with a brief explanation then completely forgetting it ever existed, as though it was of another time and space and disappeared down a black hole!

Further, it is not uncommon for a task or project to be given to someone who agrees to take full responsibility then proceeds to do nothing at all. For this reason, I have seen managers delegate the same job to three or four people in the hope that one of them actually does it! It is hoped that competition will stimulate the achievement of objectives, although the success of this approach is questionable. Once employees become familiar with this manner of delegation, they seem to be *less* motivated because there are always others who will pick up the pieces and blame!

Sometimes a fundamental sense of personal responsibility just doesn't seem to exist. It is common to call workers who then promise information before a certain time, or promise to call you back, or promise to give you a reply before the end of the day. However, come dinner time, everyone will disappear as though all responsibility and promises officially expire at six o'clock.

While at the ownership and senior management levels you will necessarily see people taking responsibility and volunteering for opportunities of advancement, the general workforce exhibits a conscious avoidance of new work and responsibility. If due to mind-numbing repetitive factory tasks, it is reasonably understandable. Sometimes it is due to poorly structured or implemented reward systems; however, logic is sometimes turned on its head in China: One factory owner related the story of how the workers in his factory, paid on a piecework basis, were doing such a good job he thought he would reward them by raising the piecework rate. He was surprised to find that performance actually fell significantly afterwards! It appeared that the workers were happy with their lot, so thought it perfectly acceptable to work less when they could get the same money for it. Issues of this nature plague and compound the difficulties faced by managers. The adaptation from a planned economy to a market economy is not in all cases a logical progression; it is hard to shake the traditional Chinese perception that bonuses are based on seniority or professional rating rather than on performance.

One thing is certain in Chinese culture: when there is a problem, everyone takes cover and no one is to be found. If they are found, there is always a creative excuse for why a job was not done, yet still there is the total absence of responsibility. If the going gets tough—for instance, you have an approaching deadline or a difficult ship date to meet—you may often find, as the pressure mounts, that instead of a spirit of "lets do whatever it takes to make things happen" or an "all hands on deck" attitude, you will begin to note the physical absence of employees. They will be distancing and disassociating themselves from the project so they don't get blamed if the worst happens (which is all the more likely because they are no longer there!). The Chinese worker prefers avoidance of potential failure than throwing themselves into a difficult situation and making it a success against the odds.

How can this knowledge translate into fine tuning our business strategy and improving our chances of success when working in China?

First, *if you want results, you must keep a constant eye on things, inspire, assign tasks, and continually monitor progress until completion.* It is not for the faint hearted. A successful project requires your energy behind it to keep things on track. If you take your eye off the ball and fail to keep up the pressure, the project will drift into oblivion and you will be left to pick up the pieces.

Second, it is necessary to judge when to exert pressure, and the level of pressure that is appropriate under the circumstances. Putting pressure on the Chinese is sometimes necessary to get a job done. However, used incorrectly or inappropriately, it can have the opposite effect, causing the employee to be off work the next day with sudden, feigned "illness". It is important to be familiar with the problem that the worker is faced with, what is possible under the circumstances, and what is under the workers control. If pressure is exerted on Chinese workers when a problem is not under their direct control, or they do not know where to look for a solution, a disappearing act is not uncommon.

Third, it is important to make sure all communication is clear, concise, and complete. Do not leave anything, even the smallest detail, open to interpretation. If you do, a common response is complete *inaction* while awaiting the missing details. This is classic work avoidance so don't assume you will be informed that details are missing. It is therefore your responsibility to make sure all information is complete. If any information is missing, whether vital or periphery to the task, just watch as new product development cycles turn from weeks into months and even years. For projects with fixed schedules or purchase orders with fixed delivery dates, this could be disastrous.

Another strategy for the average worker to avoid work and responsibility is to say that an idea or project is impossible. Sometimes when you approach Chinese workers with a new idea or an unfamiliar project, after just a cursory inspection, the response is a shake of the head and the response, "no, that's impossible." If something is "not possible" it means *there is no follow up work to do* (for this reason it is unusual to hear a response such as, "we will investigate the project and one way or another we will find a way to do it" because this means extra work for which there is no guarantee of results). Therefore, *when commencing projects with the Chinese, intimate product knowledge is a must so that you know, or have an informed idea, whether something is possible or not before you hand over a project.* Arrive prepared with viable suggestions to solve problems and overcome uncertain factors. It is necessary to be prepared to overcome a negative reception with reasoned analysis. As the reliability of information received from Chinese workers cannot be depended upon, buyers lacking the necessary product expertise are essentially unqualified to manage purchasing in China.

Related to the average worker's lack of desire to assume responsibility is that tasks are often seen as *isolated* and unrelated to subsequent or preceding tasks, meaning that the worker takes no responsibility for any other part of a continuing process. An example will more clearly illustrate the point: A metal worker was tasked with cutting large rolls of steel into specially shaped nine-inch lengths that would then form a component part to fit into the next stage of a product in a pre-defined position. After cutting more than 75% of the metal, the production manager just happened to pass by and noticed the material roll from which the metal was being cut had been placed into the cutting machine upside down. The result was that the wording, logo, and protruding parts that were supposed to fit the next piece of the product were out of line; the cut parts were therefore completely useless. The workers response? "It is not my responsibility to load the cutting machine. I just do the cutting!" It is also implied that a huge pile of scrap metal on the floor and the fact that there was, as a consequence, an insufficient inventory of steel remaining to complete the order on time was also not his responsibility.

The Chinese worker with no consideration to subsequent or previous parts of a process, treats his work as though it is isolated. It is rare for a worker to think beyond their assigned role or take a holistic view of operations. Considering what purpose his role plays and how it fits into the whole means assuming part-responsibility for it; whereas, remaining oblivious to the next task, previous task, and final product takes them out of the realm of responsibility. Such a perspective could partly be explained by the oppression of the Cultural Revolution where thinking itself was detrimental to health, often to life and limb.

This general mentality explains why pedestrians and cyclists on Chinese streets continue on their merry way, meandering in front of the other traffic and crossing the road without so much as a sideways glance. By looking sideways they must assume *responsibility* for the other traffic, and take evasive action; better just to put their head down and let the other traffic worry about them!

It is useful to look at the consequence of this lack of responsibility, and of treating work as though it is isolated, in relation to the sample development process and planned delivery dates. As information is exchanged and samples are developed, the Chinese merchandiser will focus on each step in isolation, and without any relation to the required delivery date of the order. If an error is made in relation to the sample, the merchandiser might, for instance, write to advise the customer that "the first sample was not correct so we are re-making it and will send another sample next week." It is unusual that the merchandiser will also advise you that "this will affect the delivery date, which will be a week later and therefore make it difficult for the planned delivery date to be met." When the former message is received relating only to the sample, the Western buyer is subconsciously thinking: "The sample is delayed and the merchandiser was good enough to advise me, which means everything is under control. He is aware of the delivery date, and will make sure that things remain on track to meet this delivery date." Next week, the Chinese merchandiser sends another message to explain that "we are still working on the sample but need more time to source an integral component." At no point does the merchandiser think to inform the buyer of the precise impact that this will have on the ultimate delivery date, as though these events are unrelated. The buyer often does not feel the need for concern because the merchandiser has kept him informed, understands the importance of the delivery schedule, and must therefore be assuming responsibility for it! However, shortly before the due delivery date, when the sample has finally been made and approved, the merchandiser will *then* send an email advising the buyer of a *significantly* later delivery date, as though it is of little significance to the customer. At this late stage, the buyer greets such unexpected news with shock, while the Chinese merchandiser considers it an obvious consequence. Such situations arise only partly as a result of poor planning, poor communication, or inexperience; fundamentally, they are the result of an isolated focus on the detail of each successive step, instead of a focus on each step relative to the overall task—that of completion of the order in accordance with the delivery schedule. *Western buyers must recognize this behavior and take responsibility themselves for calculating the impact and planning for the consequences of each event.* This is simply a matter of common sense. If there is any change or delay during the sample development process, it is logical that it is likely to impact the scheduled delivery date, and a buyer must plan and act accordingly. What is surprising is how often common sense goes out the window, and how often essentially unrealistic promises from Chinese manufacturers are accepted, even when they at odds with a buyer's better judgment.

The Chinese worker is also present-focused and does not seem to associate his actions with their consequences. We can again use a cycling analogy to illustrate how actions are isolated in time and space and how there is a general failure to make the causative link between actions and consequences. Suppose the cyclist is riding along with his head down, not looking left or right and he is hit by a car. The cyclist is likely to stagger home to his family and say: "Oh, bad luck today!"

If a worker does something wrong there is no point criticizing him for it as he will refuse to make the connection between what he did and the effect or outcome, literally as though once the task has been performed it ceases to exist in his consciousness. Making a mistake is not possible so your reproach will be greeted with confusion and the worker will become defensive. When dealing with Chinese workers therefore, it is better not to refer to the past or the future. Instead, frame things in reference to what they are doing right now. If they are part of a project, don't talk about how valuable their contribution is to the overall strategic goals of the organization, or how this product will improve the market share of the company in relation to competitors, or how pleased the customers will be when they get to use the product because it is meeting a need. Waste of time. Tell them instead how well they are performing their particular task. *Focus on what they are doing right now and what is right in front of them.* Nothing else is within the chosen range of perception or of much interest.

Again, it is important to recognize that not all Chinese workers are like this. There are many responsible, conscientious workers at staff and management level, yet it is necessary to recognize that this mentality exists and you must to be prepared to deal with it, limit its effects, and overcome it. It is dangerous to *assume* that everyone you give a project to will take full automatic responsibility for it. This should influence your working style: how you prepare projects, how you communicate them, and especially how you manage them (which are covered in more detail in Success Steps 7 and 8). While you are working with Chinese companies, and when Chinese workers are managing your projects, it is necessary to manage as though you are responsible for all their actions. After all, the responsibility for results is ultimately yours!

"Job Protection"

A common characteristic of Chinese companies is "job protection," although not job protection in the sense that we are familiar with. Job protection in China concerns employees keeping important information to themselves, particularly operational information, instead of teaching, delegating, or sharing that information to help and allow other people to perform the same tasks. It is as though sharing is perceived as creating competition and the behavior is in line with the Confucian bias against *horizontal* learning and sharing.

For example, if a senior merchandiser is given an assistant to share the workload and work as part of a team, instead of teaching the assistant all the relevant information he or she needs to perform his or her job to maximum effect, it is likely that the senior merchandiser will withhold vital information to ensure a state of dependency. This protects his position and ensures that job position is based on seniority rather than merit. I remember a marketing manager of a company in Guangzhou who was given three new marketing staff due to the sudden increase of sales. For a month, the new employees sat there with nothing to do because the manager wouldn't teach them, afraid that her "key" position was being eroded and her job was at risk from ambitious new staff!

This behavior ensures that the employee withholding key information remains necessary and vital to the company. It is a very primal method, borne of fear, to protect and justify their position because no one else in the organization has the necessary information to replace them or rise above them. Employees without the information must continually ask the person holding the information how to do their job. This "key" person is therefore always busy, which perpetuates his importance. Consequently, as the person is always busy through a failure to delegate, he has no time to think strategically or to implement any proper planning or training procedures. This is what is explained to the boss when the boss asks why everyone else is less effective! The situation is wholly self-reinforcing. The consequence of such failure to delegate is a stunting of the normal learning curve, leading to general inefficiency and retarded development of company procedures. The other repercussion is that when one of these "key" people leaves the company, the knowledge and information goes with him. If he did teach anyone, it was typically done informally so that no written procedures exist. It takes time to re-build the same body of knowledge and expertise.

"Creative Misinterpretation"

A trait that will be a source of bewilderment and mystification to anyone working in China is what I term "creative misinterpretation." It is when you hand over a project with specific instructions and the recipient at the factory does completely the opposite of what you have asked for, or changes things according to his own ideas.

I recall working on a project at the sample development phase. I sent the most recent sample back to the factory with the attached printed note: "material correct, color perfect, please modify size" and noted the new specifications. When the next sample arrived, the material and colors were completely different and there was no change in size. Polite enquiries as to why the sample department had not followed instructions were simply greeted with the reply: "We thought it would be better like this."

Another example: A large order for boys' sports bags in red color was placed with a factory. Production was almost complete when the cutting department realized there was insufficient material to complete the order quantity. So the cutting department manager looked in the warehouse in search of material that would enable the order to be completed. The closest he could find was a pink color. He wisely referred this to the factory manager, who thought it was the perfect solution and authorized the cutting department to complete the order for the boy's sports bags with the pink material. Unfortunately, I can't repeat the response from the importer.

In the words of a colleague, "the Chinese have a great way of giving you what they think you want and not what you've specifically asked for!" If sample development is left unsupervised, the colors and specifications chosen can at times resemble the sort of thing Aunt Maud gives you for your Birthday—presents for which we express thanks and subsequently wonder what we are going to do with! It is as though the worker sees your instructions as an opportunity or challenge to come up with something "better." We must bear in mind that products appealing to Chinese consumers (and workers) are different than those dictated by fashionable Western standards.

It can also be a case of *practicality* prevailing over the market, i.e. the result is what will be quickest and easiest for the factory to make rather than what the market wants. Such "creative misinterpretation" demonstrates a general lack of both experience with and exposure to customer-led markets. The Chinese worker generally fails to recognize that he is working for a client, in accordance to the client's specifications, that is in turn dictated to by the demands of the marketplace.

We must bear this in mind in both a strategic and operational sense. On a strategic level, it is not prudent at this point in China's economic integration to leave the function of design for global markets in the hands of Chinese companies that do not have the requisite insight. Therefore, a greater degree of guidance is necessary. In relation to operations and at the project level, it is important to make sure specifications are in an orderly, precise, structured, and easy-to-follow manner, ideally with illustrations. Make sure there are no "information gaps" that can be interpreted in an unexpected or undesirable way. If samples are going to be sent to you by courier, make sure you request digital pictures by email before samples are dispatched. Putting in this extra check will allow the more obvious deviations to be picked up and will save both time and expenses. Finally, though it can be exasperating at times, *don't look to logic to explain creative misinterpretation; accept that it is a characteristic part of the Chinese experience and allow longer lead times for projects.*

Management Selection

Following the discussion of some of the issues that face Chinese management thus far, in particular the issues of personal relations, corruption, and theft, we have some understanding of why China is such a complex environment in which to operate. Chinese managers must be adept at managing the effects of corruption in its various forms, and the ability to maintain close personal relationships with government officials is a key management responsibility in China. In sum, Chinese managers need improvisation skills and the ability to deal with challenges that are unique and with which Western managers are largely unfamiliar. Business schools might teach executives how to run a theoretical company; I don't yet know of one that addresses the gray areas that managers in China must deal with on a day to day basis.

Due to the complexity of managing an organization in China, management selection necessarily tends to be based on different criteria. Highly valued is trustworthiness, connections with the right people, familiarity with handling corruption in its various forms, the ability to develop loyalty and enforce discipline among the workforce, and the general ability to get things done. In conclusion, practical problem solving skills are rated higher than any inherent technical competence, theoretical knowledge or modern management expertise. Political skills are more highly prized than a manager's ability to optimize all processes of the company's value chain. The different selection criteria for Chinese management are borne of necessity and survival. For this reason, it is not uncommon to see employees chosen for export departments for their personal relations with customs officials instead of any knowledge of documentation, or to see family members or personal friends promoted to positions of responsibility based entirely on the issue of trust. Indeed, I know a trusted chauffeur without any operational knowledge who is director in charge of overall operations at a factory with more than 1,300 workers!

This leads to the conclusion that while management of Chinese companies may be strong in a practical sense, they often lack the education, organizational and strategic management skills normally required for professional, well-organized and efficient international companies. Organizational structure and delegation are often not at a level that allows companies to grow to their full potential. Chinese managers, particularly those at smaller companies, tend to be delegated to rather than being expected to make any strategic contribution. Problems get dealt with and sorted out, yet systems and procedures to ensure that similar problems will not occur again in the future often fail to be implemented. While the average American corporation has systems and procedures in place that act to mitigate the advantage or failure of individual managers, the absence of efficient systems in Chinese companies means that the personal and professional qualities of managers have a greater impact on operations.

In the West, jobs tend to be viewed as an income source where competence is exchanged for pay and an effort is made to keep business and personal lives to some degree separate. The Chinese tend to view their workplace as a second home and fellow workers as an extended family. Employees feel that once they are employed, even though they might not feel a high degree of loyalty to their company, they expect their company to take care of them, including the responsibility for their personal development. As personal relationships are central to the Chinese culture, the help of superiors is even expected in personal matters, such as assisting an employee's daughter or son to secure a place at a university. Correspondingly, managers tend to expect a greater *personal* level of loyalty and a deeper commitment and dedication from employees. Professional and personal lives are blurred in what might be termed *workplace-guanxi* and management is more personal in China. In China, people feel they are working for a person rather than a company and will work hard for a company only if they have a good personal relationship with their manager. This means that the style of management is different in China and that managers in Chinese companies are often chosen less for expertise and more for their personal qualities and ability to form a committed and loyal staff. It also means that the personality of the manager becomes the company culture and when a well liked manager leaves, he is often followed by a number of loyal staff and, as a result, entire departments must be rebuilt.

It is often the case that managers perpetuate and magnify inefficiency by creating their own fiefdoms of power within companies made up of friends and family members whom they can trust. Trusted colleagues and "yes" people are chosen above competence; the ability to get things done on a practical level is valued more than true leadership. The overall result is a complex structure of misaligned loyalties and power cliques within a company that distorts efficient operations. In addition, managers in China must not only make decisions by thinking solely of the company's interests but also the interests of all those with whom the company has *guanxi*—a far wider range of "stakeholders." The visiting buyer is greeted with the appearance of a company organized along efficient and professional lines although due to the informal, ambiguous relationships that exist, it is unclear where the real power or loyalties lie within the organizational structure. The scruffy driver that picks you up from the airport in an old beat-up white van could just be the chairman's brother!

Management Style

When you hear businessmen speaking of Chinese management style it is common to hear it referred to as "management around the kitchen table." Due to culture and issues of trust, and indeed because many of China's smaller manufacturing companies are family owned, it is customary for business to be discussed casually among family members and close friends. Decisions are made informally, without due consultative processes and without the benefit of high-tech strategic planning aids. While in more stable markets it is possible to outline a long term strategy, in the complicated and fast changing environment of China, meetings must continually be called to flexibly adjust plans to the situation.

For family-owned businesses, the owners then return to the companies to *impose* these decisions on the organization, leading to a management style that tends to be *dictatorial*. Middle level managers therefore have more the role of enforcers rather than being involved with policy making in any real sense; much like the armed forces, they are expected to unquestioningly and passively take orders from above. While by all outward appearances a Chinese company may appear to be organized like a traditional, multilevel, hierarchical structure, with owners, directors, senior managers, departmental managers and so on, in reality many smaller Chinese organizations operate as though they have only two levels—the owner, and everyone else. "Management by walking around" is taken to extremes by Chinese company owners, both out of the necessity to keep an eye on things, and due to the characteristic Chinese management style. There is a widespread practice of owners completely bypassing middle managers and giving orders directly to lower level staff. Staff will be told to do something or change something and their managers, who have the responsibility to the client, will be blissfully unaware of such orders. When these managers later ask why the workers are not doing as they are told, the staff simply retort that the manager's previous instructions have been superceded "on orders from the boss." This has the result of causing managers to lose face, acts as a disincentive, damages their authority and credibility, and leads to chaos. It also places the manager in a position where it is hard to give reliable information to the client. For instance, an account manager might check with the production manager concerning the progress of an order, and confirm a ship date to their customer based on this information. The boss then walks into the factory and re-arranges the production schedule according to his priorities. The account manager, who is in direct contact with the customer, is out of the loop and the customer is therefore the last to know that the shipment will be late. In the archetypical Chinese organization everyone is answerable to the boss and no one to the customer! In situations where you or your staff have given instructions to the account manager and these instructions have been overridden by their boss, you can speak as much as you like with your account manager although nothing will happen because no one can disregard the orders of the boss, regardless of whether it makes sound business sense, or if it keeps the customer happy. *With this in mind, the ability of foreign business people to get results often requires an understanding of the informal organization power structure, tactical thinking to navigate a way through it, and recognition that speaking directly with the boss is sometimes the only way to sort things out.* Consequently, the boss's time is spread even more thinly because each time customers have a problem that needs fixing they call the boss directly.

The key point to remember is that while a Chinese company may ostentatiously give the impression of a company with an organized hierarchical organizational structure, with clear responsibilities and well defined decision making power, actual decision making power—even for insignificant issues—often resides in just a few hands. The tendency to "micro-manage" by Chinese business owners leads to serious organizational inefficiencies because, as they remain involved in every decision as the company grows, their time and attention is stretched too thin. Further, as middle and lower managers are not groomed to be decision makers, the company's success relies on just one individual's perspective of the situation. The issue of succession should also be borne in mind. If the founder or owner of the company controls and micro-manages the operation, what will happen to the company when the helmsman is no longer around? The consequence is usually complete disarray within a very short time and therefore the age and health of founding Chinese business owners can be an issue of concern.

In China, a custom that I have often observed is the management use of public humiliation in response to a mistake. Like a throwback to communist party denunciations during the Cultural Revolution, it is when the owner or top management very publicly exposes lower management mistakes, demonstrating how stupid they are in front of an audience of their peers and subordinates. With professional management, when someone makes a mistake they will be summoned to the office of their superior where the problem is discreetly discussed, normally with a view to solving the problem rather than apportioning blame. Afterwards the employee may feel deflated, yet their credibility with subordinates usually remains intact, which allows them to continue to do their job. Public humiliation, however, seems to have an opposite and destabilizing effect. It appears designed to satisfy five purposes: First, it sends a clear message not to make the same mistake again. Second, it is a form of general education, sending a clear message to others not to make the same mistake. Third, it is a form of punishment. It is most Chinese people's worst fear to be humiliated in front of friends and colleagues. Fourth, it causes the person to lose self-esteem and therefore makes them more malleable and easy to control in the future. Fifth, it demonstrates the castigator's superiority and status as undisputed leader, much like the dominant male in wild animals living in packs, reinforcing the hierarchical relationship between ruler and ruled. Whatever the purpose, it certainly doesn't raise morale or rectify incompetence.

What it does achieve is to perpetuate a lack of staff involvement in decision making, stifles creativity, and fails to encourage responsibility (the person on the receiving end is less likely to take responsibility when failure could lead to public humiliation). It also results in reticence among staff, particularly when there are problems. *The Chinese worker will rarely be the first to advise you about problems* — it is best to ignore problems in the hope they are not discovered. If they are not discovered, there is a small chance that they won't get shouted at, or the loss of face is at least postponed. Top management can therefore be completely unaware when problems occur, or become aware much later. In an apparent contradiction, therefore, when problems are suspected it may sometimes be worthwhile to seek information from someone lower in the organization!

Summary

We should no longer be completely in the dark about what we are dealing with in the average Chinese company.[41] Above and beyond the standard business problems faced by managers in organizations worldwide, Chinese managers face a myriad of environmental complexities, cultural issues, and endemic organizational inefficiencies: power shortages due to economic growing pains, corruption, labor shortages, disloyal workers, workers that fail to return *en masse* after the Chinese New Year holiday, and so on.

In turn, management selection criteria and Chinese management style play no insignificant part by creating their own organizational inefficiencies and problems. Whereas the basis for Japan's "economic miracle" was largely due to its management techniques, which have been widely documented and studied by Western executives, Chinese management is one of China's weaknesses. Indeed, up until the late eighties, there were only state-owned enterprises. Modern companies are a relatively recent phenomenon.[42] In addition, many of the company owners and senior managers running Chinese companies today grew up through the Cultural Revolution and were thus part of a generation deprived of educational and professional opportunities to match their ambition. *We should bear in mind that these management problems are our problems, indirectly.*

After a brief look behind the scenes, it is possible to recognize the existence of a unique interplay between culture, economics, labor, management, even superstition. With this general background, understanding the average Chinese organization and the culture within which it operates, we can see why China has the potential to be a minefield. We can begin to understand likely causes for a container of inferior quality goods and why companies lose money in China.

It becomes apparent why a company owner in the West is out on the golf course while their Chinese counterpart is working long hours. It is not only that the Chinese place great value on hard work, sometimes to the point of endurance, it is a matter of necessity to be physically present to control and keep their eye on everything. While companies operating in more stable environments can run on autopilot with limited involvement at the executive level, firms in China need fully engaged leaders that are constantly on top of things. The complexity in China helps to explain why many Western companies who directly invest or attempt to set up their own manufacturing operations in China are prone to fail. Many of the issues are too intricate to be managed and controlled by Western educated executives.

The most important starting point for successfully dealing with Chinese companies is to acknowledge the additional complexity in China. *For those that recognize and face up to this complexity, China can be a major opportunity for competitive advantage; for those who don't, China will remain incomprehensible and unprofitable.* It is important to be familiar with the nature of the problems that exist "under the hood." Empathy can only improve the effectiveness of the management style we employ in China. Seeing things from the inside should help us to be more understanding and more prescient, rather than simply watching from the outside and wondering why things are not running smoothly. Our level of success will reflect our understanding.

It is equally important to recognize that working with Chinese companies or factories is not as simple as placing an order and forgetting about it until it is time for delivery. Part of the problems encountered by foreign business people is the consequence of uncertainty—not knowing the source of problems or what is going on around them. When we know the source we should be able to proceed with more certainty. When we understand the problems lurking behind the scenes we can modify the manner of our supervision accordingly.

In China, no news can often mean bad news. In China, you need to be more vigilant, more pro-active, more involved. We therefore need to take more responsibility for our own projects, put in checks and double-checks, and *never assume* that things are going to run smoothly.

It is true that the foreign business person has little or no influence over many of these problems unless cooperation is in the form of a joint venture over which we assume a degree of operational control. However, we are able to avoid some of the problems by changing the manner and quality of our communication; others we can avoid or influence through the more careful selection of our partners, which is the subject of the next section.

10
STEPS TO SUCCESS

SUCCESS
STEP 5

Choosing Strategic Partners and Suppliers

Choosing the right partners is crucial to success in any endeavor in China.

This statement cannot be underestimated. Working together with strategic Chinese partners is much like a marriage in that partners must be compatible and chosen with a view toward the long term. The choice between suppliers is not only the difference between a few minutes drive from the airport to reach one and a five hour drive to another. *It is also profoundly more than a one dollar difference in price, the singular yardstick used by many buyers to compare and evaluate suppliers.*

Support from the right supplier can mean the smooth flow of business, allowing your company to focus on sales and increase market share. The wrong supplier can mean endless difficulties, quality problems, and late shipments, all of which result in loss of market share (not to mention gray hair and sleepless nights!) There is a limit to the number of delays that are acceptable before your competitors have won the market or the market has moved on, and there are only a certain number of times your customers will accept late or poor quality shipments; in some industries it is only once. For smaller companies, there are only a certain number of late or poor quality shipments they can *afford*; for all companies, any inefficiency, hold-up or quality claim means you are operating at less than peak performance and therefore impacts profitability to some degree.

Many buyers tend to view Chinese suppliers and partners as entirely separate entities, not directly related to the core downstream operations of their company. However, it pays to view suppliers and partners as more integral to overall business operations; supply-side problems directly or indirectly affect the ability of a company to sell. When seasoned executives identify potential key strategic Chinese suppliers, it is not uncommon that they modify their product lines to coincide with products in which these strategic suppliers specialize. They understand that having a product line whose supply and quality is consistent is worth more than a unique product whose supply is a constant concern; how can you sell with confidence when your suppliers are not supporting you? Ultimately, it comes down to money. *Synergy and support from your partner means making money; an unsuitable partner means both loss of money and opportunities.*

It is therefore clear that the choice of suppliers and partners in China is of *strategic* relevance to operations; the choice of principal suppliers is a strategic decision. I am often surprised at the number of companies, small and large, that send out their purchasing staff to China, letting them loose to seek out new products and partners. Unfortunately, *product buyers in general tend to be too focused on individual purchasing decisions to recognize the strategic importance of the relationships they are creating.* Inexperienced buyers in particular seem to think the very nature of purchasing is to get as direct as possible to the source of the products, at the lowest possible price. Indeed, many buyers consider this their *only* objective, irrespective of other considerations. This is in contrast to a company's strategic priorities of first assessing the risk in dealing with a particular supplier and considering this in the context of the company's risk profile; second, ensuring a *consistent* supply of products at the right quality and at the lowest price *within these parameters.* Price should be a secondary consideration only after the supplier has satisfied the requirements of a more strategic nature, which are addressed in more detail below. There is little point having the world's lowest price if quality and consistency of supply cannot be guaranteed, or the inherent risk in relation to strategic objectives is too high. Key buying decisions should be made at the strategic management level or at least should receive the approval of strategic level managers.

The following discussion identifies some of the more important considerations when choosing suppliers and partners, setting parameters, and putting the selection of suppliers into a more strategic context, including what to look for to narrow your search, how to choose strategic suppliers and, more importantly, how *not* to choose suppliers.

Legal Jurisdiction

If you need to resort to legal means to resolve a problem, it is often too late for relationship building or problem circumvention, which should be the dominant focus for business people in China. Nonetheless, if China is a part of your strategy, a decision as to jurisdiction should go to the very heart of your choice of business partners.

Although the Chinese legal system is improving with increased integration into world markets and WTO membership, legal protection for companies buying from China is still quite thin on the ground, or a lengthy, complicated, bureaucratic process. If you order goods from China (without comprehensive quality control or advantageous payment terms) and the goods shipped are poor quality, in all likelihood, whether directly or indirectly, it will result in loss of money. It is wise therefore to make a conscious decision based on the size of your company and aversion to risk whether to work through a Hong Kong based[43] company with factories in China, a Hong Kong trading company or buying office, or to work directly with a company or factory in mainland China. As much of the communication is now by email, which renders geographical location irrelevant, the novice buyer often does not notice the difference or recognize the significance of such a seemingly innocuous decision. However, *it is important to recognize that the moment you step across the border into China, whether physically or through cyberspace, there are profound legal consequences and a fundamental impact on risk profile.*

Most notably, let us look at the legal consequences of the decision to work with a company on the mainland as opposed to a Hong Kong company. The Hong Kong legal system is based on the English common law system. Therefore, in the event something does go horribly wrong, there is recourse through an impartial and respected court system through which, depending on the facts, you may recover losses. The bureaucratic nature of China's legal system, on the other hand, is protracted, onerous, complicated, and the final result rarely makes the exercise seem worthwhile.

While this is obvious to most business people working in Asia, *the deceptive simplicity of moving from a Hong Kong company to a mainland manufacturer can obscure the important jurisdictional issues*; legal considerations need to be borne in mind. This is true for foreign executives who are completely new to China and those who have been dealing with China for many years. New buyers to China often don't consider the consequences since they are concerned only with products and competitive pricing, while buyers with years of experience sometimes become so comfortable with China and Hong Kong that they often make decisions about vendors without giving adequate consideration to such decisions and the potential impact on their companies. Decisions are often along the lines of, "shall I buy from Ching Yip Manufacturing at $14.00 or Wong Shing Manufacturing at $15.80?"

However, if we are to rightly consider the issue of jurisdiction, the decision should initially be: Shall I buy from Ching Yip Manufacturing (P.R.C.) or Wong Shing Manufacturing (H.K.) Ltd.? Price should be a secondary decision, subsequent and comparative to an overall assessment of both legal jurisdiction and risk aversion. Ultimately, this decision goes directly to your company's ability to absorb a financial loss in a worst case scenario. For a small company, one mistake in China without adequate legal protection could be the last. For companies that can bear the financial risk, a financial loss of one bad shipment can mean the loss of profit on the next five. Problems with Hong Kong companies can normally be resolved more expediently because they are aware of the legal contingency. *In China, quality problems often result in companies being drawn deeper and deeper into relations with less suitable factories in order to recoup losses through subsequent shipments.* Mainland Chinese companies are aware of the inefficiencies in the Chinese legal system (and foreign companies' aversion to legal recourse in China) and will play on it to their advantage.

I recall an incident that concerned a large German company that supplies products to one of Germany's famous car manufacturers. For a number of years, the orders had been supplied successfully by a Hong Kong vendor with a factory in China. Due to a small cost saving, the company decided to switch its purchasing directly to a mainland Chinese factory, with less than desirable consequences. More than 30% of the goods that arrived in Germany were rejected due to quality problems. When this was brought to the attention of the Chinese factory, the immediate response was "it is impossible because we only ship good quality!" This was followed shortly after with a communication that "this is not our responsibility," and later by a complete cessation of communication—the famous Chinese stonewall treatment. Subsequent attempts to recover the sizable costs and losses were futile. For a few cents saving per unit, they were left facing a total loss. As a consequence, the contract is again being fulfilled by the vendor in Hong Kong. It is fortunate on this occasion, notwithstanding the loss of reputation suffered with an important customer, that the German company was strong enough financially to absorb the loss on their balance sheet.

This is not an isolated example. Without correct supervision, there are numerous examples of companies that transfer money to

China and in return receive warehouses full of products that are not fit to sell. While it is getting easier to work directly with Chinese companies, we must recognize that working directly with China has attached risks. *It is useful to bear in mind that once you step across the border to work directly in China, you are automatically exchanging the fundamental protection of what is technically an English common law legal system in Hong Kong, for the "law of the jungle" in China where remedies are more difficult to pursue, the process more protracted, and outcomes highly uncertain.*

Hong Kong has historically been the stepping stone for doing business in China. However, due to the constant competitive necessity for seeking out lower prices, there is an obvious economic justification to bypass Hong Kong vendors in favor of the cheaper prices being quoted directly from mainland factories. This may be a suitable strategy for many companies, but it is not a suitable strategy for all; *such decisions should be the result of a proper operational risk-reward evaluation.* A proper analysis of risk would not only include the immediate contractual costs of a supply problem; it must take a more holistic view, taking into account the cash flow implications, disruption to operations, lost opportunity costs, potential loss of both reputation and clients. For a large company with full organizational resources to mitigate the associated risks, such as factory audit and quality inspection teams, working directly with mainland factories is more easily justifiable. If you are a small company with limited resources, the lower prices for working directly with Chinese manufacturers may not justify the additional *overall* risk.

For smaller companies, a proper risk-benefit analysis would often conclude that the risk of dealing directly with China is disproportionate to the rewards and not therefore the optimal course of action. Working directly with mainland factories may satisfy the perceived professional needs of buyers to work as directly as possible with the source of the product, yet if the inherent risks are not justifiable, they are proceeding in a manner that is detrimental to the overall interests of their company.

Whatever the jurisdiction, and bearing in mind that relationships with suppliers are of paramount importance, it is still necessary to have the legal side of transactions properly in place in the event that resorting to legal means becomes necessary. It is surprising how many business people neglect to do this properly in their haste to get projects underway, or perhaps due to the very loose relationship between purchasing and legal departments. It is advisable to ensure that contractual documents are properly drafted in advance of order placement. I have noticed that many companies allow their buyers to send orders informally, where the order details are contained within the body text of an email. The consequence of this is that the terms and conditions of the order are to all practical purposes governed by the Chinese supplier's standard sales contract, which becomes the operative document, and the product specifications (or lack of specifications) contained within it. These sales contracts typically do not contain clauses that are designed or sufficiently detailed to protect the purchaser.

If orders are expected to be placed regularly or by a number of different staff members of a purchasing department, it is recommended to draft a "Master Agreement" that contains all the most important terms and conditions that will govern the relationship and cover all subsequent orders placed on behalf of your company, and make sure this is signed before any individual orders are sent. This is all standard procedure for large corporations yet something often overlooked by smaller companies. Important terms relating to delivery deadlines, product quality and specifications should also be stated in a standard format on the Purchase Order, leaving no room for discretion for individual buyers tempted to sacrifice legal protection for speed. In addition, if trademarks, proprietary designs, or intellectual property are involved, these should be covered by separate contracts.

Trading Companies and Buying Offices

It is true that increasing global competition is dictating the demise of the general trading company, especially so in Hong Kong. Twenty years ago, Hong Kong served as the de facto stepping stone and intermediary for conducting business with mainland China when the mainland was a place where many buyers feared to tread. Hong Kong trading companies capitalized on their strategic location and made a lot of money during this time. Now that China has become more easily accessible, both physically and due to the widespread use of the Internet as a medium for business communication, the fate of Hong Kong companies providing only the sourcing, buying, and selling functions of the classic intermediary has effectively been sealed. Buyers perceive trading companies as generally obsolete and unnecessary when they can just as easily communicate directly with mainland factories. Purchasing managers consider trading companies as just another layer of fat between themselves and the source.

For the standard trading company that is not value-adding, this may be an accurate perception. Indeed, in China it can sometimes be hard to see the benefit that trading companies actually provide. Furthermore, especially at trade fairs, it can often be a challenge to determine whether a company is a factory or a trading company. This confusion is only helped by trading companies that take great pains to disguise their true nature for fear of being perceived as uncompetitive, and by small manufacturers that are so inexperienced with marketing that they could easily be mistaken for trading companies with their practice of dumping poorly related and assorted products on their shelves. In addition, some trading companies merely provide export licenses for small factories without the necessary licenses to export themselves. For a number of buyers, this confusion gives rise to a quest to cut through the jungle of trading companies to get to the treasure of hidden factories.

There are numerous buyers who consider it a measure of their ability and success, if not their mission, to cut out all intermediaries and work only directly with factories, without any consideration of the strategic role or added value that a good trading company or third party buying office could play. However, the decision of whether or not to use a trading company or buying office should be made as part of an overall corporate strategy, rather than a haphazard consequence of an inexperienced buyer's foray into the woods of Chinese commerce. While many buyers automatically consider trading companies as an unnecessary middleman and therefore an unnecessary cost, *the use of trading companies or buying offices can work out to be better overall value if considered in relation to the value and functions they provide when strategically integrated within overall operations.*

In response to an increasingly competitive marketplace and realizing that the days of the standard intermediary are gone, a growing number of trading companies, both in China and Hong Kong, are focusing on value added services to complement their trading activities and provide a competitive edge. In addition to their standard functions, such as product sourcing, consolidation of sample shipments, factory selection and audit, quality assurance, product inspections, and financing, some trading companies offer the higher value added services of design and product development, material and product testing, assembly and packing of products from various sources and locations, and warehousing with just-in-time shipments of increasingly smaller quantities to save warehousing and handling costs at the country of destination. There is also the issue of *guanxi*. Many buying offices or trading companies have long established relationships with factories that not only means smoother working relationships and the ability to secure better terms, but the ability to apply leverage through orders for their other customers to get better service in relation to your orders. Generally, the commission charged by trading companies and buying offices can range from 5 – 20% depending on the level and extent of services provided.

A decision whether or not to use a trading company or buying office should be the result of an informed strategic analysis rather than simply dismissing them as an unnecessary layer in the supply chain. Such an analysis should include these four issues: (1) a risk analysis on your company if dealing directly with a Chinese factory, (2) an overall cost-benefit analysis of the value-added services provided by the trading company, (3) how these value-added services fit into the overall corporate strategy, and (4) familiarity and expertise of the trading company with your particular product.

Different companies choose to follow different strategies. Some companies that prefer to focus their efforts on design, marketing, and sales use trading companies to manage the supply end of the business in China and will not consider working directly with a factory. This allows them to focus on their core strategic competence, while the margin earned by the trading company is offset partly by the trading company's expertise in sourcing products at lower cost and partly by the cost saving in salary, office, and travel expenses for not having to get involved with the "hands-on" management of production in China.

At the other extreme are companies that want to do everything themselves. Sometimes a low price, generic product strategy forces them to venture deep into China to secure the lowest possible cost structure, although one that also requires a high level of supervision. Other companies pursue a strategy that is a combination of both. For instance, they will work directly with their "key" partners —

companies that have met clearly defined criteria such as reliability and quality consistency — while second tier suppliers, due to concerns in relation to quality or reliability, will be managed through a trading company or buying office. Even though these suppliers are managed through a trading company or buying office, it is still possible for the company to maintain some level of communication directly with their suppliers. Third tier vendors may be wholly selected and managed through a trading company according to product and project requirements.

The key point is that the decision to deal directly with a factory or to work through a trading company or buying office is a strategic choice that should result from an informed analysis of your business needs. It should not be the result of random development or the sum of collective decisions by individual members of a buying team. It is necessary to consider what your business needs are and what value-added services a trading company can offer. What is of more value to your overall business — a ten percent lower buying price on one hand, or design capability, product sourcing, and quality guarantees on the other? How do the fixed costs associated with hiring your own staff and opening your own office in China compare to the variable costs of a buying commission from a trading company? How does the higher margin and service provided by a trading company compare to the efficiency, performance, hotel, travel, and opportunity costs of sending your own managers to China? What level of control over sourcing decisions are you willing to sacrifice by allowing a trading company to make these decisions? It is necessary to arrive at an optimal decision within the overall company strategy after considering both the tangible and intangible costs.

The individual buyer often focuses on the contribution made to profits by reductions in the unit purchasing cost alone, leading to an unbalanced preoccupation with price and a failure to acknowledge the strategic value and operational consistency that a trading company or buying office is able to provide for an extra margin. Remember, if the trading company is Hong Kong based, there is the additional safety of Hong Kong's legal system. Small companies in particular think they are saving money by working directly with factories, yet the cost of salaries, hotels, and travel are disproportionately higher when sourcing and controlling factories on their own.

Finding Factories

Finding factories in China is not difficult. The challenge is to find factories that are reliable and that provide a "fit" with your operations. Spending the time and effort to more carefully select reliable partners is an investment that pays off in the long term — just ask anyone who has lost money working with unsuitable factories in China! In China, with the emphasis on *guanxi,* connections, and introductions via intermediaries, bear in mind that it is often an expedient solution to locate suitable suppliers through existing suppliers or contacts. Upstream suppliers of raw materials are often a valuable source of information for downstream manufacturers of finished goods. For instance, if a relationship exists with a supplier of raw materials or components, it is often in their own interest to refer or recommend a manufacturer that is suitable for a project because the manufacturer is likely to order the raw materials from the supplier providing the recommendation.

Each time you place an order with a supplier you are making an investment in that supplier to deliver products on time and at the right quality, which allows you to fulfill the commitments you have with your customer at a profit. In addition, either you or members of your staff will be spending time in day-to-day communication with the supplier, and the efficiency of that communication has a direct impact on the cost and allocation of your company's human resources. Time must therefore be dedicated to the task. Some purchasing mangers work with the first factory they find, as if they were fortunate to find one at all. *In China, we must remember the buyer is not short of options, although the options vary wildly in terms of professionalism, expertise, and reliability.* In this section, we look at alternative means for sourcing and selecting suppliers.

The Internet

What I am about to say will not be good news for the new breed of computer-literate professional buyers who believe Chinese products and factories can be sourced exclusively via Internet, and communication performed solely by email. Sourcing factories and buying products in China is not like buying a CD from amazon.com. It cannot be done by the click of a mouse. *It is necessary to form personal relationships with key partners and become intimately familiar with their operations and capabilities.*

There are wildly different levels of professionalism, expertise, reliability and quality among Chinese factories that cannot be perceived from a computer screen thousands of kilometers away on the other side of the world. It is hard to believe that some business people place large orders with factories they have never seen, without any third party supervision in place.

The growing number of business-to-business websites devoted to sourcing products in China (see Appendix for some examples) has spawned a new generation of buyers who pride themselves in being able to do all their sourcing and buying from their desk. A word search on a product can result in tens, or hundreds, of Chinese factories advertising their ability to manufacture a certain product, and growing confidence with the Internet as a problem-solving tool misleads some buyers into believing that product and factory selection in China can also be performed through cyberspace. However, *it is important to appreciate that the internet can only serve as a starting point in an investigation.*

It is not only that the Chinese place considerable value on personal relationships that can't easily be built via broadband. The main problem with the Internet is that large factories and small factories, factories with expertise and small, inexperienced fly-by-night operations can, with a good web designer, all appear to be of similar expertise from only their web pages. With slick graphics, product pictures, and creative text, an enterprising Chinese worker who has just started a factory in his back yard with ten workers can look like a world expert. I know factories with small, dirty, disorganized operations with such well designed websites that lead the viewer to believe they are operating at an entirely superior level. I also know of some highly specialized, professional and experienced factories that supply some of the world's leading brands that have either no website at all, or a poorly designed and rarely updated website that does not do justice to the scope, size, or operations of the company. What the new generation of buyers doesn't fully appreciate is that they are judging the expertise of the web designer rather than distinguishing a factory that best fits their requirements. In addition, while it might be possible to get a general indication of efficiency and professionalism through a supplier's response time to email communication, such indications are superficial and mainly reflect the quality of an individual staff member at their office rather than a general ability of the factory to meet your delivery, quality, and other manufacturing requirements.

Unfortunately, there is no substitute for intimate knowledge of the operations of suppliers in China, or for building personal relations, building mutual trust and giving face to strategic partners by traveling to China for high level meetings.

Trade Fairs

China trade fairs are another useful starting point for sourcing products and factories. While there are new trade fairs springing up each year in cities all over China, the most famous fair in China is the Chinese Import and Export Commodities Fair (The Guangzhou Fair or Canton Fair).[44] The semi-annual Canton Fair, which takes place during 15-30th April and 15-30th October is the largest fair of its kind in the whole of China with companies from provinces all over China exhibiting their products. The 100th session of the Canton Fair in October 2006 boasted 14,000 exhibitors in a net exhibition area of 282,000 square meters, and more than 190,000 visitors. It is one of the best opportunities for foreign business people to get an overview of what Chinese manufacturers are capable of. However, while it is an excellent opportunity for buyers to meet potential suppliers, it can also be a veritable bazaar of business hazards.

The best advice is not to assume what you see is what you get. Many business people visiting the Guangzhou Fair for the first time act like children in a candy store; for the first time they get to see where products on brightly lit store shelves in US or European shopping malls are coming from, and the prices that are being paid. Unfortunately, many then proceed to act as though they are still in a big US or European shopping mall and conduct their purchasing accordingly. The new buyer would do well to think of Chinese trade fairs as though the aisles and booths are the set of a Hollywood western—façades of wooden buildings, shops and saloons although you can never be entirely sure if there is anything of substance behind them!

The danger for new buyers is that such ease of access to Chinese manufacturers and the ability to buy such a wide range of products in one place makes buying from China appear deceptively simple. At trade fairs you will have access to some of the most professional, experienced, specialized, reliable producers in China.

Yet these excellent Chinese companies are exhibiting alongside less experienced and less reliable companies. Those inexperienced suppliers will one day become experienced suppliers; *however, the question is whether they will be practicing on your orders, or the orders of your competitors!* There will undoubtedly be experienced companies able to manufacture your product with little supervision required, and there will be companies able to perform only with a high level of supervision and assistance. The key is to determine which are which.

So what are the complications? First of all, the buyer should be careful with the integrity of information received. As with any country, it is possible to encounter people that are less scrupulous with the information they are providing, particularly when a factory is aggressively pursuing new customers. Chinese exhibitors desiring to bring in a new customer can sometimes be quite economical or selective with the truth. It is often necessary to investigate further and judge for yourself the accuracy of some of the things that are said in relation to the nature of their business, expertise, and pricing. For example, you may be talking with a trading company or an import-export company whose manager will quite openly tell you they are the owner and operator of a factory. When asking a factory owner whether they have the expertise to fabricate a certain new product, the answer is invariably "no problem," when in fact they have no experience in such products and just hope to be able to sort it out later. The buyer, in an effort to have an indication of a supplier's expertise or the quality level of a factory's production, may ask whether the factory manufactures for famous Brand X. The reply, "yes we are working with them" is designed to instill confidence, yet it could mean the factory once made a sample for Brand X five years ago and never heard back from them again.

With regard to price, prices are often quoted at trade fairs to get buyers sufficiently interested to visit their factory or to place an order. These can sometimes bear no relation to reality. The Chinese salesman can be seen studying a potential customer's expression to see what answer he thinks the customer wants to hear, and changing the answer until he hits the "right" one. When the customer gets to the factory, or is ready to confirm the order, it is possible the price has changed or materials will need to be substituted to meet the fanciful prices quoted, now that the factory staff have had sufficient time to study costs. The buyer must share responsibility for such antics by expecting exhibitors to be able to quote accurately in the surroundings of a trade fair, without ready access to their production departments.

It sometimes pays to test the integrity of potential partners with information about which you are already well-informed, though keeping your conclusions to yourself. If you catch someone telling an obvious lie, it serves no purpose to directly confront them other than causing them loss of face. Bear in mind that replies may be improvised rather than based on fact and that some of the staff at the booths are local university students hired for the duration of the fair who are therefore not overly familiar with the exhibitor's operations and will not be around to follow up your enquiries.

In conclusion, it is necessary to be more observant and exercise considerably higher caution with respect to information received at Chinese trade fairs. A naïve buyer could find himself in all kinds of undesired situations by relying on all information received as fact. Ideal choices of partner are not based on false assumptions and erroneous information so become used to double-checking and verifying information.

It should be noted that not all the companies exhibiting at fairs are manufacturers. Trade fairs comprise an assortment of manufacturers, traders, and import-export companies.[45] It is often difficult to tell them apart by the appearance of the booth, and trading companies often do their best to obscure the true nature of their business. As booths can be relatively expensive for smaller companies, it is also common practice for two or more factories to share a booth, which then gives the appearance of a trading company selling unconnected product groups. Another idiosyncrasy of Chinese trade fairs is the manner in which booths are allocated, which is often not the most transparent method and can lead to additional confusion. Booths are allocated to companies, and whether permitted in the rules or not, use of the booth is transferred to another company and in some cases transferred yet again. This explains why the signage of a booth can read, for instance, "Beijing Petrochemical Products," although the products exhibited can be anything from bamboo, to bags or pottery. The Canton Fair's new exhibition centre at the Pazhou Complex has benefited from better organization and this situation is gradually improving.

Visitors should not be surprised if some exhibitors do not have a brochure or a price list, or anything at all that you are able to take away for later reference. Furthermore, no photographs are allowed. The potential buyer may wonder how a Chinese company is trying to develop new business yet seems unwilling to provide any marketing materials. It may be that with the fast pace of China's economic transition, some companies are just not familiar with the concept of marketing. Many Chinese companies still approach sales with an order-taking mentality. Alternatively, it may be due to lack of proper planning or procedures. Instead of preparing a price list, some exhibitors stand there with calculator in hand, calculating prices each time there is an interested party. There is also the issue of copying. Copying is so rife in China that exhibitors often do not display the new designs either for fear they will be copied by other factories, or because of paranoia as their trust has been abused in the past by foreign buyers that have taken the exhibitor's new designs and samples directly to their *preferred* suppliers to copy or place orders. For this reason, Chinese trade fairs tend not to be the best places to see the latest design innovations.[46] To see a factory's latest products and designs, it is necessary to develop a degree of mutual trust and typically arrange meetings outside the trade fair, at their office or factory.

A good strategy to employ at Chinese trade fairs is to walk fairs once very rapidly, taking notes of the exhibitors that are of most interest, and making a schedule to return to these later on. This ensures that there is time for in-depth discussions with the exhibitors that are of most strategic interest. This disciplined approach also avoids spending too much time with suppliers that *may* be of potential interest, only to come across more suitable partners late in the day when they are packing up and are less disposed to entertain you. It is also useful for the visitor to have two separate business cards with two different e-mail addresses, one for handing out to companies you want to hear from or work with immediately after the fair; the other for those whose priority is less time sensitive and which should therefore be kept separate and directed to another account. This avoids the need to sort out a deluge of emails immediately after the fair to find those of most importance.

When seeking partners in China, ideally you are looking for specialists in your field and normally these are exhibitors whose booths are filled exclusively with the product category you are looking for, as opposed to displaying assortments of different product types. The fact is, in China it is sometimes hard to tell which factories are specialists and for this reason, *it pays to spend more time finding out information about the company and operations rather than focusing excessively on products.* As the latest designs are often not displayed, it is important to view the products on display as an indication of capability or potential, rather than as an exhaustive reference. Although not conclusive, check for factory pictures and additional factory information; make a note of the size of the company, number of years in operation, export markets supplied, existing customer base, and product *expertise* (which may not be apparent from the products presented). No one wants to spend all day driving to a factory that he immediately realizes is unsuitable upon arrival when more effort could have been spent confirming relevant details beforehand.

It is also important to note a company's location and the location of its factories, if different. Trade fair booths are not always organized by region and therefore factories from Shangdong, Guangdong, Shanghai, Qingdao, Harbin or Yangjiang can be exhibiting in neighboring booths. As a consequence, some buyers fail to pay sufficient attention to location and its important practical and strategic considerations. While two factories from two totally disparate regions of China may be exhibiting identical products on two adjacent booths at the fair, the consequences for your company will be significantly different. Buying from different provinces of China is not the same as buying from different states in the US where there exists homogenous transportation networks, operational environments, and infrastructure. China is not only a vast country, the varying degrees of development and infrastructure can have a significant impact on logistics and operations. A Shenzhen factory is within minutes of a large, efficient shipping port. A factory located in an inland or a western Chinese province may have additional difficulties ranging from adverse weather conditions to logistical difficulties transporting finished goods to port and longer intervals between sailing schedules. Different provinces suffer power shortages to a greater or lesser degree, a factor that interferes with production and can therefore result in delayed shipments. If you are buying on behalf of a small company, where consolidation of shipments is an issue, it may not help to be buying from both Shenzhen and Shanghai. It is more cost-effective to ship FCL[47] from one port than LCL[48] shipments from several distant ports. If your company is performing factory certification and quality control itself, traveling to Dongguan may be quicker and cheaper than traveling to Xiamen. If you are using a third party company for quality inspections, it pays to consider whether the company has an office and qualified staff in that area of China.

It is also useful that buyers have a general awareness of which provinces or areas are known to specialize in certain product types. Pens and small plastic products, for instance, appear to be the proficiency of factories in the Ningbo area. Shanghai and Yangjiang are known for metal products such as knives, Guangdong province is proficient in the manufacture of Christmas decorations and toys, while shoes are the expertise of Dongguan, Wenzhou, and Jinjiang. Yiwu, in Zhejiang Province, is known for its small commodities markets where buyers are able to purchase small order quantities and, for products that are stocked, arrange consolidated shipments within days. Such information is useful because local infrastructure is often geared toward the product type, and component suppliers are typically located nearby meaning easier availability of materials and spare parts for manufacturers.

Rising salaries in the industrial coastal areas of China have been the impetus for buyers to look farther inland for suppliers. The Chinese government has encouraged this process with its "Develop the West" campaign that seeks to expand the economic boom into the interior. However, pushing out the "frontiers" into China's backyard comes with additional risk; factories in the less developed areas of China not only require longer travel times, but also typically require a higher level of supervision than factories located in the industrial coastal areas that are already decades along the learning curve.

For purposes of planning a future visit to the factory, make sure you get *specific* details about the location. How would you travel to the factory and how many hours will it require with and without traffic congestion? This is one way to get around excessively optimistic responses that can ruin carefully planned schedules. Business travelers to China often schedule three or four factory visits in a day, then due to traffic or underestimation of distances only manage to get to two, which sends a message to the others that they are less important and causes loss of face to the management waiting at the other factories.

As you are walking around the fair it is important to be aware of these geographical considerations. Purchasing needs to be coordinated, taking into account the overall strategic impact on your company and the operational impact on logistics. For selection of key strategic partners, trade fairs are just a starting point. It is vitally important to visit the factories of strategic partners to develop the necessary personal relationships and become familiar with their operations and production capabilities, even if a trading company or third party is responsible for sourcing and factory selection.

The Factory Visit

It has been noted that trade fairs and the Internet are just starting points in the selection of partners. Notwithstanding that a factory visit is a relationship building exercise in its own right, the buyer must also be satisfied that a factory is both a *suitable and capable* choice before committing important orders.

I have known a number of buyers who have been buying a particular product from a particular factory for some time and, while they have been generally satisfied with the quality, when they finally make the effort to visit the factory it transpires that the product they are buying is almost a side-line business for the factory rather than its core competence. This is a common occurrence in China when buyers place orders with companies without taking the trouble to visit the factory that is actually manufacturing the products. While this might not have a major bearing on operations in the short-term, in the long-term it is typically best to order products from manufacturers for which those products are the manufacturers core competence; if problems are encountered, they are solved more easily by manufacturers with experience and longer learning curves. In addition, manufacturers producing products that are not their core competence are less motivated to solve technical or other problems for periphery products that are not contributing the bulk of their revenue.

In China, it is important to find a company or factory that is specialized and experienced precisely in the type of work you need doing. *The further you stray from this principle the more risks you take.*

It is not only an issue of checking that facilities are in line with your company policies but also that the factory has the capacity and expertise to do the job. It is also important to make sure the management is not "gambling" with your orders.

The Chinese seem to have a cultural propensity to gamble. If anyone doubts this, they need only to visit the horse races in Hong Kong, which have the highest per capita betting in the world. Total wagers on race day routinely exceeds $US150,000,000—often higher than an entire year's betting on many American or European racetracks. Or look no farther than the casinos of Macau, where turnover has surpassed that of Atlantic City and Las Vegas.

There are times when this gambling mentality spills over into the sphere of Chinese business practices, and we must keep a watchful eye in relation to the Chinese companies that we select to become partners. Broadly speaking, the Chinese have three philosophies toward business: low-risk, medium-risk, and high-risk. It is important to recognize the behaviors associated with each so that an informed decision can be made with regard to the degree of risk we are willing to assume on behalf of our company, so that the approach taken toward a working relationship with the supplier is appropriate to circumstances.

The "low-risk" philosophy is associated with companies that are diligent, efficient, professional, and ethical. These companies know their business and run their business with the intention of building a successful long-term operation. They will only accept projects and orders that fit with their core competence and will tell you honestly whether your requirements fit within their competence. If not, they will advise you that their factory is not the most suitable and sometimes recommend another company.

"Medium-risk" companies are those that understand what a project, venture, or order entails; they believe they have the organizational capability to do the job; and they are willing to do it, although they are still on the learning curve and may need your help. Working with this type of company may require a higher level of involvement, supervision, or some deeper level of commitment involving training and education.

High risk companies are those that will accept a project or jump into a venture without knowing or fully understanding what is involved, or even whether they are actually capable of doing it, routinely accepting projects that are not within their core competence. They will take a chance if the rewards are great, or if they believe that your guidance will take their company to a higher level or into a new area of business with which they were previously unfamiliar. *These are the Chinese companies that will happily "gamble" with your orders.*

Time and again, I have seen orders placed with Chinese companies whose management have a gambling mentality and are eager to do business. The buyer hears the words, "no problem, we can do this for you," then the factory spends month after month making samples that are never quite right until finally they admit defeat. By this point, it has cost the buyer valuable time that could have been spent with a more specialized supplier, by which time the project would have been completed. Recognize that the gambling mentality exists at some Chinese companies and *having the discipline to cut losses at the earliest possible stage* will save a lot of frustration and money in China. Visiting the factory and determining for yourself the particular expertise of the company is the best way to look after your own interests and nothing short of a complete operational familiarity will suffice.

It is standard practice for your Chinese host to guide you around the parts he wants you to see, tell you what he wants you to hear, linger in areas he wishes to emphasize, and avoid those that he does not. While bearing in mind that a factory visit is a relationship-building exercise, it is important to remain focused enough to obtain sufficient information to enable an informed decision as to whether the factory is suitable and capable. It is recommended that a factory be investigated and evaluated in relation to 8 areas:

1. General factory standard and capacity
2. Management expertise and professionalism
3. Current customer base
4. Strategic matching
5. Product expertise
6. Procedures and systems
7. Quality control
8. Respect for intellectual property.

1. General factory standard and capacity

Before proceeding to checking whether the factory is up to standard in relation to products and processes, some fundamental issues need to be addressed. A buyer must be satisfied that the general operational standards and working conditions are compliant with the requirements of his company or those required by his company's customers. A good place to start is with factory certification. The most basic benchmark is certification such as ISO9000[49] or industry-specific documentation that will provide a general insight into operational standards. Then there are the "social compliance" or factory audits that are used by well-known companies, major retailers, and famous brands because they can't afford the resulting bad publicity if the factories they are using are found to have poor working conditions and standards. For instance, check to see if the factory is approved for production and shipping to any major brands or retailers such as Wal-Mart, Nike, or Disney. Each of these companies has their own rigorous factory auditing processes (which are discussed in more detail toward the end of this section). Check the date of the *latest* certification and the certification level. So that valuable time is not wasted on site during a visit to a factory, this documentation can be requested and checked prior to the visit; if the certification level is good, factory managers are normally willing to share this information. If the factory you plan to visit has not been certified and requires auditing by your company before orders can be placed, it is often good procedure to bring the documented requirements of the audit with you and bear these requirements in mind as you walk around. What changes would be needed to comply and how much effort would be involved to make these changes?

A fundamental question is whether the factory has sufficient capacity to comfortably service your level of business. I have seen large orders given to surprisingly small Chinese operations that have just been unable to produce the volume within the time frame needed—something that could easily have been verified beforehand. Therefore, make a note of pertinent details such as the number of workers and the output in units per day, week, and month. Make a note as to what capacity the factory is now operating and what capacity the factory expects to be operating at in future months. Check if the area or province is subject to electricity cuts or power disruptions and whether the factory has its own power generator (make sure you see the power source yourself). How long can the factory generate power to maintain production without public supply?

An issue related to factory size and capacity is the widespread practice of sub-contracting. If your orders are of little interest to the factory, if your orders are likely to be too large for the factory to handle, or if the factory is at full capacity, it is common for orders or component parts of orders to be sub-contracted to another factory without your knowledge. Materials will be delivered to another factory, or factories, and these factories will produce and deliver the goods to the factory to which you initially placed the order for final shipment. This means that while you may have spent time approving a factory that meets both social compliance and quality standards, the production is done in another factory that may or may not be of a similar standard or able to produce to the same quality level, and over which you exert no control. The practice of sub-contracting in China is a difficult issue both to discover and to control, without a high level of constant supervision.

Finally, many companies make a point of checking the financial health of Chinese companies before proceeding with any business relationship. Access to a full set of financial records of a potential partner is particularly important when large projects are involved. While several financial service companies can provide this type of information, it is often difficult to get completely reliable information in China, which has one of the least transparent financial systems of the world's major economies. It may not be possible at all for smaller, privately owned companies and therefore spending more time getting to know potential partners probably serves as the best due diligence possible under these circumstances.

2. Management expertise and professionalism

Spend time with management and ask searching questions. It is good to know the education and background of both owners and management. Provided the questions are asked sincerely and informally they will not be considered rude; in fact, the hosts will generally be flattered at your interest. A good approach is to start with questions about family—it is common for Chinese people to talk about family when they first meet—then move on to education and background.

As you spend time with management, observe how they interact with others in the organization. Do they command respect or are workers loyal through fear? Observance of such details will provide an indication of management style and professionalism. Does the senior management involve other key staff in meetings and discussions? Do they take time to translate or explain discussions to other managers? Who takes notes at meetings (does anyone take notes!), a merchandiser, customer account manager, the senior manager, or the president? (If the president or most senior person present is taking the majority of notes, this often signifies poor delegation and organization).

Ask about how the organization is structured and how each separate department is managed. It is worth noting whether the company President has surrounded himself with the best and brightest industry talent, or with "yes-men" who seem only to be fulfilling the role of enforcing discipline rather than making a meaningful contribution to effective organization or leadership.

3. Current customer base

For an indication of the quality level of which the factory is capable, ask for information about the current client base: which customers is the company currently and actively manufacturing for? This means *on-hand* orders. As previously mentioned, it is sometimes heard in China that a factory is "working with" a certain famous brand or company and sometimes you see dusty samples in the showroom with famous brand labels, yet this does not mean they are currently working with these companies in the sense that the factory is a regular or valued supplier. It is possible that the factory has produced one small order or made a few samples without any resulting order. *The most reliable indication is to take a look in the finished goods storage area and note the names of customers on the export cartons.*

It is also useful to understand to which markets a factory is exporting. Depending on the nature of the product, this can give clues as to quality and expertise, as well as an indication as to familiarity with the specifications of producing and shipping products for your market.

On a strategic level, what customers or brands is the factory producing for that might potentially be a conflict of interest for them or a strategic liability for you? The factory could be supplying your two closest competitors while you may not be aware of it. Is the company working with a competitor who may not be too pleased that you have discovered their vendor and which might lead to pressure on the factory to cease business with your company? Is it in your best interests to have the confidentially of next year's new designs in the hands of a Chinese vendor who also deals with your competition? If a factory is intended to be a strategic partner and you are competing directly against another of their customers for a particular order, your company might find itself in the position where the Chinese factory has the upper hand over pricing, being able indirectly to influence who succeeds to get the order.

Chinese managers understand these concerns. I have often witnessed factories halting production of one brand and removing any trace of it from the production floor on the day of a competitor visit. This is a tricky situation where reliable information may be hard to get if the Chinese company is privately owned. I have found that one of the best sources for information is factory employees at staff level, rather than management level. As you are walking around the factory, if you are friendly with workers they will often supply you with blatantly honest information because they have not been indoctrinated with the desired public relations responses.

4. Strategic matching

Sourcing in China is not so much about "buying" or "selling." *It is more a question of matching. It is imperative for long-term success that your strategy fits with the strategic goals of the factory, in the absence of any conflicts of interest.* Working with a Chinese vendor is slightly more complex than one would first imagine. Don't make the mistake of assuming that because you are the buyer and they are the seller they are automatically motivated to do business with you. Likewise, if you demonstrate inexperience or a lack of professionalism, you might find you are not taken seriously. In addition, the typically Western assumption that "the customer is king" does not always hold true in China. In fact, there are many influences that dictate the level of interest you receive or the service you might expect.

The most obvious influence is potential revenue. If you are a relatively small player in the market, depending on the factory's existing client base and in the absence of additional value that you may add to the Chinese operation (such as a particular expertise or unique products that the factory might offer to their other customers), there may be little interest in dealing with you. If your company is able to place orders of a size that could potentially interest the Chinese factory, yet the factory is already cooperating with the main players in your market (you may or may not be able to discover this), then again, your business might not be of much interest. Coming from a service-based market and without the benefit of complete information on the Chinese supplier and their aims, you might find it rude that a Chinese factory shows little interest in the potential business you are offering. However, before jumping to conclusions, *try to understand it from the perspective of the factory*. It is often the case that Chinese and Western companies have different agendas or definitions of success. A Western company might be seeking the introduction of automated equipment and a compact workforce to produce high quality, high margin products; the Chinese factory might be trying to gain face with government officials by creating as many jobs as possible in the local area. Some factories are not just seeking orders *per se,* they are seeking continuity of production, and in many cases this is only provided with regular large volume orders. Therefore, if the factory is big and your potential orders are small, it is unlikely your orders will be a priority. Getting straight to the point, if you are XYZ Limited don't expect Wal-Mart treatment.

Even for big companies with large potential order volumes, it is not as straightforward as one might expect. If the factory believes you are "shopping around" China for the lowest possible price and know they will be squeezed on price to the point where profit is marginal, the Chinese will quickly understand there is a small possibility of loyalty or profitability and their actions will reflect this by showing little interest in large orders.[50] The key question to ask when seeking potential Chinese partners is whether you would prefer to be a "big fish" for a small factory, or a "small potato" for a big factory? Size relativity of respective companies certainly influences the level of service you receive in China. In sum, the ideal is not only to deal with a company that is capable, but to deal with one that appreciates your orders and makes your orders a priority.

The second influence is the type of the work. If, for example, the products and nature of orders you are offering a factory are potentially more profitable, yet the factory needs to invest in or upgrade equipment and processes to meet your requirements, the management may be reluctant to work with you. If the product you make is complicated while their existing product range is simple, then again, the orders may not be of interest. Likewise, if your product is high value and entails small production runs, while the factory is geared for low margin and high volume, it is important to recognize that the factory may not be for you. I recall a small factory that was approached by a well-known brand with a view toward forming a partnership and expanding a new line of products. The project required the factory both to increase its output and improve its quality control systems in order to upgrade the level of products supplied and would earn the manufacturer higher margins. The well-known brand was even willing to invest money in training and new processes. The factory owner did not show the slightest interest. Despite the potential for growth, he was happier to keep the factory at its current size and basic quality level, having no desire to change or to have additional work. Sometimes, the achievement of a reasonable level of success in China is treated as a signal to relax. We should be aware that decision making in China does not always conform to business logic and can be unpredictable.

The third influence is the factory's strategic objective. For instance, if you are a European company and the strategic objective of the vendor, for reasons of market size or expected economic conditions, is to court US customers, you may find that your custom is not a priority. Likewise, if the vendor is looking for OEM[51] or OED[52] partners and you are in the mainstream retail industry or supply generic products, don't be surprised at a lukewarm reception.

The key to success in China is to find, cultivate and develop complementary alliances and strategic "matches." In order for there to be a win-win for both parties, your products must not only fit the product specialization of the Chinese partner's factory, but operations and goals must fit the factory's working style and strategic objectives, in the absence of any significant conflict of interest. Not all Chinese factories want to manufacture and sell to you just because you are willing to buy. The Chinese vendor is not looking for more customers *per se* or straightforward revenue potential but also ease of acquisition—the path of least resistance. In sum, this means you must make the effort to get to know the vendor, the vendors existing client base, and their desired strategic direction. It is important to know where you are in the market, understand where they are in the market, and proceed accordingly.

5. Product expertise

One of the more important judgments you make is whether a factory is not just *able* to manufacture your product, but if they are *specialized* in your product. The inexperienced buyer who has been searching the internet for weeks or walking for days up and down aisles at trade fairs to find a manufacturer for their new product idea is often only too pleased to meet a company that tells them, *"No problem. We can manufacture your product."*. After a long flight and a tiring car journey to a factory, this answer can seem like music to the ears.

However, this is where discipline is important. Don't let a factory manager talk you into business. The proclamations of a factory owner must be taken with a healthy degree of suspicion and it is necessary to take a calm look at their operation, *not one clouded by Chinese hospitality*, and make up your own mind if a particular factory is the *ideal* choice to trust your product to.

Remember, there are Chinese managers (the gamblers) that are not sure if they have the technical expertise but who will merrily take on your project with a nothing-to-lose attitude in the hope that all will turn out for the best. There are those who know this is not within their core competence but who will endeavor to help you and will ask you to help them. Then there are the professionals who know without too much study if a product fits the capabilities of their operation and will ask all the right questions. Work only with the latter type—unless you have plenty of patience, a desire to baby-sit, or the desire to vertically integrate.

When in meetings with factory managers to discuss the more technical aspects of a product, be alert to the amount of hesitation and scrutinize questions for pertinence and to gauge experience. There are obvious clues that tired buyers may not notice on a whirlwind tour of a factory, or may not wish to mention for fear of appearing rude to their host. Make sure to pay close attention to the products that are actually on the production line on the day of the factory visit. I have heard factory sales staff explain, "We are normally manufacturing products with a high degree of similarity to yours, but today we are manufacturing something different because of a rush order for one of our important customers." The key is to make sure the product you want to produce is within the factory's core expertise *and* that something very similar to your product is actually being produced when you visit.

While this may seem obvious, I have seen these simple rules broken when buyers on tight deadlines discount their own better judgment and choose to believe a shrewd Chinese salesman. Perhaps the disorientating effect of China's cultural and linguistic difference causes the buyer's familiar process of logic to function differently. I have seen the results: tents made in bag factories, orders for sports bags given to a manufacturer specializing in sleeping bags, high-end leather bags made in a factory specializing in cheap promotional nylon bags. Granted, each of these products involves fabric joined by sewing machine; however, the accumulated technical experience, the learning curve, and the mentality and training of the worker to make each different class of product is subtly yet substantially different. Workers paid by volume to churn out thousands of cheap promotional nylon bags, month after month, cannot quickly and effectively adjust to making high-end leather bags where inspections are made at each and every stage, where raw material costs are twenty times higher and wastage needs to be absolutely minimized, and where the overriding factor is quality, not speed.

These examples are variations in a particular industry sector, yet apply to all products. Even if you are working with tight deadlines, *make sure the proper time is invested in order to find a supplier that is specialized in your product.* Make the best choice, not one forced by any externally imposed time constraint or based on loose sales talk.

6. Procedures and systems

Since the source of many problems and pitfalls in China is often found lurking in the internal organization, it is important to ascertain the standard of a factory's procedures and systems.

It is possible to form an overall impression from clues from each department of the company. Is the office lined with rows of neatly arranged files, or are desks hidden under untidy piles of paperwork? Is the showroom clean and organized? On the factory floor, are the aisles narrow, untidy, and difficult to navigate, or are they wide and clean? Are floors covered with scraps and work in progress or are they routinely being swept and tidied? Are there new and clean posters on factory walls explaining rules and procedures for the workers or are they faded, outdated, and dog-eared? Is the material warehouse operating a FIFO[53] system with everything numbered and bar-coded, or does it look like the aftermath of a typhoon? How are purchasing and the quality of incoming raw materials controlled?

One of the main causes for receiving inferior quality products from China (after receiving a perfect sample) is because the factory does not have a proper sample approval system. Therefore, make sure you visit the sample department and ask specifically about the procedures. Is the factory using unique product identification references for each consecutive sample made? Does the sample department keep accurate customer records? Do all raw materials and components listed on the bill of materials and cost sheets have unique reference numbers? How is product information relayed to the production area? Ask to see the documentation and forms used to communicate between the sample department and the production floor. Are these systems computerized or informally paper-based?

While many of these things are not generally under your control or influence, at least be aware of the level of operational sophistication you are dealing with. This information should then influence the manner and format of your communication and determine your level of involvement, or the level of involvement required of a third party such as an independent quality inspection company.

7. Quality control

Take particular note of the quality control (QC) procedures and systems. Is the factory using a formal QC system, for example Acceptable Quality Level (AQL) 2.5? How is it enforced? What is the ratio of QC personnel to manufacturing line staff? Are the QC people wandering around performing their work in an informal manner, or is there a separate enclosed work area where QC is formally performed without undue influence of manufacturing departments? Who do the QC people report to? Ask to see quality control documentation and check whether QC personnel are individually accountable through identification numbers. If the factory is producing children's garments, has the factory instituted a systematic needle policy?

If a factory has a good QC system, the management will be proud to explain it to you in detail. If they don't recognize or appreciate its priority, then don't expect an explanation with too much detail.

8. Respect for intellectual property

When intellectual property is an important or integral part of your business strategy, it is worthwhile performing some informal checks during meetings with the factory owners and managers. Ask about other companies and trademarks they are working with, then sit back and see how much they are willing to tell you. Does the factory have its own design staff? Ask to see some of their own work and determine the quality of work they are producing. Ask to see the exclusive designs and samples of their other customers. See how readily or reluctantly the employees will get them out and show you. Are the more privileged samples kept in a separate restricted area? Are there any measures in place to prevent theft of samples and designs? Surreptitiously look into the possibility of placing orders for the exclusive designs of their other customers. Test what degree of modification to their other customer's designs is necessary before you are able to place orders for them.

Insights into how the intellectual property and new designs of other customers are treated will give you an idea how your exclusive designs will be treated when you are not around to watch over them!

Factory Audits: The Inside Story

Most multinationals, well-known stores, and international brands have valuable images to protect and are terrified of the inevitable public relations disasters that accompany discoveries of poor factory conditions or child labor. Resourceful investigative journalists are constantly on the prowl for headlines linking a famous brand with the exploitation of workers.

In response to such fears and to reduce the likelihood of such occurrences, many larger international companies and designer brands have their own systems and procedures for auditing factories, resulting in a factory rating or certification. These audits are variously referred to as "social compliance" audits, "ethical standards" audits, or simply "factory audits." Apart from reducing the risk of a public relations disaster (and whether through self interest or altruism) the factory audit certification process serves two other purposes: it ensures that factories are of a sufficiently reliable standard, which means less disruption to efficient global supply chains, and it has the effect of improving the lot of the Chinese worker by ensuring that factories are ethically managed, that employees are treated fairly, and that factories are operated in accordance with local labor laws and are protected by safer working conditions. This has led indirectly to the peculiar situation where capitalist corporations are taking the responsibility for improving the conditions and protecting the rights of workers in a communist country!

Large corporations, such as Wal-Mart and Disney, have their own audit teams based at various locations in China. If your company is supplying one of these large corporations, the Chinese factories manufacturing the products are subject to the respective rules and procedures of their audits. Other companies, rather than maintain their own system, use a third party auditing company to ensure vendors meet the grade. If certification is not essential for your company or its customers, factory audit certification is still a useful measure of a factory's operations and management. If the factory has been successfully audited (depending on rating, Audit Company or brand), you know the factory has the basic processes in place and is reasonably well organized.

The factory audit focuses on two main areas: the physical factory facilities and conditions, and management practices in relation to workers. An auditor will inspect all factory buildings, including the production areas, warehouses, dormitories, and canteens, making sure working conditions are acceptable and comply with local laws and regulations. A thorough auditing company will also inspect other factories carrying out sub-contract work. Audit procedures are designed to ensure that machinery and equipment are safely operated, that there are sufficient fire exits, alarms, extinguishers and medical facilities in relation to the number of workers, that there is adequate lighting and ventilation, that hazardous chemicals are properly stored and, if shipments are destined for North America, that security is sufficient to prevent the introduction of non-manifested cargo into shipments.[54] Management practices and company policies are then reviewed to ensure compliance with

Chinese labor laws, such as making sure wages and overtime are accurately documented and fairly paid, working hours are within the prescribed maximum, hiring practices are free of discrimination, and there is freedom of association. Most importantly, the audit ensures that there is no use of child or prison labor.

Factory audits involve a comprehensive review of documentation including company rules and regulations, labor contracts, and payroll records. Findings and observations are verified through interviews with randomly selected workers, which typically take place in a private room away from the watchful eyes of factory representatives.

When the audit is complete, the factory is given a rating. Wal-Mart, for example, has a four tier color-coded rating system: Green, Yellow, Orange, and Red. Factories where no violations or minor violations have been found receive a "Green" rating, which enables the factory to receive and ship orders and re-audits are scheduled on an annual basis. Where violations are observed or conditions are classified as medium risk, a factory is awarded a "Yellow" rating, while factories with violations considered high risk are awarded an "Orange" rating. Both Yellow and Orange-rated factories are normally audited again within 120 days. Where violations considered most serious[55] are observed, a factory will receive a "Red" rating. Following the audit, except for factories rated Green, a Corrective Action Plan is submitted, which sets out the changes that are to be adopted for future compliance, all of which is part of Wal-Mart's stated commitment to working with factories to improve their operations and the quality of life for their workers. For factories that receive a "Red" rating, it is possible for existing orders to be cancelled, future orders disallowed and, ultimately, the business relationship can be terminated.

The documented rules and specific requirements of the various audits give the impression of a clear-cut, infallible system. *However, while factory certification does provide a general indication of the standard of a factory, it is an imprecise science.* It is true that focusing attention on the improvement of facilities and working conditions and attempting to comply with the requirements does undoubtedly raise standards at factories. However, factories must balance compliance with the attainment of operational and economic goals and this is where objectives diverge.

When a factory is at full capacity, employees often work around the clock, seven days a week, to fulfill on time the orders on hand. This often happens due to poor planning or the seasonality of buying cycles. However, when social compliance audits stipulate a maximum of 60 working hours within a 6 day week, both the production objectives and compliance with the audit cannot be accomplished at the same time without significant commitment from the very highest levels of the organization, together with a radical overhaul of human resources.

At such a high level of commitment where change is necessary, the passing of a factory audit often becomes more a game of cat and mouse; to pass an audit when capacity is stretched becomes more an issue of covering undesirable practices rather than eliminating them. The reality can be likened to the anti-virus industry, where anti-virus companies work around the clock to keep abreast of the viruses that are created. This is what typically happens at factories. Those that have employees working long shifts to keep up with orders keep an entirely separate set of payroll records and accounts to show to the auditors. The auditors, wise to this practice, resort to clever interview methods, for instance, asking workers what television programs they were watching the previous evening in order to deduce their real working hours. The factory management, upon hearing of these tactics, begin an intensive and time consuming education process to teach workers how to favorably answer questions, financially rewarding the workers that are randomly chosen to answer them. Auditors, wise to this technique, try to pick the least indoctrinated workers and those they consider least likely to be able to answer questions favorably, in the hope they will trip up and reveal the truth. To counter this, factories reduce the size of their workforce on the day of an audit, leaving only those that management believes are capable of satisfactorily answering questions on the production floor. At times, I have seen workforces so reduced on the day of an audit that it looked like lunchtime all day! The auditor is surely acquainted with this practice yet because there is no check box questioning if a significant number of workers are missing, the auditor does his job. The whole process is smoke and mirrors, although one thing is beyond question: Chinese factory managers are highly resourceful when they need to be.

Due to the highly sophisticated methods employed by auditors and counter measures taken by factories that verge on "institutionalized cheating," many multinationals have been forced to expand their investigative work outside the formal audit process and are using more clandestine methods to monitor factories and determine the true state of compliance. It is not unknown for well-known corporations to employ the services of investigative agents who hide up in buildings adjacent to factories to observe the actual working hours of employees, or attempt to interview workers under informal circumstances outside the factory gates.

There is also the issue of corrupt practices that seep into the audit process in various guises and at various levels. Audit companies normally have strict policies to prohibit solicitation, and the offering or acceptance of any gift that may influence the audit process; in fact, the usual practice is for the auditor to place a sign on the table detailing such prohibitions. However, this does not always ensure that the parties obey the rules; it just takes the forms of inducement to a more subtle level.

There are auditors who make it difficult for a factory in order to justify some form of "gift," others that accept money on borderline cases and factory managers who lavishly use entertainment expenses to smooth the process. For this reason, audit companies try to rotate auditors, so it becomes more unusual for the same auditor to consecutively visit the same factory, and it is becoming more common to send two auditors, rotating them so it is unusual to receive the same two auditors together. I have heard of cases where auditors moonlight after hours, coaching the factory how to pass their own company's audit and even of Chinese companies that will work together with factories to prepare them for audits and that are able to "guarantee" a passing grade.

There are two important points to note in relation to factory audits. If you are sourcing a factory that does not currently have the requisite certification, although it will need to pass an audit in the near future, you must become familiar with the audit requirements and visit the factory to satisfy yourself that it first has the *potential* to pass.

Secondly, and crucially, recognize that the most important factor in passing an audit is management commitment. There are significant incentives for a factory to be certified. Passing an audit and becoming certified to manufacture and supply the leading companies and designer brands is not just financially rewarding in its own right; certification has the added advantage that factories are able to use the certification as a marketing tool to attract yet more customers. In addition, and surprisingly, the external enforcement of higher standards, while demanding, is often welcomed by factory managers that lack the knowledge and expertise to take their factory to another level without help. Sometimes management lacks the clout or impetus to improve their own organization internally, so external intervention often acts as the necessary catalyst for action and change.

However, it should be recognized that preparing for an audit, successfully passing an audit, and maintaining continued compliance can require a factory to make significant investments of money, time, and resources. The physical premises may need alterations, machinery may need to be modified, new equipment provided, workers trained, not to mention the enormous and detailed task of systematizing information processes (and sometimes preparing a second set of books!). Therefore, when selecting a factory required to pass an audit, more important than the existing physical state of the factory and existing procedures is undoubtedly *management commitment* to the process. Without commitment from the very top of the organization, it would not be possible to implement the changes necessary to become certified, or to sustain them after the initial certification has been granted.

So before you make your own investment of time and resources to help a Chinese vendor through an audit, pay a visit to the factory to determine if it has the ability, with improvements, to pass. Then sit down with the factory owner and management and make sure they are all familiar with the audit requirements and process. It is necessary to make a judgment on two things: First, what is the current client base and desired strategic direction of the vendor to decide what it would mean and *how important would it be for the vendor to pass?* Second, does the management have the *will* to implement the necessary changes and ensure continued compliance into the future? Remember, some factories fervently seek customers that will set higher standards and take them into another league without the slightest knowledge of what this actually entails on an operational level.

Conclusion: The *Strategic* Development of Partners & Suppliers

It is important to recognize that the selection of suppliers and partners in China is of a *strategic* nature. Senior foreign executives should ideally not be sending inexperienced buying teams to China that are focused only on individual buying decisions that collectively have strategic consequences.

Key suppliers and partners, in particular, must be chosen from a strategic perspective. Fundamental decisions need to be made in relation to jurisdiction; the role of trading companies must be considered within the context of your company's overall operational objectives; unit product prices must be considered from a wider perspective; *and the inherent risks of working directly with Chinese manufacturers must be properly contemplated, both in relation to your company's ability to assume that risk and in relation to operational measures taken to minimize that risk.*

However, the process does not end here. Partners that have been selected strategically must then be developed strategically. Suppliers need to be built into the supply chain step by step according to a plan. It does not mean that once a supplier has been set up in your company system as "preferred supplier" that they can be forgotten. It does not mean developing a number of new products, requesting numerous samples, and then failing to place an order for six months. Equally, it does not mean giving a Chinese factory the largest order in the history of your company as the first order. It means placing an order that tests their ability and gives the supplier a chance to prove themselves. It is not only a question of products, it is also a question of both sides becoming familiar with the system of communication and the unique way each respective side operates. Let the supplier deliver successfully and build on that success, step by step. Advise them what you plan to do, structure their expectations and then follow the plan.

If you are a company owner or purchasing manager, it is important to brief the entire purchasing team on the strategic role of each supplier within the supplier base and their particular expertise, *and then ensure that they are treated accordingly.* Furthermore, Chinese vendors need to be treated consistently throughout each contact with your company, from top to bottom. It is all too common for senior level Western executives to take time and effort to build relationships and *guanxi* with Chinese companies at the board level only to see the relationship subsequently ruined—sometimes quickly—by the actions of management or staff level employees. Therefore, be careful and selective in which members of your team are assigned to work with Chinese suppliers or are sent to China, for all behavior reflects on your organization and is indicative of your company's overall respect for the Chinese partner.

In addition, once the necessary relationships have been developed at the highest levels and a partner has become part of the supplier base, relationships must be maintained at the highest levels, not simply passed along to subordinates and forgotten. This may mean periodic or frequent visits to China, depending on the importance of the project or phase of the project.

Furthermore, try to get out of the habit of seeing things only from your company's sales and the needs of your company. Consider what the Chinese supplier needs and how you are perceived by them. From the viewpoint of a factory, with fixed overhead costs and generally fixed labor costs, regular and consistent orders are often valued more than large erratic orders. Factories have high and low seasons. It is sometimes possible to negotiate better prices if orders can be planned evenly or for production to take place during low seasons to help maintain stability. Purchasing managers sometimes mistakenly believe they are a factory's most valued customer by placing a million dollar order once a year. However, the factory is not sitting empty for eleven months waiting for that order. With buildings, machinery, and hundreds or thousands of workers, a factory needs to keep running twelve months a year. As in any relationship, understanding and appreciating the needs of the other party helps to build stronger relationships.

It is also important that suppliers and partners be closely monitored and periodically reviewed for performance, relevance, and suitability. Relationships should not just run on autopilot. When circumstances demand, the supplier base should be restructured without delay. Don't be afraid of cutting loses and ejecting a poor performing partner. The Chinese have a proverb that asserts there are no eternal friends or enemies, only interests. Long standing partnerships should not be taken for granted and costs and benefits must be re-evaluated in light of changing circumstances. The consequence of a switch from trying to work with an unsuitable Chinese partner to working with a more suitable alternative should not be underestimated and can be a significant benefit both to operations and the bottom line.

In addition, while relationships are going well with Chinese partners, it is easy to become dependent upon them; if one is not careful, relations can go beyond this to the point where the Chinese partner starts to call the shots and you become more at his mercy. If this is not recognized or addressed, it could ultimately prove to be a competitive disadvantage.

SUCCESS
STEP 6

Supervising the Manufacturing Process

A well-known company in Germany promoted a hard-working young buyer to the position of Purchasing Manager responsible for all imported products for their famous brand. Within a few months, and brimming with enthusiasm, she was soon sourcing new vendors in China and had placed her first two major orders. Her superior was impressed and this reinforced his confidence in having made the right choice for the job. Ten weeks later, and two shipments of inferior quality goods later, both of which were immediately rejected, the confidence had disappeared; the buyer had instead become a liability for her company and was in danger of losing her job.

Scenarios such as this happen on a daily basis to companies around the world and demonstrate the reality that *sourcing and buying in China cannot be considered separately from the issue of quality control*. In the worst case scenario, manufacturing in China is like a game of Chinese whispers—the game where a phrase is whispered into someone's ear and repeated down the line until the last person "repeats" the phrase out loud, which typically bears little relation to the original phrase! Similarly, instructions given to a project manager or senior merchandiser in China get "modified" as they pass from department to department and person to person. By the time instructions reach the production floor, the result can be a different product from the one anticipated. If Chinese production could be perceived in this way, the foreign buyer would proceed in a more insightful manner.

It is useful to understand why the control of quality in China presents such a great challenge, and to recognize the root causes of the problem. Quality problems have a wide variety of sources, some of which were mentioned previously in Success Step 4. For instance, poor quality can be due to a lack of internal procedures: when a sample is modified, the latest sample may not receive a new sample reference number so, while an order is placed based on the sample incorporating the latest design changes, the factory may follow a different version of the sample for production. Poor quality products can also be the consequence of poor control and questionable ethics along the supply chain: one batch of the same order for components might be the right quality while the next is of inferior quality, or a sub-standard batch of material might be mixed with a good quality batch in order to clear it from stock. When factories without strict procedures of their own receive these raw materials and components, they often become part of the finished products, resulting in sub-standard products. Experienced factories in China are often forced to perform a 100% quality control inspection on incoming materials and components as standard procedure, which adds to costs.[56]

Quality problems can also be traced to the factory lacking a properly documented or organized quality inspection process at crucial stages of assembly, or having inadequately trained or experienced staff at the final inspection stage. Sometimes it is due to the failure of workers to take responsibility, a lack of attention or proper supervision, or the consequences of a quality problem being too remote in time and place to be properly considered by workers — workers are thinking about meeting their quota and getting home to dormitories adjacent to their factory in Shanghai, not about the American consumer in San Francisco returning home with a quality product two months later.

A Chinese Quality Control Manager once mentioned to me that a product made in China will always be a Chinese product. He explained that if you had Italian designs, imported all the parts from the USA, and had German engineers and quality supervisors, it would still be a Chinese product because the average worker doesn't have *feeling* for what he or she is doing. While workers in Japan might do a great job through conscience or because they have been conditioned to believe customers remain loyal to companies that exceed expectations, Chinese workers, in general, have not yet assimilated vague notions of customer satisfaction and will do the minimum that they can get away with. Therefore, constant supervision is a necessity to maintain constant results, especially in relation to quality control.

It may be noted that many of the sources of quality problems are internal production issues over which we have little direct control, unless a project takes the form of a joint venture. We therefore need to focus more on the issues over which we can exert a degree of control.

As mentioned previously, one source of problems in China, and one that is rarely considered, is *worker unfamiliarity with the product that is being manufactured*. In the west, we often take for granted a comfortable lifestyle, the abundance of high quality products, and the frequent new product innovations appearing on store shelves. The everyday existence for the average Chinese factory worker is completely different from the average Western worker, and especially from the foreign executive traveling to China. Chinese factory workers are often unfamiliar with the high quality of products we have come to expect, or the products themselves that we take for granted.

When we are faced with what appears to be an appalling mistake or failure in quality, we typically do so in reference to quality standards that have emerged over a long period of development in our own marketplaces. To the Chinese factory worker, with a different frame of reference, certainly without the benefit of the Western consumers' frame of reference, a product that we would consider a reject is often seen as perfectly acceptable; indeed, the Chinese worker would be proud to take it home as a gift for his family! This difference in perception is often the root cause of manufacturing problems in China related to consumer products. When we demand high quality standards, a Chinese worker is left wondering what all the fuss is about. When we are ranting and raving about poor quality, it can be a bewildering experience for a factory worker. Our requests for seemingly unnecessarily high standards can be met with incomprehension.

I was once involved in a purchasing project for a European company that specialized in equestrian products. After a series of quality problems, the buyers involved traveled to the factory just outside of Guangzhou and sat down with the factory management and the workers responsible for quality control. With red angry faces, the buyers were trying to explain how stupid their choice of materials had been for a certain key component. With frustration and disbelief, they couldn't understand why an inferior material had been chosen for part of the product that would be subject to heavy rain, gusty winds, under high stress conditions when a horse is galloping around a field. Across the table were the puzzled expressions of the workers who had no concept what the buyer was referring to. They had never ridden a horse. In fact, it is quite possible that many of the factory representatives at the meeting had never set eyes on a real life horse, let alone contemplated the product specifications required to meet real life conditions.

The first thing to overcome in China therefore is a fundamental difference in perception and not to assume that because something is logical to you is also logical to others. We must not assume basic knowledge of a product—this is true for Chinese workers and consumers alike. The buyers' presentation in the example above could have been more effective had they stopped for a minute and identified with their audience, recognizing that the personnel in charge of quality control might lack any real life experience with the products in question. To all intents and purposes, show jumping might just as well have been a sport practiced on another planet.

In China, an approach based on empathy leads to better outcomes than the standard "I can't believe you did that" type of response that is commonly heard in China and which leads nowhere. To get the best out of people in China requires more of an influencing, teaching, or coaching style. It is not only necessary to teach workers to do things a certain way, it is also necessary to teach people to *understand* why it makes sense to do things in a certain way. Without such an understanding, workers are just as likely to go back to doing things their way despite what you say. Knowing a better way to do things does not guarantee that people will completely change their style of working. Working in China is about changing *your* approach until you get things done the way you want them, not by forcing your definition of reason onto workers without the frame of reference required to assimilate the information. Blame in China is energy wasted.

It must be recognized that the quality control process starts from the very first communication. All specifications must be sufficiently detailed and included in purchase orders and sales contracts. We must make sure that instructions given to a supplier are clear and precise and that drawings are used wherever possible. The Chinese tend to process information in a more holistic manner due to their pictographic language; therefore, pictures can be far more effective than a sequence of words for explaining requirements.

In addition, symbolism can be used to great educational effect in China, particularly where quality is concerned. Take for example how the Ruimin Zhang, CEO of the Haier Group, China's largest home appliance manufacturer, solved quality problems on their leading line of refrigerators through the unorthodox use a dramatic and symbol act. After a customer visited the factory to complain about a faulty refrigerator, Zhang ordered that all inventory be tested and discovered 76 defective products. He had them all lined up and labeled with their faults and the names of the workers who had produced them. He then had the entire workforce assembled to watch as the respective employees were made to smash the faulty appliances with sledgehammers, many of whom were in tears because each refrigerator was worth close to two years of the worker's salary. This harsh symbolic act paid off. Only four years later Haier won China's top quality award and even surpassed the quality of its German partner.[57] While it is not advocated to start smashing things up in front of our Chinese partners, we should bear in mind that the use of symbolism can have a powerful and long term educational effect; a single act is sometimes the equivalent of a thousand words or a whole series of lecture-style training sessions that don't engage the emotions of sleepy participants.

We also need to ensure systematic and continued compliance with specifications at every step from sample development through to manufacturing, double-checking and safeguarding for mistakes that the factory may not observe or be aware of. In this process, we can learn from the world's leading stores, brands and companies that have years of experience working in China and have more or less surmounted the learning curve. *Successful companies working in China systematically manage each and every step from sample approval through to shipment.* Samples are initially approved by the buyer. "Pre-production" samples are sent for in-house testing or to a third party laboratory to test for size, material specification, components, performance, chemical content, color fastness, conformity with industry standards, legal regulations, and various other specifically defined product or country-specific criteria. Then "Production" samples made with the materials delivered specifically for the particular order, together with any labels and packaging materials, are also sent for testing, and to the purchasing department for final production approval. Samples are signed with tamper-proof, non-removable labels and these samples are used by the factory to follow in production and for quality inspections at the factory which are performed in accordance with formal procedures and sophisticated statistical sampling methods. Major and minor defects are carefully defined and documented. Test reports and product inspection documentation then become requisite documents allowing orders to be authorized for shipment.

When an order is placed, it is important to take a pre-emptive and objective approach to quality control. This not only brings peace of mind but provides certainty to operations when you know at the point of shipment that the goods are of the required standard. In China, it is essential to have quality inspections before the goods are shipped. For new suppliers or those with which you have experienced quality issues with previous orders, it is prudent to put in additional inspections, ideally at the early stages of production which allows time for any mistakes to be rectified in time and avoid shipment delays. To put things right at the factories is exponentially less expensive, complicated, and damaging to your business than after the arrival of a shipment, or worse, after the products have been sent on to the final customers.

The question is who will provide the level of certainty where you have confidence that professional responsibility is taken for quality control? Is your Chinese partner proven, experienced, and reliable enough to provide that certainty? Or is it in your company's best interests to send your own trained staff or engage the services of one of the various independent testing and inspection companies (examples of these are noted in the appendix) that augment and confirm quality control at the factory? An alternative strategy is to place ultimate responsibility for quality in the hands of a trading company with its own quality inspection teams. I am often surprised at the number of foreign companies that leave quality control unquestioningly in the hands of the Chinese supplier without asking these questions.

If the decision is made to use an inspection company, it is essential to make sure the inspection company has the expertise with your particular product to be able to supervise quality to the required level. It is also necessary to work together to formally document the key points for inspections, denoting what constitutes a "major" or "minor" defect, according to business and marketing priorities.

If the product is particularly complicated or if proprietary knowledge is involved, it may be prudent for your own company to retain responsibility for quality control. Some companies send their own quality assurance teams to China to set guidelines, to teach quality control staff and to supervise inspections. However, it often requires more than just sending your resident experts for a week then returning home again satisfied that the newly trained workers will maintain the standards set. In China, learning is not always cumulative. It is possible to give new instructions and implement new procedures and ten minutes later workers are doing the same things as before, or performing it according to another idea they have. There is often a lack of consistency; one day workers will follow procedures, the next day they won't. With quality control in particular, changing the habits of Chinese workers can be like wobbling a jelly; the moment your team leaves the factory and are on the flight home, procedures and standards wobble back to their previous form! Taking responsibility to manage your own quality control systems in China requires *long term* commitment.

Deciding the optimal method of providing certainty of quality and the appropriate level of involvement depends on the circumstances, the supplier, and the product type. For each Chinese vendor it is necessary to make an informed judgment, and it is always best to err on the side of caution. If a product is new, the vendor unproven, or there are doubts about an existing vendor (and the vendor is not managed via a trading company responsible for quality control), it is at a very minimum necessary to engage the services of an independent inspection company to perform a "Final" inspection before shipment is authorized. If the product or circumstances dictate a higher level of scrutiny, it may also be prudent to arrange an "Initial" inspection at completion of ten percent of production, a "During Process" inspection at fifty or eighty percent of production and then a "Final" inspection before shipment.

If the vendor is experienced, professional, and proven it may sometimes be justified to leave full responsibility for quality control to the vendor, although only after a full consideration of three issues. These three issues are: product flow, operational protection, and protection of financial interests.

Product flow is a consideration of deadlines for particular orders and stock levels for particular products, and whether your company can afford the delays associated with receiving a poor quality shipment and the time required for a replacement shipment. For instance, if an order is custom-made for a fixed delivery date to a customer, then no delay is acceptable. On the other hand, if an order is for replenishment of stock, then there may be flexibility in relation to ship dates.

Operational protection is ensuring that products are of the required standard of quality before they leave the factory for shipment. If an independent inspection company correctly performs their inspection role and shipment is only authorized by an inspection "pass," both operation and financial protection are satisfied; there is certainty concerning the quality of goods and financial protection because the vendor is not paid unless the goods have passed inspection. In case of doubt, and as an additional precaution, it may pay to use an additional document, referred to as a "Shipment Release Agreement," that the supplier needs to sign before shipment. This agreement states that while the goods have been inspected and passed, should any subsequent defects or problems be discovered, the vendor retains liability and responsibility for costs, consequential loss, and for the replacement of goods,.

In the circumstances where the vendor is given charge of their own quality control, you are trusting the supplier with the responsibility for providing operational certainty. However, even the best factories make mistakes. Therefore, we need to consider the effect of a quality problem that is not picked up at the factory. The buyer must not only deal with the consequences of the breakdown of operational certainty, but in addition, the protection of the buyer's *financial interests*. If the shipment has been paid for, the buyer has lost significant control over the outcome of any negotiated settlement or claim. The buyer must rely on the vendor's guarantee or good faith to rectify problems, which is not the strongest position in to be in when working with Chinese companies.

In relation to the protection of financial interests, it is therefore necessary to consider two additional factors when vendors are left to verify their own quality control. First, the buyer needs to consider the vendor's payment terms. If payment terms with the vendor are longer than the time it takes for the goods to be shipped, received and checked upon arrival, then the buyer still maintains a degree of financial protection. If the goods are faulty, the vendor can be informed, payments withheld, and the vendor therefore bears the financial risk until proof of quality or resolution of the problem. Second, the buyer must note whether any other forms of financial incentive simultaneously exist that would put the vendor in a position where it is unequivocally in his interests to make good on quality claims, and whether such incentives are sufficient. For instance, if the vendor has other orders on hand from your company for which the vendor has ordered materials and is in the process of manufacture, the vendor risks the cancellation of these orders and therefore the incentive exists to resolve quality issues on orders already shipped. It should be noted whether any orders on hand are custom orders, i.e. are they made specifically for your company with modifications or branding that would make it difficult to sell to another buyer should the parties fail to resolve the quality issue, or whether the orders are for generic products for which there are many potential buyers, which reduces your respective bargaining power.

Therefore, due to the inherent vested interest that exists when the vendor has final responsibility for quality and no independent third party inspection or trading company exists between buyer and seller to verify quality, the buyer must recognize there is no financial protection unless (1) payment terms are sufficiently long that quality can be confirmed before payment, and (2) the buyer has determined the existence of sufficient financial incentive for the Chinese vendor to honor any claim (due to sometimes irrational decision-making this should be underestimated rather than overestimated).

It should be noted that even when a settlement is negotiated, the buyer often ends up bearing some of the costs. In terms of time, resources, relationships, and money it is worth repeating that it is eminently more sensible to get quality right at the source than to resolve issues after shipment. The ideal, both operationally and financially, is to independently and objectively verify quality *before* shipment.

When considering *product flow,* even with the existence of financial protection, it is still unwise to leave operational protection solely in the hands of the supplier. This is especially true when any delay will have serious consequences for deadlines imposed externally by customers, when other parts or processes are dependent on the timely arrival of a certain shipment, or if it is of strategic importance to get an order right within a certain timeframe.

Each of the three issues—product flow, operational protection, and protection of financial interests—must be properly considered before the optimal strategic solution for quality control for each supplier can be determined. It is interesting to note that the world's largest and most successful companies do not leave ultimate responsibility for quality in the hands of a Chinese vendor under any circumstances. *They understand that ultimate responsibility for product quality is the buyer's and to be successful in China you must have in place consistent procedures and systems to compensate for those that factories generally lack.*

The optimal strategy for avoiding quality problems is to *monitor and control* orders at every step from the product idea, factory selection and audit, all the way through sampling and manufacture to final shipment. The more you depart from this model, the more risk you are inherently accepting in China. The more checks and balances left out, the greater the risk of poor quality shipments, which in turn, regardless of the financial consequences, hinders the overall efficiency of operations.

For small companies buying from China that don't have access to the resources of a large company such as in-house quality control and inspection teams, it is necessary to evaluate the level of risk and determine the *minimum* level of quality control necessary. It is just not prudent to leave full responsibility for quality to a new Chinese vendor in the hope that what you specified is *exactly* what will get shipped. It is surprising how many companies learn this the hard way. For small operations, one bad shipment from China can have disproportionately negative consequences. At the very minimum, a "Final" inspection should be conducted by a third party inspection company and, while this may not be a panacea, it is the closest you can get without pitching your own tent at the factory!

For purchasing managers at medium sized companies, a systematic approach is needed to properly supervise the supplier base in China. It is necessary to periodically review the performance of all vendors. Check whether vendors are new or current vendors. If current, analyze their past shipment history and any claims related to quality. Note the product type with reference to the level of complexity. Then note the payment terms, the nature of past cooperation and any other financial incentive that exists for the vendor to resolve quality issues. Finally, based on this information, grade them and determine the most appropriate quality control arrangement for each and systematically apply it. This approach will dramatically improve results over the long term and eliminate or reduce incidences of financial loss.

Remember, failing to adequately supervise the entire manufacturing process in China, in particular, to take a systematic approach to monitoring and control of quality, is worse than disregarding the existence of Chinese whispers. *It is nothing short of playing Chinese roulette.*

SUCCESS
STEP 7

Staying One
Step Ahead

Developing a
"Mindset of
Anticipation"

While this is the seventh step, if a foreign business person buyer wishes to successfully work with Chinese companies, *this is perhaps the most crucial of all the Success Steps.*

It must continually be borne in mind that in China we are not dealing with the typical American or European company. Working in China is more complicated and the cultural and environmental setting creates a unique set of management problems. We must recognize that to work successfully in this environment therefore requires a different approach and a different set of skills; in short, a different mindset is needed. That mindset is the *mindset of anticipation.*

Success in China requires that you are constantly anticipating problems and are consistently one step ahead of the game. It is almost as if the moment you are leaving home to visit China or start working with Chinese companies, you must flick a switch and turn on the China mindset!

The first place to start in developing the correct mindset for China is to take the phrase "I am sure everything will turn out well" and delete it from your vocabulary! This is *hope*, which has no place in Chinese business. *The business person must get used to the idea that he cannot sit back and wait for things to happen in China; the business person in China must make things happen, or supervise things until they turn out well.*

Working in China is like teaching a child to ride a bike. You make sure the child is prepared, sit him on the bike, stand behind him, give him a push, then run alongside to make sure he doesn't fall off; if he falls, you are there and can help put him back on. Like the project manager that passes a project to China or buyer that places an order in China and expects everything to proceed without mishap, the parent that gives the child a big push then stands back hoping everything will be ok is courting danger.

It is a fact that most new buyers and project managers in China spend an inordinate amount of their time and energy solving problems and correcting mistakes *that they didn't anticipate.* They give projects an initial push then sit back and expect things to turn out as hoped. They fail to anticipate where things might go wrong. They fail to supervise, to check progress, to double-check, or get involved where necessary. Newcomers to China are continually caught off guard, always on the back foot, always running around solving problems *reactively*. Consequently, successful execution of projects in China remains a mystery; yet it is not—the answer simply resides in the detail.

To understand the practical significance of taking care of details in China, it pays to refer to discussions in previous Success Steps. Two crucial factors were mentioned in Success Step 4: the general failure of the average Chinese worker to take personal responsibility, and reticence in response to problems rather than taking action to solve them. Sometimes projects that you have initiated will run into an obstacle, or missing details will cause a project to come to an immediate halt without the factory making any attempt to notify you. *If there is a problem, you will normally be the last to know.* The project will be put aside while workers get on with the hundreds of other things that *can* be done—the upshot of a culture predisposed toward the practical. If you don't call or request an update on the status of a project, the worker will automatically assume it is not urgent and will forget about it. A project can be given to a worker and they will accept it with a "yes, no problem," simply because they prefer not to make themselves feel unhelpful by saying "no," or for you to feel bad, then proceed to take no action at all.

As mentioned in Success Step 5, in relation to choosing strategic partners and suppliers, there are companies that accept projects in which they have no expertise, and companies that accept orders from customers that are not an operational or strategic priority. The same section also referred to the issue of corruption, the integrity of information provided by Chinese companies, "creative misinterpretation," lack of proper procedures and systems, "job protection," and the failure to effectively delegate. Recognizing that these issues exist will have a direct bearing on a Western business person's ability to anticipate problems and stay one step ahead of the game in China. There are endless reasons why projects become problems, fail, grind to a halt or end in disaster. Appreciating the existence of the aforementioned issues alone, and taking effective measures to counter them, will double your chance of success in China.

It is imperative that the business person dealing with China is constantly abreast of everything, constantly monitoring and supervising all ongoing projects, proactive in all aspects, anticipating the Chinese partner's requirements and his next step, making sure he takes that step and that the outcome is satisfactory; if not, it becomes a question of working together to find a solution and making sure it is implemented. This proactive, anticipatory approach to China is the only approach that works. China may appear complicated and success often eludes those trying to comprehend their circumstances or those looking for a complicated answer to their problems; yet success simply requires the mindset of anticipation, which depends on staying one step ahead and paying attention to detail. A mindset of anticipation is the mindset for success in China.

Success in China is not a mystery; it is based on the deceptively simple, mundane principles of diligence, discipline, consistency, determination, and tenacity. Disaster in China is often the combination of an unprepared business person encountering an unforeseen problem, while success is simply meeting challenges and opportunities with preparedness. Any complacency can lead to disaster. The danger for the reader is that he may fail to appreciate the wisdom veiled in such simplicity.

Those who wish to work successfully with Chinese companies must follow the example of experienced buyers in China who are proactive in anticipating problems on two levels: problems relating to projects and orders, and problems relating to strategic choice of suppliers and supplier relations.

Projects and orders

To take proper control of a project or order, the first stage is to make a complete chronological schedule of individual events that go together to accomplish the objective. This allows the process to be correctly supervised and facilitates the anticipation of problems.

A chronology of events is essential for managing and controlling any project, although it is surprising how many buyers or project managers fail to do this properly. These buyers and project managers start projects with Chinese companies assuming the best case scenario, usually without any clear concept of each separate process or without any clearly defined schedule of events. Inevitably, projects fail to be completed in time, or fail to be completed at all, which can be particularly disastrous for time sensitive projects, orders for fixed-date promotional events, or products that must be in-store for particular sales periods such as Back-to-School, Valentine's Day or Christmas.

For the development of a new product, a chronology might start with the concept idea, through design renderings and sample development, include several modifications and versions, and end with the finished product. For an order, it will start with confirming the order details, include the approval and confirmation of samples, production and shipment.

Many buyers seem to have a tendency to simplify lead times, such as using a 30/30 rule—thirty days for production and thirty days for shipping. In reality, after losing days in correspondence to clarify order details, together with the time spent sending and confirming approval samples and overcoming unexpected delays, such rules do not reflect reality, especially with weekends, Chinese public holidays, and when different time zones are involved. Such simplistic thinking consistently results in orders being last minute and labeled "urgent" to the point where the word "urgent" loses all meaning because everything is urgent! This also puts constant strain on manufacturers who are rushing to meet unnecessarily tight deadlines that are the result only of poor planning on the part of the buyer. Manufacturers and buyers alike are then forced to cut corners to meet deadlines, which in turn encourages mistakes.

Proper planning requires first an exhaustive list of all the events to be put in sequence. For example, the events associated with the buying procedure might include sending the order by email or fax (day 1), supplier review of order details and reply covering any questions (1-2 days), buyer's response to questions (1 day), vendor confirmation or preparation of sales contract (1 day), checking and signing the contract (1 day). Unless one or more of these steps are eliminated, one working week (5-6 days) has effectively been used just to confirm the contract.

Continuing, for the purposes of illustration, with a simple consumer product such as a Nylon backpack, the process continues with the confirmation of the order in the vendor's system, the checking of the stock of materials in the vendor's system, and the generation of purchase orders to the vendors respective material and accessory suppliers (1—2 days, plus an extra 1—2 days if the order quantity is large and requires meetings with suppliers to negotiate prices), manufacture and delivery of materials and accessories (10—

25 days, plus 10—15 days if the materials are being shipped to China from Taiwan or Korea), receipt and checking of materials (1 day), cutting of materials (1—2 days), production and packing (10—30 days). So depending on circumstances, the lead time for a common consumer product, not taking into account the factory's production schedule, could be from 17 days for a standard small order for which the factory has materials in stock, to 68 days for a non-standard, large volume order, and 83 days for a non-standard, large volume order with materials produced and shipped from Korea. These lead times do not including sample approvals, laboratory tests, or inspections. Apart from demonstrating the wide variance in lead time for different products and order types, this illustration exposes the overly simplistic view that many inexperienced buyers have of Chinese production.

To be able to properly identify potential problems and proactively deal with them, once each of the separate events have been listed, together with the number of days that each event will conservatively require to be completed, it is necessary to start at the bottom with the required delivery date, "in-store" date or "event date," and work backwards in time through each event on the list, noting the corresponding calendar dates for completion of each event, until arriving at an order placement date at the top; the date when the order must be given to the vendor. To enable progress to be monitored as an order progresses, actual completion dates can be recorded in the last column. Figure 1 shows an actual example that was used to manage a stationery order for a well-known US retailer.

Event	# Days	Cumulative # Days	Event Date Completion	Actual Completion
Send purchase order	1	1	28 June	
Vendor review of PO and reply	2	3	30 June	
Respond to questions	1	4	1 July	
Sales contract confirmed/sent	1	5	2 July	
Sign sales contract	1	6	3 July	
"Pre-Production" sample making	4	10	7 July	
"Pre-Production" sample lab test	1	11	8 July	
Lab test / approval	5	16	13 July	
Allowance for sample re-test	(10)	26	23 July	
Order materials and packaging	15	41	7 Aug	
"Production" sample making	2	43	9 Aug	
"Production" sample for lab test	1	44	10 Aug	
Lab test / approval	5	49	15 Aug	
Production	15	64	30 Aug	
Final inspection	1	65	31 Aug	
Container load and to forwarder	1	66	1 Sept	
Vessel "on board" loading	3	69	4 Sept	
Transit time by sea	20	89	24 Sept	
Customs clearance	4	93	28 Sept	
Inland transportation and delivery	2	95	30 Sept	

Figure 1

This schedule is not suitable for all products or industries, or in any way exhaustive, but it is indicative of the thought processes of the buyer. For this order, the final delivery date was September 30th, which after scheduling each separate event leading up to this date meant that the buyer needed to place the order on 28th June. With the benefit of experience, the buyer also included 10 days for the making and re-test of "pre-production" samples in the event that the initial samples failed for any reason (indicated by brackets so the buyer can see where the "cushions" are). It would also be prudent to place the order in advance of this date to allow some extra days for any other problems or delays. Placing the order in this example on 21st June would give the buyer an extra one-week allowance.

As Chinese holidays have the potential to affect production and shipping schedules, it is also necessary to cross-check dates with a Chinese calendar. Factories are typically closed for the three major holidays in China, which are Chinese New Year (falling at the end of January or beginning of February) and the other two "Golden Weeks"—the Labor Day holiday (at the beginning of May) and the National Day holiday (in the first week of October). Chronological schedules need to be revised accordingly to take account of their impact.

For example, to illustrate the effect of the Golden Week Holiday in May and to see how this might affect the overall order lead time, let us suppose the previous example had a final delivery date at the end of May, instead of the end of September. Production would fall at the end of the one week holiday and the production schedule would therefore need to be revised to ensure production is completed and shipped before the holiday. To be on the safe side, production should be finished and containers loaded and delivered to port several days before the start of the holiday. It is therefore necessary in this instance to start from the holiday dates which are May 1st—7th and then work forwards and backwards to fix all the other events. The dates would change according to Figure 2.

Event	# Days	Cumulative # Days	Event Date Completion	Actual Completion
Send purchase order	1	1	18 Feb	
Vendor review of PO and reply	2	3	20 Feb	
Respond to questions	1	4	21 Feb	
Sales contract confirmed / sent	1	5	22 Feb	
Sign sales contract	1	6	23 Feb	
"Pre-Production" sample making	4	10	27 Feb	
"Pre-Production" sample lab test	1	11	28 Feb	
Lab test / approval	5	16	5 March	
Allowance for sample re-test	(10)	26	15 March	
Order materials and packaging	15	41	30 March	
"Production" sample making	2	43	1 April	
"Production" sample for lab test	1	44	2 April	
Lab test / approval	5	49	7 April	
Production	15	64	22 April	
Final inspection	1	65	23 April	
Container load and to forwarder	1	66	24 April	
Vessel "on board" loading	3	69	27 April	
GOLDEN WEEK HOLIDAY MAY 1-7				
Transit time by sea	20	89	17 May	
Customs clearance	4	93	21 May	
Inland transportation and Delivery	(10)	103	31 May	

Figure 2

As shown, the vessel is now scheduled to be on the ocean during the holiday. Due to earlier arrival of the vessel this now leaves ten days instead of two for inland transportation and delivery, which means either early delivery to the customer or storage. Delivery on May 31st requires the order to be placed on February 18th which is now an overall lead-time of 103 days, instead of 95. If a buyer had failed to compensate for the Chinese holiday, it is quite likely that the order would not have been delivered on time in accordance with the stated delivery date.

As previously mentioned, factory closures during Chinese holidays can significantly affect project completion dates and order delivery dates, especially at Chinese New Year when factories can be closed for several weeks. In the previous example, the difference in lead time is estimated at eight days. If the order is one for replenishment of warehouse stock, a difference of eight days may not be noteworthy. However, if the order is for an event to be held on a specific date or a delivery date that has penalties for late arrival, eight days can mean the difference between successful completion and financial loss. It is not unheard of for shipments to be four or six weeks late due to the impact of Chinese New Year, particularly if your orders are not considered a priority by the factory and at a time when other customers are putting pressure on the factory to get their delayed orders produced first after the holiday. Neglecting to allow for the impact of Chinese holidays is a common source of stress and frustration for buyers. It also helps Chinese vendors spot the more inexperienced buyers.

The best way to retain control of a project in China and allow problems to be anticipated and dealt with precipitously is to use the chronological sequence of dates for each event as *check points*. When the overall project is broken down into a sequence of separate events, it is then possible to monitor each one and ensure it is completed on time, thereby ensuring that the scheduled final objective is on track. Each date becomes a trigger point, triggering a phone call, email, or some other form of check to confirm the completion of each event. The *actual* completion date can then be noted next to the scheduled completion date, which tells a project manager immediately if the project is ahead or behind schedule. This information adds to the learning curve and leads to more informed and accurate estimates for subsequent projects. It is all part of the process of developing a proactive approach, which is essential for managing projects successfully in China.

It is advisable for buyers to adopt a system similar to the ones illustrated in these examples to be able to plan ahead and properly manage projects in China. For larger companies, purchasing software systems should take account of the integral steps in the purchasing process together with holidays of the Chinese lunar calendar. Overall lead times should then better reflect reality and improve decision making throughout the company.

To enable a project to be managed from initial concept idea, through sample development, order placement, manufacture and shipping, a product development schedule can be combined with an order planning schedule similar in nature to the example. It is important to recognize that each step is sequential in that any delay with one step puts all subsequent steps on hold. For example, if a sample is not approved or fails a test, materials cannot be ordered; with no materials, production cannot start; with no production schedule, vessels cannot be booked. Once one step is late, it becomes harder to squeeze all the other steps into the time remaining before a deadline and increased pressure to meet deadlines tends to lead to more mistakes. In this sense, mistakes and delays are cumulative. Successful operators in China tightly manage each stage of a project, respond swiftly to problems and nip them in the bud. Unsuccessful operators take their eye off the ball, allow problems to escalate or deadlines to slip until events are beyond their control. *Success in China is the accurate execution of a series of small and incremental triumphs, which alone are insignificant, but taken together mean the completion of overall objectives.* It is necessary to keep the objective in mind, while simultaneously maintaining a laser-like focus on the detail.

Another common mistake that buyer's make in relation to orders for new products is to assume factory lead times commence from the date of order placement, while most factories are operating on the assumption that lead times commence on the date that the final sample is formally approved. This can and does lead to misunderstandings and indeed is often a source of conflict. Again, the source of such a mistake is the failure of buyers to put themselves in the shoes of the manufacturer; if they did, lateral thinking would make clear the absurdity of their assumptions.

To be able to properly plan and manage projects in China, a buyer needs to be familiar with each step of the process and have a realistic understanding of the time required for each step. The process of project and order planning is significantly enhanced if the buyer has a greater practical familiarity with the manufacturing process, which is another reason to visit the factory. *Rather than spending more time on the internet sourcing new products and suppliers, the effective buyer would do better spending more time understanding the intricacies of the manufacturing process.* A hands-on operational familiarity greatly enhances a buyer's ability to do his job and enables both reliable information and realistic timelines to be provided to other departments. If a buyer understands why a small re-order of a standard product in stock colors and materials can be turned around in weeks, and is intimately familiar with how and why large, more complicated orders in non-standard colors and materials affect and impact lead times, he would become more of an asset to his company's sales and marketing departments that rely on this type of information. Appreciating the multitude of sources that can cause delays and other problems that are peculiar to production in China also helps a buyer to judge the extra number of days that should be built in as a cushion for each particular order, product, or project. Product expertise and familiarity with the manufacturing process in China is practically a form of *self defense* in that it can prevent being misled into accepting versions of events that accord with the motives of the Chinese supplier. If you are not familiar with what is going on, it is easier for a supplier to invent any believable explanations that are more suited to their underlying motives, rather than in accordance with your own objectives. For instance, a supplier can advise you that a certain material is the most suitable for your project, not because the specifications are superior, but because it is easier for the supplier to work with, or happens to be in stock at that particular time.

Many of the problems encountered in China can so easily be avoided. I recall a European industrial product designer who traveled to China for the first time to develop products from the three dimensional color drawings he had produced. He had already signed contracts for the supply and delivery of these products. After a meeting with the sales manager of the manufacturer he had sourced, during which all the specifications were imparted and discussed, the sales manager estimated molding and product development would require 12 weeks. The designer returned home and advised his customers of the estimated delivery schedule based on this information. Twelve weeks later he duly called the manufacturer and after some confusion was eventually informed that absolutely nothing had been done!

What was the excuse? There is no need for an excuse in China. The fact is the designer *assumed* all would go according to plan and didn't once call to check on progress, which is asking for trouble in China. For the record, what actually happened was the sales manager "delegated" the project to a colleague and left on a business trip the next day. The colleague was busy with other projects at the time, projects that he was under pressure to get completed, so the paperwork in question was put aside in the "to do later" file, which is where it remained for the next 12 weeks! To the colleague, the project was just a piece of paper. Since he had not personally met the designer, there was no *relationship* or personal leverage to get things done and therefore no loss of face involved with the designer. In China, delegated work often collapses in this way because of a lack of personal leverage.

A similar situation typically occurs when an employee leaves a Chinese company and his work is passed to another employee. Foreign buyers must recognize this as a critical period that requires a higher level of vigilance. The transition is rarely smooth because the person taking over is rarely familiar or experienced with the account, in addition to having no personal connection that would assist continuity.

In China, it is necessary to check and confirm every detail. Such a high degree of thoroughness is the only way to avoid misunderstandings, problems, and delays. *Leaving anything to chance is for amateurs.* For example, if you send a sample to a Chinese company, make sure it is received. This doesn't just mean using the internet to track the package, it means making a courtesy call to the recipient to make sure they personally received the sample and that they understand what needs to be done. If the turnaround for a standard sample is five days, check on the fifth day that the sample is ready. If development of a new product sample is twelve weeks, check on progress at three, six, and nine weeks. If production takes twenty days, check on progress on the seventh and fourteenth days and for completion on the twentieth. Checking everything must become the accepted practice. It must become second nature, the way you think and the way you conduct business. It is the mindset for China. Supervising Chinese vendors is a constant dialogue, not a one-time handing over of instructions. *The China hand must get out of the habit of passive waiting and into the habit of active waiting, ready to pounce the minute something is going off track.* This not only ensures things keep on track, but allows him to deal proactively with problems. It also allows him to deal proactively with his customers by notifying them early if project dates change. Using chronological dates and checkpoints for each stage of a project and constantly monitoring them allows potential problems or *"blockages"* to be flagged immediately. It is wise for the buyer to take the view that there are no "problems" in China, only impediments to objectives!

When issues do arise, as they invariably do in China, the next issue is the manner in which they are dealt with. When a blockage is identified, maintaining a dialogue and keeping a maintainable level of pressure on the manufacturer often leads to a satisfactory and timely solution. The Chinese are best at overcoming problems that are of a *practical* nature, or problems that can be circumvented by "greasing the wheels."

However, sometimes progress comes to a halt and an approach based on dialogue and constant pressure alone will not work. If this is the case and things are not going according to schedule, it is necessary to find out *why*. If there is a problem, cut through the excuses and standard responses and find out exactly what it is. In short, it is necessary to get involved with a solution.

I remember a buyer who placed an order with a factory in Dongguan. With the order documentation were material specifications including the words: "materials must comply with European Legislation in relation to heavy metal content." For two weeks, the sales documentation from the Chinese factory confirming the order had not materialized despite several requests by the buyer. It transpired that the office staff were trying in vain to find out details about the legislation, making inquiries to their material suppliers, going back and forth, all the while reluctant to demonstrate their inexperience and unfamiliarity with industry requirements by asking the customer. In the third week, the buyer made a telephone call to the factory and the situation was explained. In response, the buyer downloaded the whole 12-page legal text of the European Directive and faxed it to the factory. With this, the buyer thought the problem had been resolved. Another week passed. Page after page of detailed legal information was, however, proving too difficult for the language skills of the Chinese office staff. This point coincided with a business trip the buyer had planned to China, so naturally a visit to the factory was scheduled and the material requirements were discussed face to face. The buyer read through the Directive and extracted the specific information relating to the material that was relevant to the factory. Finally, the information was in a form the Chinese workers could readily understand and pass directly to their material supplier. The problem was solved; the blockage removed.

This oversight by the buyer had cost the best part of a month. If the buyer had taken the time to consider the requirements from the vendor's perspective and had instead provided information in a form they could be readily processed and directly passed to their raw material supplier, it would have allowed the project to move along without any delay. Instead of extracting the relevant details at the very beginning and noting them on the initial order documentation, the buyer had simply passed the job to the factory to research it themselves, or hoped that the factory was familiar with it already. To be honest, the buyer hadn't fully understood the legislation himself, so had passed it to the Chinese vendor for whom the task of sifting through the information proved exponentially more difficult.

In China, the key is to identify the blockage at the earliest possible opportunity *and get involved in a solution that moves things promptly to the next stage.* Thus, if a product requires, for instance, materials meeting FDA[58] food safety regulations, it is not sufficient for many Chinese factories, particularly factories with which you have not built a successful trading history, to simply be advised "material must comply with FDA food safety regulations." In addition, it is probably best not to send bulky copies of the legislation from which the Chinese can infer the relevant and important points. The best approach is to take the time to identify the key requirements and summarize them as succinctly as possible into action steps the factory must take, for example: "lead content of material must be less than 0.5 mg/kg (milligram per kilogram)." Then, assist the factory to arrange third party testing of the materials, or at a minimum oversee that the factory arranges third party testing of the materials to objectively make sure that the regulations will be met. Such differences in communicating requirements can make a big difference to the manner and speed with which orders and projects proceed.

There is also an inherent cultural logic to getting *personally* involved. Indeed, there are five main reasons:

(a) getting involved immediately when an obstacle is discovered helps to maintain momentum. When a problem that is difficult to solve halts progress, the project is often put to one side in favor of jobs that can be done. Once the project is stopped and put aside it is more difficult to get it going again. In China, it pays to keep things moving—strike when the iron is hot;

(b) if you are calling the people responsible to make sure everything is on track, it reinforces the importance of the project or order. If you don't call it can't be that important, which therefore makes your project easier to put aside in favor of other work;

(c) working together to overcome an obstacle demonstrates that you are "in this together" and reinforces that it is a mutually beneficial endeavor. It is better to be a piece of the puzzle than a hammer on a nail;

d) it makes sure things get done, especially if the job requires thinking outside the box or creative solutions, where it is not prudent to leave such tasks to a Chinese worker who would rather concentrate on routine tasks providing immediate outcomes;

(e) finally, a constant dialogue, provided it is courteous and friendly, is an opportunity to build personal relationships, an opportunity that would be missed if a stand-off approach is taken.

Monitoring supplier relations and strategic suitability

In addition to anticipating problems that may arise with regard to projects and orders, it is also necessary to be alert to both the changing nature of supplier relationships and the *strategic* suitability of suppliers. This means monitoring communication between the Chinese supplier and your company; *reading between the lines to gauge sentiment and your perceived value as a customer*. If a request is sent and no reply received, it could be due to a public holiday in China, or that the contact person is away from the office, or you may have inadvertently offended their "face." Alternatively, it could mean the factory lacks interest in your project, and so it is not being treated as a priority, or the factory does not have the ability to handle your request and is therefore not a suitable choice for your project. A negative response from your Chinese counterpart could just mean that he is having a bad day or it could more ominously mean that he has received specific instructions, or even an informal comment from senior managers, that he should not put too much effort into your project.

A failing of stubborn buyers is that they prefer not to see the signs or see responses in context, continuing with the hope that all will turn out right in the end. *It is important to develop a feeling for when relations with Chinese suppliers are not quite right and take action accordingly.* I am not recommending that executives jump to conclusions if a reply to an email is not forthcoming within two days; it simply means being aware of signs and being perceptive to trends in supplier relations.

Equally, I am not advocating a sudden and acrimonious end to a relationship, although with sufficient evidence there may be a case for starting to consider other alternatives. It might make strategic sense to locate and take the necessary steps to develop a second supplier so they are in a position to take over in case of insurmountable problems or an unsalvageable breakdown in relations. It may be necessary to instruct the purchasing department to take action to resolve an issue with a vendor, while at the same time making moves to share orders with other vendors or move production elsewhere.

It is important to determine whether problems are tactical and solvable, or more strategic. The solution to a problem may just require a change in the manner that your staff is using to communicate with the supplier; other times, niggling problems may signify that a visit by your company's senior executive may be due to reinforce the importance of the relationship.

Being proactive in relation to suppliers also means monitoring supplier performance as an indication of strategic suitability and anticipating events strategically, alert to the possibility that a supplier may not be the most suitable for the project, rather than stubbornly soldiering on with the expectation of improvement. In China, it is necessary to be one step ahead with regard to reorganizing the supplier base in anticipation of problems, rather than in response to them.

For instance, during new product development, examine samples received from a more strategic perspective. Are the samples a good interpretation of your concept and specifications? Do samples demonstrate an obvious expertise in that product type or is it clear from the outset the supplier will be incapable of achieving the required standard? Is it best to persevere or cut losses and immediately begin locating a more suitable supplier? In relation to prices, if you have been working with the same vendor for ten years, it is necessary to cross-check with other vendors to make sure prices are competitive? In relation to quality, keep abreast of any quality issues and the percentage and frequency of claims in relation to total shipments. Note the lead times that are being advised by the factory—long lead times could mean the factory is exceptionally busy; equally, it could mean your orders are not a priority for the supplier and are therefore left until last.

Strategically staying one step ahead in China also means looking ahead from a wider macro political and economic perspective, keeping alert to issues and abreast of trends that could endanger China's so far relatively smooth economic transition and affect our business interests in China. Continued good relations with the United States will continue to be important to China's growth. While both nations have an obvious self interest in maintaining friendly relations[59], there are potentially conflicting interests at stake. While China views its meteoric economic success as a "peaceful rise,"[60] the US meanwhile—long used to being the dominant global superpower—considers China's integration into the world economy as a potential economic threat that it would like to contain. Notwithstanding the trade deficit for which America considers the unfair Dollar-Yuan exchange rate a major contributing factor[61], there is China's aggressive quest for raw materials to fuel its rapidly growing economy. The commodity boom caused by Japan's industrialization was driven by a population of 150 million; China's commodity boom is driven by a population almost ten times that size. Competition for oil is illustrative of the issue. China's consumption of oil exceeded its production in 1994 and, according to the US Energy Information Administration (EIA), China accounted for 40% of the growth in oil demand over the past four years.[62] This is putting the world's two biggest consumers of petroleum products — China and the U.S. — in direct competition for oil supplies and China is not hesitating to build alliances with countries frowned on by the U.S.[63] The question is whether this rivalry could lead to hostility and protectionist alliances to ensure supply for their respective economies.

Perhaps the issue with the greatest potential to disrupt the Chinese economy is major social unrest due to a widening wealth gap between China's urban rich and rural poor together with regional disparities in income. The Chinese economic story so far has been both a staggering success but also an unequal boom that needs to be carefully managed by central government.[64] It should be remembered that as the economic prosperity and purchasing power of the average Chinese citizen increases, so too does the thirst for more political and democratic accountability, which must be properly managed. Foreign executives also need to keep a watchful eye on the increased unionization of Chinese labor, which may or may not lead to a rise in industrial action; Wal-Mart's (forced) support of labor unions at its Chinese stores marked the beginning of a trend for foreign companies operating in China. Executives must also keep abreast of changing legislation with regard to import duties, special taxes,[65] and labor rates that can tip the scales of competitiveness in favor of some provinces within China over others, or countries in relation to each other. These and other issues may lead some to conclude that things might not run as smoothly as anticipated. Setbacks are inevitable and it may therefore pay not to put all eggs in one basket, or at least to have contingency plans prepared, perhaps involving other ASEAN[66] countries.

Summary

In China, problems are so clear after the fact; their source so obvious in retrospect. In China, where problems and their magnitude are often unpredictable, the key to success is to be continually and actively anticipating problems and threats so that once they arise they can be quickly and effectively dealt with. The ash heap of foreign companies that tried to do business in China is overflowing with the remains of those who sensed or spotted problems but failed to respond to them in an adequate or timely manner.

Some degree of paranoia, a *sixth sense* or the ability to see around corners is a virtual necessity for survival in China! If your intuition is telling you something is wrong, it probably is. In China, it is typically not a case of *will* things go wrong, it is a question of *when,* and how best to put things back on track. It is essential to have a proactive mentality—a "mindset of anticipation"—together with the *discipline* to monitor and supervise every stage of a project or order. Having a proactive rather than a reactive stance, in conjunction with the use of check points along the progression of a project, allows us to anticipate, intercept, and solve problems. It is a way to minimize risk and a method of working that we must adopt to eliminate issues before they have the opportunity to grow into bigger problems.

Whenever there is a blockage to progress, the foreign business person must be prepared to get to the root of a problem and get involved to help with the solution. Strategically, it is necessary to continually be alert to the possibility that a supplier is not the most suitable choice and proactively cut losses, instead of letting relations drift into a downward spiral of deteriorating service.

These are the simple yet essential business skills for mastering China, which must be developed and incorporated into your repertoire. Foreign business people must train themselves to flick the switch and go directly into "proactive China mode" whenever they are dealing with Chinese companies.

In China, you must be one step ahead, or you will always be ten paces behind and running to catch up!

10
STEPS TO
SUCCESS

SUCCESS
STEP 8

Mastering
Presentation and
Communication

Preceding chapters have provided a body of knowledge about the average Chinese operation and some of the mechanisms that should be in place to properly protect our interests when dealing with them. It is now time to turn our attention to the way we present ourselves and our companies when in China, in particular the image of our company we leave with the supplier after meeting for the first time. It is also important to look at the manner of our communications to make sure they are not creating problems of their own.

This Success Step is divided in two parts. The first part looks at the presentation and the issues that should be borne in mind during preparation; the second part takes a look at communication and discusses how the approach we take to giving instructions and working together substantially affects the successful completion of a project or order. We should be aware of the relatively minor adjustments we can make that will radically change the results that we achieve.

The sum of the presentation we give and each individual communication thereafter contributes to the overall impression our Chinese partner holds of our company. We must realize that this professional image is a strategic asset and should be groomed for the outcome that we desire.

Mastering Presentation

The way that you present yourself and your company from the very first meeting structures the future manner of your reception, the level of service, even the prices that you are subsequently quoted. In China, providing good service and acting in the best interests of the customer are not forgone conclusions; to get what you want it is often necessary to appeal to motivations the Chinese more readily understand, such as the sincerity of the relationship, loyalty, and long term profitability and cooperation. It is necessary to start from the general and work towards the specific. For this reason, the quality of the presentation is a strategic asset and it is therefore vitally important not only that the forces at play are understood, but that the requisite effort is put into planning the presentation to achieve the desired results.

I have seen presentations so compelling and vendors so inspired that they will do virtually anything to assist the attainment of the goals of the buyer because of a belief in the long-term vision and partnership. The approach and manner of a presentation can completely transform a relationship. A good presentation can result in a small company receiving service superior to that which would normally be warranted, or obtaining the same or similar pricing as a much larger company. It can result in a buyer's orders taking priority over those of his competitors, or getting samples in two days while other customers wait two weeks.

The presentation is an opportunity for the buyer to influence and control the formation of the Chinese partner's opinions of the buyer and the company he works for. It is not something to be taken lightly in China, particularly when personal relations and appearances are more important in this part of the world.

This section discusses eight issues that should be borne in mind when planning and preparing the first meetings with Chinese suppliers:

1. Brand and company recognition
2. Buyer's arrogance
3. Visual impact
4. The gloss
5. Leveraging personal rapport
6. Professionalism
7. Emphasizing loyalty
8. Credibility

1. Brand and company recognition

Unless your company is a well known multinational or a global brand name, it is unlikely that a potential Chinese supplier will be well informed about your operation. *The initial meeting and presentation is therefore crucial in structuring their understanding and perceptions.* The impression that the Chinese supplier forms of your company from the outset is likely to endure and continue to influence the level of service you receive for some time in the future, modified only by subsequent performance and information received by the supplier through the "industry grapevine." It is therefore important to control this impression to your advantage.

One common mistake of business people traveling to China is to assume that because their company or brand is well-known in their country, it is also well known in China and nothing therefore needs to be said, and consequently nothing prepared. If the brand is Nike or Coca-Cola this may be a reasonable assumption, yet for second tier brands and companies it is not. Even if the company for which you are purchasing is globally famous, the Chinese partner is more likely to have a vague familiarity with your company rather than the necessary operational understanding that will allow the Chinese company to work effectively with you. The leading Chinese vendors in an industry will, of course, be intimately familiar with the main foreign players in the market; most smaller vendors will not be.

It is quite possible that a well known company or brand in your market is an unheard of name for the person you are about to meet. It is also necessary to be aware that in order not to lose face or appear less knowledgeable, Chinese employees will sometimes admit to knowing a company or recognizing a brand they have never heard of. Before the recent opening of the Chinese economy, China had been a relatively isolated market, and staff at lower management level had not had abundant opportunities for global travel. Therefore, unless your brand or company is world famous or has a major marketing campaign on the Chinese mainland, it is best to assume a low level of awareness.

A well-planned presentation is a good way to anticipate and avoid misunderstandings. At least prepare information about the size and structure of the market, your company's positioning within the market, what your plans are in relation to China, where the Chinese partner fits into the picture and what you expect of them as a supplier. If you don't prepare any information about your company and market, or have no brochure to leave with the vendor, you will be sending the message that he is not important or worthy of your time, whether this is intentional or not. Just the fact of having prepared something for a meeting with a Chinese vendor demonstrates to him that he is important and gives him face. Leaving a glossy brochure may be a throw-away gesture for you, although it can be like a trophy for the vendor; something that may help him gain social capital in the office after you leave.

2. Buyer's arrogance

Buyer's arrogance is an issue worth mentioning that relates to the perceived importance of the buying function. Company sales and marketing teams tend to have glossy brochures and professional presentation materials. However, the purchasing department's presentation materials are often viewed as less important or unnecessary because there is no contact with the final customer. The result is hoards of buyers turning up in China with poorly prepared presentations that don't adequately inform the Chinese of their operations, or leave a lasting impression. At times, the extent of a buyer's presentation is no more than a copy of the company product catalogue, which they are reluctant to leave with the supplier. So while three dimensional computer graphic product drawings are created by marketing departments for use by sales presentations to end clients, buyers often arrive in China with nothing more than a spiral bound notebook and pen, explaining product modifications to their Chinese supplier by way of hand drawn sketches.

For reasons of professionalism, however, quality presentations should not only be the domain of the sales side of a business, thought should also be given to adequately planning and preparing presentations on the buying side. *The Chinese are judging the manner of your presentation not only as a gauge to professionalism, but also the desirability of cooperating together and whether it is possible to improve their organization by working with you.* I have often seen large professional foreign companies give such hurried, mediocre presentations to potential Chinese suppliers that suppliers dismiss them as struggling companies and are left wondering whether it is in their interests to cooperate with them at all.

Another common misconception among purchasing staff is that because buyers are in China to buy and vendors are there to manufacture and sell, then all vendors will be falling over themselves to attract their business. The result of this misconception is that buyers pay little attention to the image they are portraying, neglect to prepare a presentation adequately explaining what their company does and what their requirements are, and assume the buyer's presence itself is sufficient. Admittedly, there are many Chinese factories that are desperate to court business in any form, although there are also many others for which this is not true at all. Some small Chinese factories might do anything for a chance to grow their business. Established companies, however, by the very fact of being established, already have a client base and are likely to be more selective about who they work with. *Buyers would do well to bear in mind that although China might sometimes give the appearance of a bazaar, not every potential seller wants to sell to every potential buyer.* For smaller companies in particular, it is often necessary to "sell" their strategy or idea to an experienced supplier to generate sufficient interest for the supplier to want to deal with them.

A well-prepared presentation is therefore a useful tool to assist such companies to attract a supplier base of a sufficiently high caliber. The arrogant buyer treats Chinese vendors as desperate, while in fact, though they will rarely mention it, most are selective. Although both types of vendor might accept your business, the difference appears in the level of attention and service buyers subsequently receive!

Finally, there are buyers with an over zealous preoccupation with products to the exclusion of human relations. These are the buyers that arrange meetings with vendors and walk straight into the showroom to select products, virtually ignoring the Chinese sales staff as if they were not humans but robots at hand to serve them. It is understandable that some buyers may have busy schedules and are tired after having traveled long distances on Chinese roads, yet *there is no excuse for ignoring the human element and the development of personal relations in China.* At least take the time to drink tea together, use this time to learn something about their operation, outline your requirements and develop some relationship capital. All meetings should be perceived as an opportunity for *both* parties to learn and to gain something from the experience.

3. Visual impact

An integral part of any purchasing trip should be to prepare presentation material for potential Chinese vendors, preferably something for your counterpart in China to keep when you leave their office. If, for copyright reasons, you are reluctant to leave the latest product design brochure with the supplier, prepare a corporate brochure. The good news is that most Chinese company owners, managers, and employees are both busy and more practically inclined, so page after page of facts, figures, and detailed written documentation is probably unnecessary. A brief, corporate overview is typically adequate, including company history, number of years in business, number of employees, product range, customer base, revenue (if appropriate), what makes the company different and what it expects from vendors, both ethically and operationally. Most importantly, mention where the Chinese vendor fits into the picture and why the supplier would benefit strategically from working with you. In China, developing partners is more than just buying and selling.

It is advisable to design the presentation for visual impact, making good use of pictures and easy to understand at-a-glance charts, newsletters, and PR material. During the meeting, the Chinese side will be taking more time studying you than the details in the presentation booklet, which will be read later. At the outset, the Chinese side is trying to get an instant indication of your size, prestige, and sincerity.

4. The "gloss"

Presentations in China should not be exclusively about facts, figures, and business; *it is also about public relations.* While opening a meeting with your company brochure is a good professional introduction, bringing out a newsletter that features a picture of your company president with the US President, British Prime Minister, Spanish Royal Family or Arnold Schwarzenegger becomes a talking point. Bear in mind both the human element and the significance of "face" and make the presentation more memorable and interesting by mentioning glossy facts, such as your company retains famous celebrity X for advertising, or is a supplier to the Queen, or the fastest growing company in the industry. These are points that distinguish you from the vendor's other customers. After you leave, the glossy facts are the topics informally discussed by colleagues at the office and become conversation pieces in front of the Chinese manager's friends at the Jockey Club. While other customers' business is just about buying and selling, it can give your company an initial service edge. The fact that your company is memorable is helpful when your office is 12,000 kilometers and 12 time zones away on the other side of the planet.

5. Leveraging personal rapport

When your office is located 12,000 kilometers away on another continent, you can't get on a plane each time there is a problem. *The initial meeting and presentation should therefore be recognized as a valuable opportunity to establish personal rapport with the people you meet, with a view to building long-term friendly and effective working relationships.*

This applies equally to senior management staff that receive your requests and those in the factories that execute them.

Meetings and presentations in China are an opportunity to make your face and your company memorable. After you leave China, personal meetings are replaced by faceless emails, faxes, and documentation where, for recipients, your company is just another letterhead at the top of the page and your name is just another name at the bottom. Bringing a touch of personality to the meeting therefore serves the purpose of planting and associating personal attributes in the mind whenever a communication is received from your company. Therefore, bring along family photos and photos of the staff with which the Chinese employees will be communicating in the future. Provided they are given sincerely, gifts also help to break the ice (although don't expect them to be opened in front of you).

Establishing personal relationships in China are crucial to the manner in which your company's inquiries and communication are subsequently handled. I know a friendly and happy Swiss buyer who gets support and service completely disproportionate to his company's level of sales. In contrast, I know buyers at large companies who struggle to get a response because they did not place sufficient effort to cultivate relationships. I know another whose communications are often ignored until last because he offended someone at the Chinese office and remained unaware of it. The Chinese may wear serious expressions but they are not made of wood. Making the effort to build friendships in China is an investment that makes life so much easier.

6. Professionalism

The Chinese are not just interested in sales volumes and profit *per se*. Chinese companies like to work with customers from whom they can learn and customers that will directly or indirectly help them to raise the standard of their operations, which in turn can lead them into new markets and to long-term increases in revenue. Therefore, even if you believe your business is not that interesting to the Chinese vendor in absolute terms, *providing the opportunity for the vendor to learn can prove to be an indirect way to get better service*. There is a long tradition of valuing education in China.

For example, a Chinese factory will appreciate it if you are able to make a valuable contribution to their development, either in relation to internationally recognized business or industry practices, or through the supply of useful competitor or market information. It may be a short-term strategy, but in the meantime it can give you time to increase market share and become a more important customer in the future. While potential sales volumes for the vendor may not be large, new ideas and designs, manufacturing processes, technical know-how or industry information that you can also bring to the table may compensate and be of more strategic value to the vendor. Therefore, when structuring your presentation, bear in mind that it is not only about sales, you could also be presenting yourself as a cutting edge expert in the field that can help to take the vendor to a new level. *Think of the value that you can bring to the table; don't only think in terms of sales.* The inverse is also true: bringing nothing to the table except standard orders may become of less importance to a Chinese vendor that is offered other opportunities for upgrading.

Chinese vendors are also noting your conduct and manners as an insight into your sincerity and professionalism. Making appointments in advance instead of at the last minute is not only more professional but also demonstrates your sincerity and that you value the vendor strategically. While this is standard practice for most buyers, there are some who are in the habit of calling a day or two before to schedule a meeting that fits in with their other appointments. The Chinese understand that last minute appointments are often made with those suppliers that the buyer has put on his schedule to visit only if he has time after the most important meetings are settled. This may work for small factories eager for business but less so for large, established suppliers with busy schedules themselves.

It is also easy to spot the inexperienced business people in China; they are the ones who underestimate China's size and, consequently, make more appointments than can possibly be kept. China is huge and even with substantial investment in new highways, travel times between factories usually exceeds the most liberal estimates, especially with congested traffic conditions. Locations can also be hard to find unless the driver has local knowledge. It is therefore important to set realistic schedules by confirming travel times in advance and taking the worst case scenario. Times provided by your contacts at Chinese factories are likely to be optimistic estimates without traffic so as not to prematurely deter visitors. I have known one buyer's last meeting of the day to have taken place in a taxi on the way to the airport. While this may work for the buyer, it doesn't leave the other party with a lasting impression of professionalism, or with the feeling they are the most valued vendor. In addition, due to long flight times and time differences, make sure you do not miss appointments due to jet lag. Inexperienced travelers often oversleep appointments after a long flight. If you are flying east, try to avoid making appointments early in the morning; if flying west, avoid late evening appointments.

With China becoming the centre for global manufacturing, Chinese businessmen are in daily contact with executives and professionals from every country in the world. Educated Chinese business people generally know more about the West than Western professionals know about China and are able to conduct business in two languages (how many Western executives speak Chinese to a level at which they can comfortably conduct business in Chinese?). Don't therefore believe that you can get away with behavior of a lower standard than you would consider acceptable at home, or that the Chinese expect less because they are a developing economy. If you want to be taken seriously and get things done in China, make sure your conduct and presentation is professional at all times.

7. Emphasizing loyalty

The Chinese value loyalty. Loyalty to a manufacturer means working together as partners for the long term. Chinese manufacturers prefer consistent orders that assist with cash flow and increased stability on the production line, instead of irregular, one-off orders that need to be shoe horned into the production schedule. While it may be driven by competitive necessity, the disloyalty inherent in presenting the image that you are shopping around China for the lowest possible prices and switching suppliers for a small cost saving is anathema to the Chinese—almost a betrayal. *Therefore, whenever appropriate, make loyalty a theme during a presentation and emphasize the desire to build relationships with preferred vendors.*

It is erroneous to assume that a large corporation or famous brand name *automatically* commands deferential behavior or preferential pricing. Speaking sincerely of long term relationships and co-operation is a better way to negotiate more competitive prices, in stark contrast to the one-off deal where a vendor will price to ensure a profit. If relationship-building is the stated aim, it is surprising the extent to which prices can fall or the level of service improve.

If you are just buying and selling, then you can expect standard prices. If you are sincere about working together and change the dialogue accordingly, it is possible to expect "relationship" pricing. Therefore, instead of the standard buyer's dialogue of "we need to buy Product A at $50," better prices can be achieved through more general and informal discussions along the lines of, "we are adding a new product line and prefer to keep our supplier base small by consolidating our purchasing on a select few preferred vendors. If we work together and can achieve our target price for Product A, we can start the new product line together and build our *mutual business*."

Instead of emphasizing the product, emphasize the relationship. For example, instead of dialogue such as "we are developing this product line so we can be the market leader," emphasize partnerships, co-operation, and mutual benefit, for instance, "if we can cooperate on this product, with your factory supporting us in production and our company managing sales, we can increase business and lead the market together." Make sure to take the broader view in presentations and involve the supplier in your strategy. *Start from the big picture of mutual cooperation and supplier relations, then gradually lead and narrow the conversation to individual issues, such as prices or terms. The discussion of individual issues then takes place within the context of the overall relationship.* Talking of partnerships and the promise of future business is the best incentive for the Chinese partner to help and support your company.

8. Credibility

The presentation you give the first time you meet with a new vendor is important in creating a favorable impression of your company and for laying down the building blocks for a future relationship based on mutual support. However, all the planning and hard work will be wasted if subsequent action taken is not in line with what was promised. *For the Chinese in particular, it is important to make sure your words and acts are congruent.* In short, it is essential to "put your money where you mouth is," which builds credibility and sets in motion a virtuous cycle.

This is particularly true with regard to the potential size of business that you represent. From the minute you sit down with the Chinese you are being evaluated on your potential for sales volume and profit. This, in turn, determines the level of interest you receive, including who will meet with you, from the boss to the secretary.

If you are a small company, it is better not to exaggerate the level of business you represent. If you give the vendor the expectation of millions of dollars in business and afterwards only do a fraction of what was promised, you will quickly lose credibility. It is better to start with credibility and retain it by acting congruently with what you discuss, than to talk big at the beginning and lose credibility and face thereafter. While it might be flattering to the ego to be met by the Chinese company president, it is better to keep to the truth and deal with a member of staff corresponding to the size of the business that you represent; if orders grow in size, the Chinese company president will quickly become more involved with your business. However, if it is apparent you are talking bigger than your size, the boss may attend the first meeting but will disappear very soon after! Starting with 'big talk" followed by disappointing results tends to lead to a downward cycle in relations. If your account is initially perceived as having great potential and the light subsequently fades, the best staff will be re-allocated to manage more promising projects and less experienced staff will be allocated to manage your account, which makes the potential of projects even more difficult to realize. *When starting relationships with new suppliers, it should be imagined that there is a window of opportunity to establish credibility after which it becomes an uphill battle.*

Honesty and sincerity is the best approach. Speak realistically about sales volumes. If prices are negotiated and the Chinese vendor meets the target price, place the order as soon as practicable. If a project is discussed and an agreement reached, start as soon as possible. It is a rare company in China that has patience to wait six months or a year before the realization of a project or receipt of an order, unless this is specifically communicated at the outset. Even if it requires a test order to commence business, this should be communicated at the beginning to avoid false expectations or disappointment. Unless the expectations and time-line for product development are very specifically stated and understood by all parties involved, you can find that projects quickly lose momentum after a time delay and it may take concerted action at more senior management levels to get things going again. Take action; demonstrate that you mean what you say and that your words can be relied upon. The Chinese will appreciate it and reciprocate accordingly. If not, you will lose face.

With regard to product development, bear in mind the ratio of the number of samples developed to the number of orders placed. It pays to keep a formal record of sampling activity for each vendor. If you start with an inspirational presentation, then request samples, then more samples, and no orders follow, it is only a matter of time before your credibility expires. Chinese factories are not running sample-making businesses and make samples only with the expectation of orders. If you are serious about working with a vendor, be acutely aware of the work/result or sample/order ratio.

The key is to build credibility from the beginning. Inspire the Chinese partner with your vision then follow through to give them confidence that you are able to achieve what you plan. When you commit to something in China you must do it to. *That way you earn respect.* With the Chinese, it is far more preferable to start small and build both credibility and face slowly, than to overcome the effects of a grand entrance followed by a less than spectacular follow through.

Summary

It pays the visitor to keep in mind that China is an environment without perfect information, where the customer is not always king, and decision making does not always obey the rules of rational market decision-making. *The large corporation or buyer representing a famous brand name is not guaranteed the best prices or service; the buyer for a small, unknown company is not guaranteed the worst. Much depends on how you present yourself.* We must recognize that a well-planned and implemented presentation plays an important role in structuring a potential Chinese partner's perception of your company to your advantage. With imperfect information and Chinese suppliers that sometimes lack exposure to global markets, the consequent level of service your company receives reflects the information imparted, and the manner in which it is imparted.

The initial presentation is an opportunity that shouldn't be missed to communicate your intentions, build rapport with key members in the Chinese organization, and structure the business relationship as a long-term partnership. A *good* presentation can save a lot of time and preclude countless subsequent discussions relating to the negotiation of prices or conditions. A *great* presentation should change the relationship from one where you are asking the vendor to do something for you, to one where the vendor is actively looking for an opportunity to help you to achieve your goals.

Mastering Communication

With such wide cultural and linguistic differences, communication in Chinese is fraught with challenges. It is therefore essential that the importance of communication to the success of projects in China is recognized and mastered to the point where your communications —whether face-to-face, by email or fax— are serving your interests rather than causing problems of their own. *There are enough cross-cultural and operational difficulties without adding to them with communication problems!*

It is not long before the business visitor to China becomes familiar with the Chinese phrase méi wèn tí (momentai in Cantonese) which means "no problem." When someone says no problem in the West, it can usually be taken at face value and a signal that we can relax. In China, on the other hand, it could mean no problem to big problem, or anything in between. It can stand for "I understand" or "I don't understand." It can signify that "the instructions are very clear and I will get to work on them," or "I have no clue what was just discussed but I don't want to appear stupid and ask again." In China there is an inherent cultural reluctance to say "no," which effectively means that person is of no use to you; the Chinese generally prefer to say "yes" in reply to everything and work out what is possible later!

When we are working with China we must be consciously aware of the fact that we are not at home and not dealing with our compatriots. Communication cannot always be taken at face value and it must be recognized that *fundamental differences exist in organizational culture and working style.* For instance, in American corporate culture it is common to fire off an email with a quick response to questions and copy half a dozen other people involved in a project, where each person understands their respective role and gets things done. With the general tendency for avoiding responsibility in Chinese companies, requests and instructions must be more direct and more precise. Successful communication requires that we go back to basics. A person doing business in China would do well to consider the analogy of the fax transmission report when sending a fax that confirms that the fax has been communicated and received. In China, each time instructions or information are exchanged, the foreign project manager or buyer would be wise to check that their receipt is both acknowledged and understood.

This section provides some down-to-earth common sense advice that will go a long way to overcoming communication problems. This advice alone is enough to avoid many of the problems characteristic of business in China and saves a great deal of frustration. Again, due to the simplicity of much of this advice, the reader is more in danger of failing to recognize the exponential effects that such small and subtle changes can have on Chinese operations.

For purposes of clarity, the discussion is arranged under two headings: Personal and written communication.

Personal communication

There are a number of advantages to communicating personally in China, not least of which are the ability to build rapport, develop personal relations, and immediately address and clarify misunderstandings.

The first thing to do when meeting the Chinese, which many buyers overlook, is to focus one hundred percent of your attention on *people*. Establish personal bonds and show sincerity as you shake hands by maintaining eye contact and make sure you have pronounced each person's name correctly. Have your business cards accessible and give one to each person using both hands (running out of business cards on the last day of a trade show is understandable; arriving at a meeting without them is less acceptable). Taking a business card without giving one in return is a mild violation of the law of reciprocity.

Before launching into a discussion of business, sit down and take time to talk about things on a personal level; ask what each of the people's jobs and duties are and talk about your trip. Speaking to each person also enables you to gauge their level of English (if this is the language used to communicate) which in turn may require you to modify the manner and speed of your presentation. Informal chat builds a friendly energy at the table and dissipates the nervousness Chinese workers often feel when meeting a foreigner for the first time. Mention your experience in China. If you have several years of experience working with China, divulging this at the beginning can thwart any intention to take advantage of inexperience, which prevents later loss of face on both sides.

In addition, make a point to discuss the Chinese operation, and their customers and strategy, which shows sincerity and provides the opportunity to glean information that may cause you to modify the items on the list to be subsequently discussed. It is also advantageous to set an itinerary for the meeting that includes, if appropriate, a tour of the factory, lunch or dinner, and time for discussion before returning to the hotel. Despite being in both parties' interests to discuss projects, it is all too easy in China for most of the allocated time to be used up walking around a factory, driving to a restaurant and eating, leaving insufficient time for a detailed discussion of business issues. In fact, due to the emphasis on relationship building and non-task oriented discussion, the Chinese often prefer to spend more time getting to know you and to provide you with the big picture than to get down to any specific discussions.

If you are in China to educate counterparts or to present important information, pay attention to the time. Lunch in China is normally at midday and the further you talk past this point you may find the less attention and concentration you will receive; workers will be fidgeting, looking at their watches and thinking about their stomachs rather than listening to you.

When in product development meetings, get in the habit of being systematic and avoid hopping around from topic to topic which tends to be the working style in China. If this working style is allowed to dominate, the likelihood of confusion and of details being overlooked increases. Start on a topic or product, discuss it, take notes, then make sure everything is clear and understood before moving to the next item. *Get used to giving specific instructions, making specific requests and clear decisions.* Do not be tempted to leave anything open to interpretation, which could invite "creative misinterpretation." Avoid saying, "I'll leave that to you," and make sure to decide everything down to the last detail before proceeding. If you are not sure, ask for advice but supervise the decision-making process until a decision is made and ensure that all parties make a note of it. If materials are not on hand to make a decision, it is best not to leave it to come back to later; instead, wait while materials are fetched, then make the decision before proceeding.

During discussions, read between the lines of responses. If your Chinese counterpart says "no problem" or "I understand" make sure their body language and facial expressions are congruent. If "no problem" is accompanied with a look of total confusion, stop and explain. Deal with any uncertainty or confusion immediately. This is the best way to overcome misunderstandings. *Get in the habit of asking the other party to repeat back to you their understanding of what has been agreed at each stage of the meeting.*

If a number of issues, products, or projects are discussed, it is vitally important to set priorities; if not, they will be completed according to their ease of completion, without regard to any strategic importance or consequences. Without specific priorities in China, what gets done first becomes a question of maximum visibility, minimum effort!

For each point, it is also a good idea to set completion dates or deadlines. Don't set deadlines arbitrarily. *Make sure completion dates are realistic and that there is a compelling reason to complete them on time, otherwise they become just dates on a piece of paper.* It is therefore important to understand the process involved and to be intimately familiar with the work to understand what is possible. The other party is likely to give you varying estimates, from the excessively optimistic bordering on the impossible, to the ultra-conservative to give themselves plenty of time. It is good to get the middle ground. Beware of stating unrealistic deadlines in the hope of getting things done more quickly; if deadlines are not realistic you risk losing credibility. In addition, if deadlines are physically impossible to meet, it will not improve the completion date. In fact, the work is more in danger of being put aside because they know finishing on time is impossible. At the other extreme, if deadlines are too relaxed and too much time is provided for completion, it often means the project will be put aside while other work is done instead. There is then a mad rush at the end and the project is often late anyway!

When the subject matter is appropriate, make sure accurate notes are being taken in meetings. From the informal chat at the beginning, you should be familiar with each person's comprehension of English. Check that the person taking notes has sufficient ability and comprehension to be able to properly do the note-taking and that he or she is sitting closely enough to hear. Although this may seem obvious, I have seen a number of examples where staff sit as far away on the periphery as possible so as not to hear, and which consequently allows them to avoid responsibility for any follow up. The system of note-taking also provides an insight into the operational organization. Remember, if the company President is the principal note-taker this often indicates an excessively dictatorial management style or unreliable staff, which means extra supervision may be necessary. Make sure the notes taken are sufficiently detailed and if appropriate ask for a copy to assist with your follow up (a forewarning that you will ask for a copy of their notes later helps to ensure they will be sufficiently detailed!).

When issues arise, try whenever possible to take a problem-solving approach and avoid taking an adversarial stance. Use language such as: "we note that X hasn't occurred as scheduled. What can *we* do to avoid a problem?" It rarely pays in China to look around for someone to blame, or someone you can call stupid to make yourself feel better. *Whenever things are not going according to plan, go immediately into problem-solving mode.* There is always a reason that things are not going as scheduled and it is this reason you need to look for so that you can deal with it. It is better to get to the bottom of things in an atmosphere of collaboration. If something is not working out, try changing *your* approach to get things back on track. It is a common reaction of foreign business people to *blame* the Chinese worker for problems. However, we must understand that we are dealing with people of a different culture, with a different educational background and with a decision-making process different from ours; we must therefore modify our management and communication style to suit the situation. The very worst thing you can do in China is vent your frustration or anger, which will result in loss of face, defensive behavior, and immediately bring an end to effective problem solving.

After the meeting, it is assumed the majority of communication will be conducted by email, fax, or telephone. The meeting should therefore be seen as an opportunity to set the scene for smooth future communication. Identify the contact person for future correspondence, and also the person who will manage things when the primary contact person is not at the office. Make sure you have correct contact details for each person. State that you expect responses to emails within twenty-four hours (other customers may not ask for this and will therefore not get it, especially when they are busy). Finally, reiterate that all the points should be followed up according to priority and the completion dates agreed.

Written communication

To minimize mistakes and misunderstandings, follow up after personal meetings should be conducted, where possible, in writing, rather than by telephone. *The use of the telephone for dealing with Chinese companies should only be considered under five circumstances*: to build and maintain personal relationships; for high level private or strategic discussions with senior personnel; to gauge reaction or emphasize the importance of a topic; to discuss in advance written communication you are about to send; to follow up on written communication and make sure everything has been understood.

Detailed information should not be communicated by telephone due to the fact that English is not the native tongue for the Chinese party and also because if a point is not understood, the cultural response is often not to admit it and continue with the conversation based on, at best, an incomplete understanding of what is being discussed. In addition, there is the issue of accountability; should a person not follow through with your instructions, there is no documentary evidence and no recourse. If there is a mistake, the absence of documentation will be used as evidence that you failed to properly advise them.

Documentary communication, whether by email, fax, or courier, is in itself a veritable breeding ground for cultural misunderstandings and it is therefore vital that it is approached in the correct manner. Once again, *we must bear in mind that we are not firing off an email to a person in the same office, company, or country; our communications are crossing time zones and cultural boundaries*. When we are writing correspondence to Chinese companies, it pays us to stop and consider our objectives, rework and reword the message to make sure it is in the clearest possible form, conveys the meaning we want to convey and will illicit the intended response. We need to be sure our communication will get the job done without creating more confusion and at the same time without hurting the recipient's feelings or causing them to lose face. In other words, we must weigh our objectives within a cultural context.

To avoid mistakes, delays, and misunderstandings we must make sure at all times that written communication is clear, precise, orderly, and structured. Leave no room for misinterpretation. Ensure that information is complete and that there are no information gaps that can be filled or interpreted in an unexpected or undesirable manner. Whenever possible, organize information into prioritized numbered steps that need to be followed. Unless you are searching for information or opinions, don't ask open-ended or vague questions. Ask specific questions and give specific instructions. Instead of sending paragraphs of complex information, try to condense the information into specific details. If you are asking for answers and information, get in the habit of using forms and take the time to design a form where the recipient needs only to tick the relevant boxes or fill in the empty spaces.

However, to ensure that things run smoothly in China, project managers must go further than making sure information is clear. When passing projects to China, buyers must get in the habit of double-checking details for the "obvious." While details or interpretations of details might seem obvious to the sender, details are often open to different interpretation due to the different cultural or educational background of the receiver. It pays to step back and look again at a project to identify any *assumptions* that you might have made or details that you have omitted because you are taking them for granted. If you have omitted a detail "because it is obvious" it will help to avoid problems by going back and actually specifying the obvious. It is often the one detail that you fail to mention that will hamper or delay the project.

I have seen many cases where a foreign buyer receives a project from his customer or sales department, and because he is busy or unsure, forwards the project in its entirety to his Chinese contact person and expects him to figure it all out. This form of "passing a hot potato" may work if sending emails to people in your own department or to someone thinking on the same "wavelength." However, it is not the best course of action to use with Chinese companies and normally results in the buyer having to get involved shortly thereafter to sort out the mess, which is even more time-consuming. When busy, it is invariably better to wait until time is available, do the groundwork properly, sort out the relevant parts, and then break the project into specific steps and instructions before passing any details to China. *The golden rule is to do the value-added work yourself and send only the specific instructions that the Chinese side needs to follow.*

Similarly, if your client asks you to come up with a new concept or design solution, don't make the mistake of simply forwarding the email and asking your Chinese supplier to think for you. *Don't expect creativity unless it is creativity they are selling, or in which they specialize.* In my experience, Chinese workers handle and reply first to specific communication—the easy to answer or fill-in-the-box type—leaving the "creative thinking" type to last, or consign it to the bottom drawer, or use it to line the trash bin. Or, it will be delegated to someone else who will leave it to last, consign it to the bottom drawer, or use it to line *his* trash bin. Get the point! Be clear, concise, orderly, and specific with the instructions and information you send to Chinese companies. In addition, as discussed in Success Step 7, follow up on all communication to avoid delays and preempt misunderstandings.

Using diagrams and drawings is a good method to overcome language and cultural differences, which can also save time and circumvent numerous questions. A picture says a thousand words, especially in China when those thousand words need first to be understood then translated into Chinese so that factory workers can get to work on them! For this reason, many companies have bi-lingual staff at the head office so that projects can be discussed and translated before being sent to Chinese suppliers.

The use of well-designed forms and computer graphics to more clearly present information and specifications not only facilitates smoother communication, but also reflects your level of professionalism. Avoid hand sketches not only because they leave more room for "creative misinterpretation" but because of the image being communicated of your company. In conclusion, the more organized and better presented you are, the easier it will be to get things done and the better and more professional impression the Chinese partner will form of your company, which will reflect on the level of service you receive.

It is also necessary to consider the issue of "face" with written communication. Choose words carefully because it is equally possible to cause loss of face to your Chinese counterpart by email or fax.

Try to avoid aggressive requests borne of frustration or blaming people for mistakes, or pointing out in a righteous manner that things have not been done well or on time. The most likely response in these situations is no response. Bear in mind it is possible that communication intended for office staff is read by the manager, and visa versa. If there is a problem, adopt a disciplined problem solving approach. Get on the phone to add a personal touch. Due to the distances and time zones involved, the very last thing you want to do is sour a relationship with your Chinese counterpart.

With regard to email etiquette, it appears to be common practice, particularly among the ranks of American buyers, to send curt one sentence email replies without a "Dear..." at the top or a "Best Regards" at the bottom. This is clearly the product of extreme communication efficiency, yet it can be construed as rude by other cultures; certainly it does not lend itself to enhancing personal relations. It may seem expedient for cyberspace dialogue in real-time or tapping out a quick response before getting on a flight, but bear a thought for the Chinese person arriving at the office in the morning to an inbox full of instructions without even being addressed by name. *Building strong relationships and communication channels is essential to getting things done successfully in China.* Bearing in mind your Chinese counterpart normally receives only emailed instructions or complaints, sending an occasional and simple thank you email can make a positive difference.

Under tight deadlines, or when particular information requires emphasis, it is also common practice for foreigners to highlight paragraphs of text in red color, often accompanied with an increase in font size. It should be noted that while this may merely be considered to be adding emphasis and helping to draw attention to important information, writing in red color is considered rude, even insulting by the Chinese and should not be used. If highlighting is desirable, use blue, green, or lilac—any color other than red.

There is also a growing trend among buyers to send out "bulk" email inquiries to multiple factories. These emails are the type that have no recipient or personalized message, and are sent to an email address within their own company and copied to twenty factories in expectation of the lowest quote in return. Unless it is done periodically for research to gauge market-pricing levels, this approach in China is flawed for several reasons. First, it runs counter to the Chinese propensity for loyalty and does nothing to foster the building of relationships. Second, the best factories are not so hungry for business that they would spend time competing for business in this way. Third, and most relevant, it assumes that Chinese companies are efficiently organized and run along customer service-oriented lines. Don't be surprised to receive rapidly diminishing replies from bulk email inquiries.

Summary

Face-to-face meetings provide the best opportunity for clarifying misunderstandings, building personal relationships, and setting the tone for future communication. To have good relationships with Chinese counterparts is an asset. Whereas poor relationships can act like a patch of mud that causes projects to stop in their tracks, good relations can be like hot grease to a project's wheels.

Thereafter, it is important to do the strategic, value-added organizing of work on your side before sending very clear and specific instructions to China to be actioned. The overriding principle is to use accuracy to get work done with maximum efficiency and minimum delay. Attention to detail is crucial to success, and the best practice is therefore to put everything in writing, ensuring that instructions are clear, complete, precise, and prioritized, using pictographical presentation whenever possible.

Finally, remember that your emails and faxes are crossing time zones and cultural boundaries so the expediency of communication must be tempered with recognition of cultural sensitivity.

SUCCESS
STEP 9

Negotiating
in China
Hidden Variables
and Future Value

Negotiation is an area of complexity in any situation. With the additional cross cultural element and language barrier, the area becomes considerably more complex. China in particular presents a unique challenge, and without an understanding of the broader context of Chinese culture and values, the foreign executive can find the process of negotiating with the Chinese to be both daunting and mysterious.

A basic familiarity with Chinese culture and a superficial understanding of Chinese values will only get the foreign executive so far. It may serve the foreigner well enough to get through the introduction and perhaps the initial business transactions, but a deeper level of understanding is necessary to meet the demands of long term associations with the Chinese and to prevent deals falling apart at the negotiation table.

Negotiations in China need to be approached in a more thoughtful manner and cannot be undertaken reactively or emotionally. It is all too easy to go to China and fail to come to agreement, or achieve the desired outcome while upsetting the other party to the point where no further relationship is possible. The key is to resolve issues, come to an agreement, and get the outcome one wants, all the while maintaining personal and professional relationships. This Success Step therefore proceeds on the assumption that the negotiator desires a satisfactory agreement *and* values the ongoing relationship with the Chinese party.

This Success Step focuses on some of the more important issues we need to be aware of when negotiating with the Chinese to recognize the source of much of the confusion, create the right atmosphere for negotiations, and facilitate more favorable outcomes. For ease of presentation, the discussion is organized under the following nine headings:

1. The role of presentations in structuring negotiations
2. Bridging the cultural divide
3. Negotiating style
4. Future value
5. External pressures
6. Face in negotiations
7. Unaccountability

8. Hidden variables

9. Using target pricing

1. The role of presentations in structuring negotiations

Success Step 8 referred to the important role that face-to-face meetings and presentations play in building relationships and setting the scene for subsequent communication. Meetings and presentations also set the scene for future negotiations. In any business relationship there are countless opportunities to negotiate on issues such as the structuring of ventures, payment terms, pricing, and the resolution of problems or claims that arise during the course of operations. If the initial presentation is well planned and executed, it can preclude the need for future negotiations, or at a very minimum, transform the tone of exchange from a hard negotiation to something that more closely resembles a friendly chat. Following a good presentation, issues with important operational or strategic implications can be discussed and decided both more expediently and informally.

Face-to-face meetings and presentations should therefore be considered as the first stage of any future negotiation, regardless of the subject matter. Presenting yourself at the outset not just as a customer but as a company with a strategic vision that your Chinese partner wants to be part of, enhances your ability to achieve more desirable outcomes and more favorable terms in any negotiation. For example, in a negotiation that concerns pricing, if you have successfully communicated a desire to work in partnership for the purposes of building market share or entering a new market, the Chinese partner will try to give you pricing that furthers these mutually beneficial objectives, without you having to engage in hard negotiations to achieve lower prices. In the case of a negotiation in which the subject matter is a claim, if you have clearly communicated an intention to build a long-term strategic partnership, instead of being a difficult negotiation, the settlement of a claim becomes something that is dealt with fairly and amicably so the partnership can continue with business.

The initial presentation you make upon meeting a Chinese vendor is an opportunity to structure their perception of your company and set the tone for the ongoing relationship. Taking the time at the beginning to cultivate personal relationships and convey the impression that you desire to build a strategic alliance will pay dividends in negotiations later on. Therefore, communicate your strategy and explain the vendor's role in that strategy. Create a vision of your long-term strategic cooperation and plant it firmly in the minds of the Chinese partner. *If more time is spent proactively shaping the big picture, and structuring perceptions of the relationship as a whole, you will find that you can get most of what you want, most of the time, with less time needing to be spent later in the relationship on the negotiation of individual issues, such as prices.* I recall a presentation by an American purchasing manager that so inspired a Chinese supplier with his vision and his appeal to work together as strategic partners that while all the supplier's other customers were having a difficult time negotiating any reduction in prices, this American purchasing manager simply got on the phone personally, stated the price that he needed and the Chinese counterpart would agree with minimal hesitation.

Once the big picture is established, it will shape the outcome of all future interaction. In sum, the purpose of the presentation is nothing less than a complete *role reversal*. From that day forward, instead of asking the vendor for something, you are *providing the vendor with the opportunity to help you and further mutual objectives.*

2. Bridging the cultural divide

When we are negotiating with the Chinese, we must remember that we are straddling two different cultures and two different business environments. The Chinese way of negotiating is deeply influenced by cultural factors, which are the source of much mystery and confusion. When the Chinese style of negotiation is compared with the conventional Western style of negotiation, we are not merely referring to cultural differences, we are speaking of differences and methods of interaction that are in many cases diametrically opposed and therefore also the source of much tension and incomprehension.

While we may be using wide brushstrokes to paint a picture when we speak of the "Chinese style" and "Western style," we are generally referring to styles that are based on differences with very deep cultural roots. For instance, while the Chinese tend to be relationship-oriented, indirect, and value the harmony of the group, Western culture tends to be information-oriented, individualist, direct, and impersonal. While the Chinese have a respect for status and hierarchy and prefer a formal, long, drawn out courtship process, Western business culture is characterized by a respect for ability and a preference for short, informal, straight-to-the-point meetings. The Chinese personality is patient, indirect, and questioning; the Western personality is impatient, aggressive, and direct. Such different approaches generate a great deal of mutual distrust during cross-cultural negotiations. Western negotiators often view the Chinese as inefficient, dishonest, and rude, while Chinese negotiators view foreigners as emotional and disrespectful. It would be quite understandable should participants on either side come to the conclusion that such contrasting approaches are virtually incompatible; it is the meeting of opposite mentalities. What is beyond question is that cultural misunderstandings have soured many promising deals.

To be able to work and negotiate successfully with the Chinese, it is first necessary to understand and respect these differences, take them into account and incorporate them into your fundamental approach to negotiation and negotiation strategy. *With the Chinese, it is important to develop the right atmosphere for negotiations. This means approaching negotiations with the right attitude and taking the time to develop personal relationships and trust before negotiations begin.* Western business people tend to want to get straight to the table and straight to the point. I have seen countless times American business people walk into the office of a Chinese company, sit down and directly start to negotiate prices, while the Chinese business person sits back and wants to talk about the global economy, market trends, and the well being of their respective families.

When negotiating with the Chinese, it is important to establish harmony and sincerity before any specific matters can be discussed or resolved, which may require spending more time on a personal level, for example sightseeing or taking dinners together at suitably expensive restaurants. While Western executives focus on the objective, or *end*, the Chinese place equal emphasis on the process, or *means*. The foreign executive's haste to get the deal done is hard to understand for the Chinese, for whom getting down to business without first establishing the basis for a relationship is both clumsy and rude. As Graham and Lam explain:

"In the final analysis, trust and harmony are more important to Chinese business people than any piece of paper. Until recently, Chinese property rights and contract law were virtually nonexistent—and still are inadequate by Western standards. So it's no wonder that Chinese business people rely more on good faith than on tightly drafted deals."[67]

With good faith, and the right attitude and intentions, the difference to negotiations can be surprising and the Chinese will often overlook mistakes and oversights. Conversely, with the wrong attitude, the Chinese can be unforgiving, and mistakes are taken as an indication of stupidity or unprofessionalism. With good faith, even if the going is tough, the Chinese will take a "let's see what we can do" approach and work hard to find solutions. With bad faith, the Chinese will use the slightest obstacle as an opportunity to call off negotiations or cease work on a project.

Another facet of Chinese negotiation that causes much confusion for foreigners is the apparent haphazard manner in which the negotiation proceeds. Foreign executives are accustomed to working their way methodically through the issues under discussion and once all issues have been discussed, participants understand that a settlement is drawing near and the negotiation close to being concluded. The Chinese, on the other hand, view the negotiation as a whole and will discuss a number of issues simultaneously or switch rapidly from one issue to another, in no systematic order. *In other words, nothing is settled until everything is settled.* For a foreigner used to settling one issue before moving to the next, the Chinese negotiation style can be disorientating, particularly as it seems that no issue is being settled at all as the negotiations proceed. So while Western negotiators are more familiar with a sequential approach to negotiation, the more holistic approach of the Chinese needs to be recognized and respected. When such an approach is expected in advance, much of the confusion and frustration will evaporate. Some indications that the negotiation is drawing to a close can be sensed by a relaxing of their stance on certain issues, more detailed questions, or a higher level of intimate discussion between the Chinese participants which signals decision-making on specific issues.

There is also the issue of the Chinese characteristic of indirectness that must be anticipated and recognized. Rather than directly express or state their disapproval of a particular aspect of a negotiation, the Chinese will often skirt around it or create delays or difficulties in relation to other issues until the aspect is modified to their liking. The foreign negotiator must therefore learn to read between the lines of Chinese demands and try to gauge the underlying message that is being sent. This is often not something that comes naturally for a no-nonsense, direct-dealing Westerner, although it can be learned with patience and experience.

For busy, efficient, and impatient Western executives used to getting straight to the point, the patient approach of the Chinese can be frustrating. It is important to leave the straight-to-the-point attitude at home and be prepared to settle in for the duration with Chinese negotiators. Taking time to build relationships, trust, harmony, and switching back and forth between issues with no apparent progress being made is a process that cannot be cut short. The game must be allowed to take its course. *Any demonstration of impatience or frustration will not be understood by the Chinese and will be taken as a sign that a problem exists.* It is likely that negotiations will be halted until harmony can be restored, or for more serious incidences that might result in loss of face, negotiations might abruptly end. Foreign negotiators must also be aware of the use of brinkmanship; the Chinese will see how far they can push you in order to test your breaking point. At such times it is important to remain focused and composed. *There is no room for temperamental foreign negotiators who are unable to remain calm and friendly for the full duration; any lapse of friendliness could be fatal.*

I recall a senior American executive that on the second day of negotiations lost patience with what he perceived was unnecessary delay and vacillation. He completely lost his cool and launched into a barrage of complaint. There was a stunned silence at the table. He got up and walked to the window to regain his composure, but it was already too late. The highest level Chinese participants had already left. After saying goodbye to the lower level participants who remained, and making a brief and vague reference to continuing the discussion another day, the participants never sat down together again. Any display of anger or aggression usually results in *mutual* loss of face. Hence, any consideration of the use of anger or visible frustration as a negotiating tactic is doomed to failure.

The Chinese also tend to take a great deal of time to respond to offers and proposals, which contrasts with Western expectations of an immediate response, or an immediate reciprocal concession. Chinese business people also take more time during the negotiation for broader consultation of additional information, oftentimes away from the pressures of the formal negotiation setting, which significantly lengthens the duration of the overall negotiation. Then after some time, instead of coming back with an answer or agreement on a certain issue, the Chinese return with numerous other questions, some of which are seemingly unrelated to the issue just discussed. This can be quite frustrating for Western executives, although again, if it is expected, some of the frustration can be circumvented. In China, Western business people must learn to wait. Etiquette demands that matters of importance be approached with gradualness.

In addition to apparent delaying tactics, the Chinese are also comfortably skilled in the use of silence. Patience is a virtue that the Chinese seem to possess in more copious amounts than their Western counterparts. While the Chinese are comfortable pondering information or just sitting there in silence for no apparent reason, foreign executives often feel they must say something, or worse, grant concessions in an effort to move things along. It is important to note that silence does not signify that negotiations are faltering, or that there is a sticking point that needs to be remedied with a premature counter offer or concession before things can continue. Western negotiators simply need to emulate the calm pace of their Chinese counterparts and be more patient. The Chinese will respect this. *Impatience can be fatal to negotiations and if urgency is sensed by the other party, the balance of power can immediately shift in their favor. Alternatively, impatience might be interpreted by the Chinese not just as a weakness but as suspicious*—either you are making a weak offer or trying to sweep something under the carpet and therefore your proposal requires even greater scrutiny. The effect of demonstrating impatience is to further prolong the process!

Another distinguishing factor is a general cultural difference in approach to business. While Western executives tend to think in absolute binding terms, the Chinese approach is characterized by a *"practical flexibility."* Western business people see prices or agreements on terms as contractually binding and therefore providing a fixed basis upon which secondary agreements with customers further along the supply chain can be made. The Chinese, however, take a more practical approach and consider agreements binding only so far as conditions remain the same. If anything subsequently changes that might affect their ability to supply or even to fulfill their obligations at the same level of profit, the Chinese will feel at liberty to attempt to revise any promises or agreements that have been made. *Agreements are not perceived as cast in stone; instead, they are guidelines that are contingent and subservient to the changing needs of the respective parties.* A "look-see" approach is taken. More emphasis is placed on the harmony of relationships than on the details of agreements. For example, if you agree a pricing structure should be valid for twelve months, a Western executive will consider this a fixed issue and use it as the basis for an annual plan. However, should there be changes in the market that might affect the Chinese party's ability to maintain a consistent profit margin, the Chinese will simply argue later that prices will need to be revised, or in severe cases, cease supply until a new price structure is agreed upon. Another example might be in relation to order quantities: If the order is stated as 50,000 units but the manufacturer had problems with production or the supply of raw materials, the foreign purchaser would be expected to demonstrate flexibility by understanding the Chinese manufacturer's situation and accept a reduced quantity. Arguing on a point of principle without recognition of the other party's predicament would be perceived as looking out only for your own interests. Being flexible and accepting quantities according to what the manufacturer is able to supply under the circumstances demonstrates a commitment to the manufacturer and that the relationship is valued.

The main point is that decisions in China may not be final even when they appear final. This makes it significantly harder for Western executives to plan ahead with certainty, particularly if locked into agreements with third parties that cannot be altered without penalty or loss. When negotiating with the Chinese, therefore, we must be conscious of their practical and fluid perception toward agreements. Verbal or written agreements with the Chinese do not necessarily mean a deal has been irrevocably sealed. To avert such practices, we must not only "lock-in" prices contractually with the Chinese but also reiterate the importance of adhering to agreements and the consequences of later changes. In addition, wherever possible, we must protect ourselves with flexible contractual clauses with third parties.

To negotiate with the Chinese also requires the cultural interpretation of words, body language, and facial expressions. *When an offer or a proposal is presented, the Chinese will rarely respond with a negative response.* Poor offers or bad ideas are typically greeted with words such as "let's take a look" or "let's see." I recall that each time a German employee of a Chinese company entered the Chinese President's office with a bad proposal, he would always be dismissed with the words "ok, let's see" before the proposal was tucked away at the bottom of a pile of papers in a corner of the room, for ultimate disposal when a politely sufficient length of time had passed. Rather than respond with an outright no, which the Chinese see as offending someone's face, the Chinese are more likely to change the subject, ask an unrelated question, or respond ambiguously with a subtly negative remark dressed up in a positive response, for example "seems fairly ok" or "seems not too bad." Without the benefit of a deep cultural understanding, foreign negotiators can completely get the wrong idea, or find it hard to know what is going on when they believe a proposal has been positively received yet no further progress is apparently made.

It is not only necessary to pay attention to verbal responses but also to study the body language accompanying such responses. During negotiations it helps to remember that when the Chinese smile, it often means you have put them in a position where they understand there is a need to compromise in order to deal with the situation and you can therefore expect some movement in your favor. *Laughter in negotiations, however, typically signifies that the Chinese are angry rather than happy.* It is likely to be a forced laugh as though seeing an imaginary joke that would allow the Chinese to save face at an awkward moment.

Under such seemingly complex circumstances, it is a great advantage to have a Chinese speaking member on your team who is better able to read and understand the subtleties of Chinese expressions, intonations, moods, and other facets of communication. Such a cultural understanding can be invaluable to avoid misunderstandings that can cause potentially successful deals to collapse.

A final point should be made on the need to understand cultural differences and ways of doing things, assimilating them into your approach to business in China, yet not assimilating them to the extent where you lose objectivity or become more malleable for your Chinese hosts. When immersed in such a culturally distinct environment, the foreign business visitor, in an effort to fit in and not rock the boat, often adapts his approach to the local "way" of doing things — in short, he "goes native," In this new identity, and with these unfamiliar and new behavior patterns, it is easier for the foreigner to become more easily persuaded and manipulated, even to the point of ignoring the priorities for which he is there for. It might be considered a variation of the "Stockholm syndrome," in which captives identify with their hosts and begin to defend them! *In China, it is important to respect other cultural norms and behavior, and to recognize the other party's objectives, yet not to lose sight of your own.* It is necessary to stand your ground on some issues or principles. Other objectives can be modified in light of new information but just ensure that it is not through getting sucked into and under the "cultural quicksand."

3. Negotiating style

During more than a decade in China, I have been present at a lot of meetings and have seen many different styles of negotiation used with the Chinese. There is not one single approach to negotiating with the Chinese that is effective in all circumstances, or another that is completely ineffective all of the time. However, it soon became apparent what styles were more successful than others, more of the time. It became evident that *the best way to approach negotiations with the Chinese is through collaboration and co-operation*, which has been a consistent theme throughout this book.

Negotiating techniques that are generally less effective in China include "zero-sum," "hardball," and the "adversarial" approach. The zero-sum approach is when the pie is perceived to be fixed and whatever you win the other side loses, so you are trying to get as much as possible, while leaving the other side with as little as possible. It may be possible for the negotiator to succeed with this approach, although in reality the Chinese often win more of their formally agreed "share" later through the use of hidden variables, which is discussed below. A better outcome is usually achieved on one issue by linking the negotiation with other issues. In a price negotiation, it is easier to achieve lower prices by agreeing to place higher volume orders at a later date, or by promising to place orders for additional products, for instance: "if we agree to place orders for five other products in the product line, will you accept our target price for this product." If one side is perceived as only looking out for its own interests, it generates a great deal of mistrust and the Chinese are likely to become very inflexible in their response. In the unusual situation where the pie is truly fixed, it is necessary to refer to an external justification for a particular price rather than to be seen as gaining an unequal reward in comparison with the Chinese outcome.

Hardball negotiating is taking an inflexible position, refusing to move on major issues, and expecting the other party to make all the concessions.[68] It is "win-only" instead of "win-win." Taking this approach or attitude with the Chinese invariably leads to the Chinese also digging in their heels, a failure to get what you want, and often the ruin of the relationship. A senior purchasing executive for a famous European household consumer brand was in Hong Kong to negotiate prices for several of the products in his product line. Several weeks previously, due to rising raw material prices, the Chinese supplier had sent a message mentioning that price increases were inevitable. The executive had arranged to meet the owner of the Chinese company on the day of his arrival to discuss the issue. The company driver duly collected him from his hotel to take him to the company's office where the parties sat down together at the table. The owner of the Chinese company proceeded to explain the situation in some detail with regard to raw material supply and the result, regrettably, was that prices would need to increase to maintain supply. The purchasing manager could see the wisdom in the argument, yet stuck to his guns, adamant that once prices had been quoted they were fixed. The two sides failed to reach agreement and arranged to meet two days later at the lobby of the European executive's hotel.

At the appointed hour, the purchasing manager waited in the hotel lobby with his colleagues. Half an hour passed. Then an hour. After an hour he was wondering whether he had noted the wrong time or place and called the company owner. He said he was stuck in traffic and was on his way. An hour and a half later an assistant of the owner arrived, explaining that the owner was otherwise engaged. Quite simply, the Chinese owner had accepted another engagement and did not consider the executive's tone conciliatory enough to warrant another meeting. The price discussion then continued at a lower level on both a less compromising and less amiable basis; the owner's assistant had been briefed with prices that were to be communicated on a take it or leave it basis.

The executive, who with several years' experience should have known better, had broken several unwritten rules. First, he took for granted that his communication was direct and on a personal basis with the company owner. Second, he had failed to prepare properly. Had he been properly briefed, he would have known that increased global demand was causing raw material prices to spiral higher, the extent of those rises and the impact this would have on particular product prices. By not appearing to be knowledgeable about the changing macro-economic circumstances and the situation faced by his vendor, he himself had lost face and was not perceived to be negotiating at the same level. Third, his negotiation technique was competitive rather than based on mutual long-term cooperation; without thought to Chinese cultural considerations, he clearly valued short-term product prices more than the overall relationship. In China, it pays to approach negotiations from a wider perspective. Unless problems are insoluble through dialogue and events are past the point where issues are able to be resolved amicably, negotiations are taking place within the context of a continuing relationship. *It is therefore important not to focus on individual issues to the expense of the overall strategic relationship.* Fourth, he took a "hard-ball" stance to the negotiation, expecting the other party to accept his viewpoint and prices without giving *anything* in return. His steadfast refusal to move on price was not properly explained or empirically justified. He didn't express his understanding of the Chinese party's dilemma or seek to discuss a creative mutually acceptable solution. By taking a hard-ball approach and failing to appreciate the situation faced by the other party, the personal relationship with the owner had been soured, with the result that he was no longer dealing at the highest levels with his vendor.

The adversarial approach, anathema to the Chinese, is where parties approach negotiations as though they are on opposing sides, rather than as parties with mutual long term interests. This approach is commonly taken by foreigners when the subject matter is a claim when negotiators attempt to establish who did what and when in an atmosphere of blame, as though fault forms the basis of settlement. In China, it typically doesn't. While such an approach might produce good results in certain circumstances, it is not the best approach to get what you want while maintaining good relations.

With their keen sense of justice, British business people tend to be the worst culprits. Below is an example in the form of a correspondence from a company in the United Kingdom to their Chinese supplier in relation to a claim for a shipment of goods of sub-standard quality. In an email, after the details had been outlined, the correspondence ended:

> *"The problem was clearly your fault and therefore we fully expect that you should pay to us the full value of the order, plus the costs of shipping, the labor charges for the inspection carried out in the UK, and an amount to cover for the loss of business we suffered, or we will not do any further business with you in future."*

A threat is unlikely to put the Chinese party in a receptive state where they are willing to resolve the issue quickly or favorably for the claimant; it is more like shooting yourself in the foot. In relation to claims, it is highly unlikely the supplier will admit to being at fault and simply return your money. This would mean the supplier has made a mistake and loses face. In reality, the issue would need to be approached in a more indirect, adversarial manner. If you judge the supplier to be subsequently able to meet your standards and you want to continue business, it is often necessary to explore creative, face-saving solutions such as credit against future orders, replacing a percentage of goods, manufacturing an agreed quantity of replacement goods at a lower price, or returning the goods for repair at the supplier's expense. What such an approach is doing is recognizing the business relationship is more important than the particular claim.

Hard-ball negotiation may be suitable in some situations, although a more collaborative, "win-win" approach leads to more successful conclusions when the frame of reference is the overall long-term business relationship and you are working within that framework to get the best possible result. If, on the other hand, you refer to ending the relationship in order to get what you want, such as in the example above, it sends a clear message that the relationship is not considered important and puts the Chinese side in a corner from where they will fight tooth and nail *not* to settle on favorable terms, the question of right or wrong is largely irrelevant. *Negotiations in China are not based on principles of natural justice, right or wrong, or legal niceties—it is simply a question of focusing on mutual commercial gain and getting the best deal you can in a vacuum of conscience.*

Unless you are willing to accept the risk of terminating the relationship and see legal action as a viable prospect, neither the hard-ball, zero-sum or adversarial approach to negotiation is the best way to proceed with the Chinese. Collaboration is likely to produce much better results and should be the preferred method, at least initially. In the absence of effective and efficient legal recourse, even if the Chinese party is at fault, there is little choice but to adopt a respectful, cooperative approach from the outset. With the Chinese, it is better to stress the importance of a continuing relationship and future business opportunities, then move on to discuss the details of a solution that works for both sides. The example above would have been better approached along the lines of:

> *"We are happy working with you, value our continuing relationship, and have a significant number of orders that we expect to place with you in the near future. We have just received a shipment that we are unable to sell due to the condition of the goods [explain the quality problem in a neutral descriptive way, including photographs where practical, and offer to send samples for reference in order to demonstrate sincerity]. Please advise the best way to resolve this issue?"*

This approach makes no reference to terminating the relationship and gives the Chinese partner an opportunity to suggest a solution. The non-confrontational tone also avoids any loss of face. The length of time the Chinese side takes to get back to you, and the solution that is offered, will clearly indicate how much they value your business and in turn help to indicate the best way to proceed. Depending on the supplier's response and the supplier's relative importance to your business, it may then be necessary to continue the discussion noting the actual sums of money involved or prudent to offer to apportion the loss in some way. Such a settlement is far superior to no settlement at all and an end to the relationship. While the supplier may have been completely at fault, it often does no constructive good to blame or steadfastly refuse to accept anything less than total compensation for loss. Such an approach will only work when you also have absolute negotiation power.[69] The important issue to be aware of in China is if you do not fall into the Chinese supplier's "most valued customer" category, or are unsure of your bargaining position, don't expect 100% of your demands to be met. It is often necessary to compromise to some extent as a face saving gesture, for instance, by linking a compromise on the claim to a lower price on another product. *The Chinese will often see an attempt to get every last cent out of a claim as petty in the context of years of partnership and support.*

If you are not going to get 100% of your demands, it is often advisable to use the compromise as a strategic opportunity to demonstrate "the value that you place on the continuing business relationship," which can pay dividends in the long-term.

4. Future value

In the West there is a general expectation of fairness and justice. This is due to a combination of decades of familiarity with democratic institutions, the support of legal systems that are reasonably efficient, fair and consistently applied, and ever higher levels of customer service becoming the norm in increasingly competitive markets. The notion that the "customer is king" pervades Western collective consciousness. When consumers experience poor service or buy a product that is faulty, companies are expected to bend over backwards to correct the situation and keep customers happy. In business, similar expectations exist; legal contracts encapsulate the parties' respective expectations, the parties are expected to fulfill their obligations, and if not, they will do their best to rectify the situation. In capitalist markets where an independent media is quick to expose wrongdoing, efficiently operating stock markets where prices are based on a free flow of information and that quickly adapt to news of poor performance, and properly functioning legal systems providing a level playing field for commerce, there is a prevailing expectation of fair play.

In China, similar forces do not exist to coerce participants to play by rules of fair play—China is less of a level playing field and more a potholed quagmire! The framework that typically exists in more developed economies—such as a well developed and implemented rule of commercial law, and customer-oriented markets where success depends on providing superior customer service—either does not exist or fails to provide sufficient incentive for participants to operate according to a higher standard or code of ethics. Instead of the usual checks and balances that provide the foundation for smoothly operating capitalist economies, the equivalent Chinese institutions offer uncertain protections as they are running to catch up and stay abreast of change. Companies in China are therefore embracing the opportunities to profit from relations with foreign companies and exposure to global markets, without the corresponding institutions that impose similar rules and ethical practices on their operations.

Furthermore, while a legal system exists that governs commercial relations in China, it is a cumbersome, bureaucratic monster rather than a fair and efficient system that allows foreigners to operate in China with the feeling that their interests are adequately protected. Foreign executives are reluctant to resort to legal means in China due to a lack of familiarity with the process and higher uncertainty regarding the outcome. The role of negative publicity that plays a role in keeping business operations in check in more open economies does not exist to the same extent in China. Although China is becoming increasingly integrated into the global economy, there continues to exist a sense of isolation in that Chinese managers do not feel sufficiently connected to the global marketplace to concern themselves with the consequences of poor publicity. In the case of disputes between Chinese and foreign companies, there is very much a sense of "them" and "us" and the likelihood of damaging their reputation is unlikely to compel the Chinese side to seek a more equitable solution.

The first issue to contend with when negotiating with the Chinese is to put out of mind the expectation that resolutions will be based on fairness and justice. It is important to recognize that the Chinese approach to negotiations, and in particular disputes, is not with reference to any pre-conceived notions of fair play; it is with reference to your perceived future value as a customer. It is strictly about business, not principle.

For example, if the issue under negotiation is a quality claim, the general response in the West is *let's get to the bottom of this, fix the problem, and find a way to satisfy the customer.* In China, the initial response is usually an expression of surprise, followed by denial and avoidance of any responsibility. A complete cessation of communication is not uncommon. The issue that led to the quality problem will be fixed to avoid future problems, yet they will feel no obligation toward the customer that suffered loss. *If there is a solution, it will be based firmly on the perceived future profit potential of the business relationship and completely unrelated to fault.* If your company is a ten million dollar account for the Chinese supplier, there is a good chance of a fair, equitable, and reasonably expedient resolution. If you are a small account or placing a one-off order, don't expect too much after sales service. In such situations, without good relationships, it is harder to negotiate a fair outcome.

With claims in particular, the first concern for the average Chinese supplier is to consider your future value as a customer. This takes into account both formal and informal considerations, for instance, the cost of settling the claim balanced against any payments outstanding,[70] the future business that can be expected if the claim is satisfactorily settled, or the loss of future business should the claim be disputed.

In the absence of an innate sense of justice or any ethical considerations, and due to the key role that perceived future value plays in structuring the Chinese negotiation response, it becomes vital to manage and structure the Chinese partner's perception of your strategic business potential from the outset of the relationship. The more valuable the other party considers your continued business relationship, the more fair their approach will be and the closer to an acceptable outcome you will be able to settle.

The dialogue that you use should therefore reflect your desire to influence your Chinese supplier's perception of the future value of the business relationship. In relation to claims about quality, refer to future orders and opportunities once a particular quality problem has been acceptably resolved. If you feel the supplier is able to make improvements and meet the required quality standard in the future, place new orders as a tactic, then discuss what can be done to resolve the current quality issue (sometimes it is necessary to go beyond the mere promise of future orders and actually use a tangible incentive). In price negotiations, use language such as, "if we can meet this price for this order then we can significantly increase business with you in the future," or "if you are able to meet our target price for this item, we will consider switching the manufacture of other product lines to your factory."

The key to negotiation in China is to recognize that you are making business contracts without the coinciding moral obligations of fair play. If there is a problem, don't expect a customer-service type response. Don't take a moral viewpoint and expect a problem to be put right because the other party made a mistake. Don't expect the return of your money or an equitable solution because the other party is at fault. Forget fairness, sentimentality, and justice. In the absence of the international media and a fair and efficient legal system, having "right" on your side is not going to get you very far in China, and screaming about fair play or ethics just makes your position look weaker. In such an environment, negotiation with the Chinese is more a game of chess, where you must structure your pieces and stack the odds proactively in your favor to force a settlement that is to your advantage. Remain constantly aware of the reality that the outcome is monetary-based and agreement in your favor is strongly influenced by your ability to shape the other party's perception of your *future value as a customer*.

5. External pressures

Whenever possible, particularly with price negotiations, structure the negotiation in a way that what you are asking for is being forced on you by environmental events *or external factors that are beyond your control.* This gives the Chinese side the opportunity to help you achieve your aims, reduces the potential level of confrontation, and avoids creating a tense atmosphere. It is, in effect, framing the negotiation as an opportunity for the Chinese side to join together with you to fight an external threat.

Instead of framing your demands in the manner of "I need this..." or "we want that..." become used to framing requests in relation to external references. For instance, in price negotiations, don't simply request better pricing. Instead, refer to the fact that lower pricing by competitors is forcing you to lower your prices to compete in the market, or provide market research detailing the maximum price consumers will accept, or present documentary analysis of the price levels where you need to be to achieve a certain volume of sales or market share. *It is necessary to be prepared with a compelling, well-constructed external justification to support your requests.* The more specific the information provided in relation to the external justification and with a rationale grounded in business logic rather than emotional hype, the more compelling and effective it will be.

The reason for using external events to support your position is particularly appropriate to negotiations with the Chinese. Asking for something with no external reference is essentially pitting parties against each other to see who can get the best respective outcome. In price negotiations, it structures the negotiation as a zero-sum game where one's gain is the other's loss, giving the other side the impression that you are simply trying to push prices lower to secure a greater profit for yourself. In any type of negotiation other than price, their sacrifice is essentially viewed as being made solely for your benefit.

By framing requests in relation to events that are external and beyond your control helps to avoid confrontation and protect relationships. It changes the nature of the negotiation, providing the parties with an opportunity to work as partners and the Chinese to gain face by helping you. If the Chinese are put in a position where they are able to help you, you are providing them with a psychological feeling of superiority, which gives them face. Provided that what you are asking for is within the bounds of reason, for example if a certain situation or price level is forced upon you externally leaving you with no other viable option, it leaves the Chinese side either with the possibility to help you and gain face, or in the position where they are unable to help and where they could potentially lose face.

I have witnessed the "external threat" approach used to great effect by a company owner in South Africa. After a long and reasoned explanation in relation to a new competitor in the market, in conjunction with an inspirational vision of future business potential, the owner managed to achieve the rare result of getting his Chinese supplier to sell below cost (and I know it was below cost because I was doing the calculations!)

6. Face in negotiations

Face has already been discussed in relation to its general importance in personal relations in Success Step 3, which emphasized treating people with respect and the consequences of causing Chinese counterparts to lose face. In this section, we are more interested in the relevance of face in a negotiation setting.

The issue of face in relation to negotiations is not just about showing people respect or phrasing issues to avoid causing the Chinese side to lose face; face should influence the fundamental approach to a negotiation, determine the choice of people who represent your company, become part of your negotiation strategy, and even determine some of the issues that are brought to the table.

A consideration of connections or *guanxi,* which was discussed in Success Step 2, should also be an integral part of your approach to the issue of face in negotiations. The personal connections that you have with the Chinese side should rightly influence the choice of people whom you bring to a negotiation, even if they have no direct involvement in the subject of the negotiations. Those with good personal relations with Chinese counterparts often prove invaluable to create the right "atmosphere" for negotiations to proceed. The pre-existence of interpersonal familiarity, positive feelings, and trust transmit to the atmosphere of the negotiations and bind the participants together with a sense of mutual purpose from the outset. If negotiations were likened to starting a car on a cold winter morning, it is the difference between leaving the car out on the street to be covered in ice or having parked the car overnight in a warm garage. *The pre-existence of trust and friendship allows negotiations to move forward straight off the ramp and avoids the necessary thawing out and sizing up period when negotiators start as strangers.*

If the connections were established with the help of an intermediary, it is often wise if the intermediary is present at negotiations to add to the level of trust and cohesion. In addition, due to the cultural complexity and the potential for misunderstanding, the intermediary is often a powerful asset to the negotiation. An intermediary might be the most suitable person to commence a negotiation by introducing the matter to be discussed, is often better able to gauge and interpret the mood of the negotiation and, by continuing in the role of go-between, might more effectively communicate potentially sensitive points between the parties that the parties would find more difficult to say to each other directly.

In China, it is also important to consider the status and seniority of participants in a negotiation. The Chinese have a deep rooted sense of deference and respect for superiors. Western executives are more used to working with people on the basis of merit; however, the age and status of colleagues chosen to meet and negotiate with the Chinese must also be a consideration. A more harmonious atmosphere and greater cooperation will be achieved if there is a "meeting of equals." For instance, a Chinese company President would expect to discuss matters with someone of the same or similar rank in the foreign company; sending anyone lower could jeopardize the negotiation. The Chinese will quite possibly find it insulting if a foreign company sends a young, low level representative to discuss issues with senior level Chinese delegates.

I recall a number of instances where American companies in particular have sent young and inexperienced sales representatives to discuss high level matters with senior Chinese executives and the affront was clearly evident in the demeanor and body language of the Chinese participants. It is important to recognize and respect the significance of rank and the informal currency attached to it when dealing with the Chinese. In extreme cases it can prevent the most senior Chinese participants from attending or cause a negotiation to fail before it has even started.

Likewise, if an initial meeting starts with high level participants on both sides and lower level representatives are then sent for subsequent discussions it will be perceived as an insult and cause loss of face. It is much the same at the state level; if a government wishes to express disapproval at the actions of another government, the President will be "unavailable" for a visiting head of state, or will send the Secretary of State in his place; it is a subtle way to downgrade relations. It is similar in business in China and the level of the people that are sent to discuss issues speaks volumes and will be interpreted accordingly.

It is important for continuity of personnel to be maintained in negotiations. As personal relationships are important, sending different people to consecutive negotiations can lead to a breakdown in trust or a cooling in response and momentum. For negotiations at the highest level, it is often necessary for senior executives to make several trips to China to maintain the level of trust rather than delegating the task to others, which might be a more common procedure back home. If the president or chief executive of a foreign company makes the effort to personally meet the Chinese side, it emphasizes the value placed on the relationship, demonstrates the importance of the matter to be discussed, and gives enormous face to Chinese counterparts. The gesture speaks on its own.

It is useful to note the presence of the most senior Chinese participant during a negotiation and its ulterior significance. If the most senior Chinese participant or the Chinese company President leaves the room, this need not be perceived as a bad sign. The most senior Chinese participant is often there to evaluate the relationship and the level of sincerity as a whole, rather than be part of the actual negotiation which is not considered their role; their perceived role is more as figurehead whose task is to create and maintain the overall harmony. The most senior Chinese participant will often have provided clear guidelines to the other Chinese representatives, who may then only need to refer back for final approval of the agreement. The presence of the Chinese company President later in the negotiation is therefore a sign that negotiations are progressing well or are near a successful conclusion. It is as though they arrive in the final hour as a show of sincerity to put their personal seal of approval on the proceedings. Negotiations are then typically followed by a lavish dinner where the President can resume his role of endorsing the agreement and upholding of the harmony of the relationship.

It is also necessary to be aware of cultural differences relating to formality. While Americans especially are known for the casualness with which they conduct business and for a preference to work on a first name basis—the relaxed "just call me Tom" manner—the Chinese with their strong sense of deference to social structure could find such informality offensive, particularly if the relationship is in its infancy. Therefore, while the intention of a casual approach may be to fast track the personal relationship, it can often backfire in China. The danger is that the Chinese will find such an approach disrespectful and could result in mutual loss of face. Remember that relationships in China take time to form—the process must run its course naturally. It is best to respect Chinese formality—err on the side of caution by using first name terms at the invitation of the

Chinese, or only when you perceive the relationship has acquired some degree of personal depth, at which time suggest the more informal title in private with a Chinese counterpart rather than in general discussion in front of subordinates.

It should be borne in mind that the phenomenon of face is two-sided. It is not only Chinese face that you need to be concerned with; you must also maintain credibility and *keep* face. This is all too often forgotten as Western executives shuttle around China performing their tasks with a strict adherence to their own cultural values. Some degree of compromise is often necessary to function properly and in a manner the Chinese will consider appropriate. If you are unprepared, unprofessional, disrespectful, or if you break promises, you risk losing face, and the Chinese may not want to deal with you.

In the West, it is common to negotiate, reach agreement on issues, sign, and get on with the respective obligations agreed upon. However, in China, one must be careful that in successfully getting what you wanted you may also have succeeded in pushing the Chinese beyond the point at which they considered the outcome to be fair. It means that while you must push for what you want, be careful that you are not pushing too hard and causing the other party to lose face.

If you push too hard for what you want without due respect for the Chinese position, act too aggressively, cause the dialogue to become heated, or lose your temper (the greatest of all sins), and consequently cause your Chinese counterpart to lose face, the atmosphere of the negotiation is likely to change completely. If agreement is reached, when the parties leave the table the Chinese side may uphold the letter or substance of the agreement but not the spirit, which can make things extremely different. *It is therefore important to create or steer a solution whereby the Chinese side not only considers the outcome acceptable but also maintains face and feels good about it.* To facilitate this, it is important that the right *approach* is taken in negotiations and that the atmosphere of the negotiations remains agreeable. There are two other ways.

One way is to structure the negotiation and lead the Chinese to the outcome you need, although allowing them to arrive at the decision themselves. This allows the Chinese side to take credit and ownership of the idea. The technique is to discuss the various options and their respective consequences, *emphasizing* the desired or "right" course of action, then letting the other side make that decision. It is technically similar to forcing the other side into a corner, although it is done gently and you leave a face-saving way out. It also differs significantly in tone from a hard-ball negotiation where you bully the opponent into giving you what you want. Hard-balling the Chinese rarely produces the desired outcome. If the Chinese are forced into a position, the result is loss of face. It is therefore crucial that the Chinese are not seen to be forced into taking a particular course of action but taking that action by their own will. In particular, if the negotiation is on the international political stage, it is better not to leave the Chinese only one choice and force them to agree with it, which means a public loss of face; it is necessary to leave the Chinese space where they are able to give the appearance that *they* deliberated and decided that a particular outcome was in the best interests of both parties.

Another way is to make sure to leave something on the table. It is important that the Chinese side walks away with something that allows them to keep face. Failing to respect the law of reciprocity is not merely bad manners in China, it is virtually considered immoral. In China, the negotiating style where you exploit a superior bargaining position by squeezing the very last drop from the other party does not produce the best results and is certainly not conducive to building good relationships. The general spirit in which negotiations are conducted and the atmosphere in which you leave the negotiation are often as important, *if not more important*, than the negotiation itself. It may be necessary to resort to creativity in the solutions that are offered, or to recognize something of value to the Chinese that may not be of great cost or loss to your company. If you don't have too much movement on the topic of negotiation, try creatively linking issues, for example on future projects or other orders. I recall an instance when a German company succeeded in meeting their target prices on every single product once they had agreed to allow the Chinese to use their brand name and logo for the purpose of advertising on the back of their own product catalogue, which they perceived would give them the ability to attract a higher level of customer and was an issue of face for the company owner. Achieving the target prices was of considerable importance to the German company, yet what they gave in return was of no direct cost to them. The important point to remember is to make sure the other party gets something, which provides the opportunity to save face.

During a discussion of issues or terms, a Chinese negotiator might reply along the lines of "if you don't give me more, I will lose face." It is important that Western business people understand the significance of these words. Granted, there may be times when the phrase is simply a ploy to drive a better bargain or obtain a better price; however, when you hear such a phrase or reference to face it is typically necessary to reconsider the issues under discussion in more depth. There may be issues involved that are of higher value in terms of giving face than in actual or monetary value. For instance, if part of the deal is a reciprocal arrangement to send Chinese staff for training at a foreign facility, this can often be more highly valued as a face gaining exercise for the Chinese negotiator than increments in price. It is important to recognize issues where face may be a factor, and as these are "weighted," it may be possible to trade them disproportionately in relation to their true value.

7. Unaccountability

It is useful to bear in mind that when negotiating with the owners of many smaller Chinese factories and companies outcomes can often be unpredictable. The Chinese are known for being shrewd business people but remember that businesses are often informally managed. Many Chinese businesses are family owned, or controlled by one powerful individual who manages according to "dictatorial whim". There is a general lack of management expertise in China. *It is necessary to be conscious of the fact that you will not always be negotiating with owners that are accountable to shareholders in a traditional sense or professional managers carrying out a "fiduciary duty in the best interests of shareholders."* Therefore, don't expect business decisions always to be decided along the lines of sound logic, prudence, Harvard Business School best practice, or even with etiquette. Much decision making in China is not the consequence of logic or even in the best interests of the companies. Actions can at times be emotional and unpredictable.

The interplay between wealth and power can lead to illogical or emotional decision-making. If the Chinese owner has a big factory and drives around in a new Mercedes, it is likely he is reasonably wealthy. If he is already wealthy he does not *need* your money.

Consequently, if you arrive in China with a new project or idea, it may not be evaluated on strategic or financial merit. If the owner has earned enough and doesn't want more stress, an apparently good opportunity is likely to be declined, just as likely as a poor idea that will enhance social status or recognition might be accepted. Similarly, if a reasonable offer has been made but the negotiation has been approached with an incorrect "attitude" or face has been offended, it will be declined. If there is not sufficient interest, the Chinese can sometimes appear flippant in response to serious and well planned proposals, or inflexible in price negotiations. This is not a negotiation tactic—if you push too far you will either be ignored or receive completely unrealistic pricing. In extreme cases, if a deal is made, you can end up with high prices or poor service with a Chinese partner lacking any real commitment to the project.

It is therefore important in China that you gain the other party's trust and respect, approach the negotiation with the right attitude and take time to understand the Chinese party's operation and needs. Find out if your idea fits in with their desired strategic direction. Is there a *strategic match*? Is the factory currently running at full capacity? Don't assume that because you have a good idea the Chinese will recognize the potential or because you have money to spend a company automatically wants to work with you. Do your homework, build relationships, gauge sentiment and make sure your interests are aligned before you negotiate.

8. Hidden variables

In negotiations it is common to expand the number of variables that are on the table and compromise on some to facilitate the achievement of those that are more important. In the West, negotiation is generally about variables that are brought to the table and openly discussed. Compromise is made on one issue to get movement on another; one issue is dropped to effect change on another. The negotiation is concluded when agreement is made on the whole package of issues. In the East, however, it is often the case that variables are concealed. Just as in any other negotiation they are present and change as discussions proceed, *yet they are not out in the open*.

The most common example is with price negotiations. In the West, when we negotiate the price of a product, we are typically negotiating each party's respective profit margin, or finding creative solutions around the perimeter of the pricing issue to add perceived value to the bargain. The quality variable tends to be fixed, unless various quality levels are offered at different price levels. In China, you might think you are negotiating on the price variable only, *but behind the scenes, specifications are changing without you being aware of it.* You think you are negotiating the profit margin while the quality standard is fixed, yet as the price is squeezed, so too is the specification. An inexperienced buyer might leave a meeting with a big smile and think they are clever having negotiated a price reduction, while the Chinese party are still at the office and have called in engineers to discuss how best to reduce the product specification so they can make the same profit on the newly negotiated price! The buyer assumes he is getting the same quality, while the Chinese company has now removed some internal components or replaced material meeting US or European legislative standards with a lower grade recycled material containing every toxic chemical know to man. The buyer is not made aware of these changes and will not discover them unless through his own diligence. *This is the reality of negotiation in China.*

Behind the scenes changes in quality and material specification help to explain the diminishing prices and often unrealistically low prices quoted at Chinese fairs. When you are walking down an aisle at the Guangzhou Fair, the price for a product may start high and by the time you reach the end of the hall the price of the same product has dropped by thirty percent without any visible difference in the product. This just means the lower-priced suppliers are better at reverse engineering! In China, it is sometimes hard to get truly comparable pricing due to the existence of so many different levels of quality. It is a common problem for inexperienced buyers that negotiate lower prices for a product. The Chinese supplier agrees with the new price and promises to send a sample to confirm. The buyer then returns home and three weeks later a sample arrives bearing little relation in quality or specification to the original subject of negotiation. The buyer is frustrated and thinks the Chinese company is dishonest. The Chinese, meanwhile, think they have done a good job—the customer asked for a lower price, which they were able to meet through modification; it being inherently obvious to the Chinese that a lower price means lower quality.

To avoid such misunderstandings, therefore, ensure that quotations are accompanied with a detailed list of specifications, especially when providing target pricing. This at least allows decisions to be made on comparable products or with disclosed modifications. It is useful to remember that the Chinese rarely lose money (unless an error has been made in calculation and they are held to that price, or strategic pricing is being used for market entry). Like formulas in Excel spreadsheets, if you change the number in one cell, the contents of other cells are automatically adjusted. In China, be aware that if you negotiate one variable, others may also be changing but you are not necessarily being told about them.

In negotiations where this could happen, it is important to discuss issues in fine detail. Don't be afraid of asking many questions, repeating the same questions, or asking the Chinese side to explain their answer twice. The more the issues are discussed, the more likely potential problems will be exposed, or Chinese unspoken intentions uncovered. Try to bring out as many of the hidden variables in relation to components and specifications as possible and document them. If specifications are not documented, the Chinese will feel free to change them without notification. If they are documented, the Chinese may still change them with the excuse that they didn't notice the small print. It is therefore best to document them, personally discuss and confirm them, ensure that all details become part of the formal sales contract and that quality inspections specifically address these issues. In many instances, this requires intimate product knowledge, so if you don't possess the requisite knowledge bring someone with solid technical expertise with you.

9. Using target pricing

The Chinese are notoriously thrifty in relation to money, with a cultural propensity to work hard and save hard. In business, this means price negotiations can become lengthy affairs and concessions will be granted with great reluctance. *It also means that the Chinese often open negotiations with padded prices, or make counter offers that appear completely unreasonable.* While Western business people are used to setting prices that can be empirically or logically justified, Chinese price setting and negotiations can sometimes resemble haggling, much the same as if you were at a Middle Eastern bazaar.

By starting with a high opening price, the tactic being used is an initial structuring of the negotiation range with the objective of upwardly revising mental expectations in relation to the possible outcome. Therefore, instead of getting angry or frustrated, once you are familiar with this Chinese tactic, it is possible to question the assumptions behind stated prices to expose flaws in rationale and get prices back to a more reasonable level.

When on the receiving end of what you consider an unreasonable offer price, remain calm and ask the Chinese details of how they arrived at that price. Use comparisons with other products or suppliers, and go into more detail on materials, specifications, quantity. If prices are unrealistic, at some point the flaw will be revealed, and recognizing the point of difference provides the Chinese with a face saving way out to recalculate costs and prices.

To achieve the required price or lower prices, many buyers use the strategy of target pricing. When using target prices, it is necessary to clearly define specifications (to avoid the problem of hidden variables) and have a well-prepared external justification. Without target prices, it is unlikely a Chinese vendor will bring to bear their utmost creativity to obtain the lowest viable price. However, the target prices provided to Chinese suppliers must be realistic or obtainable through defined modification and it is often necessary to work closely with Chinese suppliers, making specific suggestions, to meet target prices in an acceptable manner. If target prices are unachievable or unrealistically low, not only will you lose credibility but there will be no effort at all put into solutions for achieving the prices. Don't forget that when a factory accepts an order, due to the inherent complications in China, the factory is taking a risk and must be compensated for that risk. It is a good strategy to request prices from two or three preferred and trusted vendors, then to use these quotations to judge an achievable target price, and then communicate this price at the next stage. Instead of attempting to unilaterally impose prices on a supplier, enlist the supplier's cooperation in the achievement of a lower price by using language such as: "The price we need is X. Please look into modifications and solutions that will help us to achieve this price," and make sure that any changes or modifications are accurately documented.

Bear in mind that when comparing prices from different regions or suppliers in China, especially suppliers with which you are unfamiliar, you are not always comparing apples with apples. As mentioned above under "hidden variables," there are often different levels of quality that are not readily apparent or identifiable, especially when receiving quotations by email. Some pricing that you receive from China may not be realistic and is based either on a miscalculation, or is pricing designed to "catch" a new customer. Once the order is placed, or even after the order is in progress, the supplier will admit to making a mistake and ask for more money. Sometimes you might find the pricing you received was for the first order only; when a second order is placed, the price has increased significantly. Local officials often promise more than they are able to offer to win projects and many state-subsidized manufacturers are uncertain how to properly calculate costs or price at ruinous levels because they do not need to show a profit to survive.

It is important therefore to be cautious of suppliers quoting the lowest prices, *which not only need to be substantiated but must also to be viewed in context of the potential extra supervision that may be necessary.* It is also important not to demonstrate inexperience by asking a supplier to match the lowest *unrealistic* quotation. If one Chinese factory has used the lowest possible specification of material to obtain the lowest possible price, it is unrealistic to expect another supplier to meet this price using higher quality materials.

With regard to building a case for achieving certain prices, there are several principles that should be adhered to. With the Chinese, it is not advisable to threaten termination of the relationship itself, for instance by using tactics such as "if you don't give me the price that I want, I will give the order to another supplier." Much like arguing with your spouse, it is not conducive to blissful marital relations to use ultimatums such as "if you do that again, it's all over between us!" *The Chinese value loyalty, so the use of such tactics will be viewed as a sign that the partnership is not sufficiently valued.* As a consequence the level of cooperation may decline, rather than positively influence the achievement of your pricing objectives.

Referring to the quotations from competitors of your Chinese vendor is an effective strategy, yet one that must be approached in the correct manner, which is circumspectly. If you give a Chinese vendor the impression that you are shopping around China for the lowest priced vendor, it gives an impression of disloyalty since the supplier instinctively knows there is little possibility of a long-term strategic alliance.[71] When business is solely decided on price, it is more difficult to build strategic partnerships, which are valued by Chinese companies. Therefore, the best approach for utilizing comparative quotations is not "we have had competitive quotations from ten different vendors and this is the price you need to beat if you want to do business with us." The best approach to take is not that you are actively and aggressively seeking quotations from numerous potential suppliers, but to indirectly use competitive quotations to demonstrate your familiarity with the market. *This subtly alters a request for a certain price from being a personal requirement to a price externally-imposed by the market.* Dialogue structured along these lines can be quite persuasive: "We have been on a recent trip to Ningbo (Shanghai, Yiwu, Wuhan or Xinjiang, etc) and the prices that are being quoted are very competitive. Many companies there are trying very hard to attract our business and each week I receive numerous unsolicited emails asking what they need to do to commence business with us. Of course, we prefer to work with you on this product, so if you can match this level of pricing we hope that we can continue to give the orders to you. This way, we won't attract any unnecessary attention from my superiors/shareholders."

What you are indirectly saying is *I know the market and therefore I expect you to give me your most competitive pricing.* This is all done in a non-threatening, cooperative manner which provides the supplier with the opportunity to make the decision. The relationship should be treated as beyond question and you will only move to another supplier if forced to do so. Once the supplier knows their competitors are breathing down their necks, they will be more creative in finding a way to help you get the prices needed. By using price comparison indirectly, you are communicating that you are familiar with market pricing and don't want to be disloyal to your preferred vendor unless forced. In effect, the vendor is given the opportunity to meet pre-defined pricing, so disloyalty is therefore the vendor's responsibility.

Ultimately, the best negotiators in China achieve the lowest prices without having forced prices on the supplier. The main point in price negotiations is not to be perceived as unilaterally forcing the Chinese to accept prices, but giving the Chinese the opportunity to help you achieve the prices you need and making them believe that achieving these prices is ultimately in their long-term best interests. *It is important to approach the negotiation in the correct manner and ensure that price requirements are adequately rationalized so that by giving you what you want the Chinese believe they are also choosing the most strategically beneficial course of action.* As discussed above in "the role of presentations in structuring negotiations," once perceptions and expectations of the overall relationship have been successfully structured, when you need a lower price subsequent negotiations are less of a challenge; if you present yourself as an alliance partner, you will get alliance treatment. Chinese vendors will help to give you the prices and conditions you need to support mutual objectives. It becomes less of a negotiation and more akin to advising the prices that you need. This is the art of negotiation in China.

Summary

Negotiating with the Chinese is different. It is important to recognize that while negotiations may be about specific issues, they are taking place within the broader context of a different culture with different values. These differences are deep rooted and must be understood, respected, and incorporated within your approach to negotiations. Western business people more used to a no-nonsense, straight-to-the-point approach must learn to slow down, sit back, and appreciate that successful negotiating operates on different principles: before getting down to business, the right atmosphere must be cultivated, trust and personal relationships developed, and negotiations approached with the correct attitude.

The Chinese approach to negotiations is based on deep rooted *cultural* values, and interactions with the Chinese will remain mysterious and confusing unless Western negotiators recognize these values in action. The Chinese personality and approach to negotiations is in many ways *diametrically opposed* to the Western way of doing things and, to be successful in China, Western negotiators must not only understand these differences but adapt their tactics and strategies accordingly. The ability to create the "right" atmosphere for negotiations is important, together with the ability to adopt traits that are more typically considered "Chinese," such as patience and the ability to deal with issues in a more haphazard manner. Yet while it is important to respect Chinese cultural characteristics, it is equally important not to compromise your objectives by doing so.

As in any negotiation, the goal is to get the result you want, yet subtle changes in your strategy will get rewards where other approaches fail. It is necessary to recognize the nuances and collateral cultural considerations and to use intelligence rather than dominating force. *Most importantly, don't waste time appealing to morality; remember your overall negotiation power is determined not by abstract appeals to fairness but by your future profit potential as perceived by the other party.* Therefore, the initial introduction and presentation should be regarded as an opportunity to structure the relationship and the other party's perception of your business potential. The ultimate objective is to set the scene and reverse the roles from asking your vendor for something and instead providing the vendor with an opportunity to help you. It is a good investment to spend time negotiating the big picture in advance to avoid fighting over smaller issues later.

Negotiation in China is always within the context of a relationship. It is not possible to just focus on the issues and desired outcome. It is necessary to pay attention to the relationships between parties and personal relationships that together form the overall business relationship. *The overall relationship should be valued more highly than the outcome of singular negotiations.* The approach to negotiation should therefore be less adversarial and based more on the cooperation necessary to face external pressures that will lead to success for both parties. Push for what you want while at all times bearing in mind cultural sensitivities. Maintain your own credibility while avoiding courses of action or communication that may cause the other party to lose face, which would undoubtedly impact your ability to achieve your desired outcome. Demonstrate your familiarity with market pricing indirectly, which respects the value that the Chinese place on loyalty. Make sure to do your homework on the company and management to understand what their needs are, and don't expect all responses to be dictated by business logic. Recognize the potential existence of hidden variables and bring them out into the open before carefully documenting the agreement.

The clever negotiator in China gets what he wants and, at the same time, the Chinese go away thinking they have done the right thing. If it is a dispute or quality claim, the Chinese will agree to satisfactorily rectify the situation and will do so because they believe it is in their long-term best interests. Likewise with prices, you achieve the competitive price you need and the Chinese side leaves knowing they have a good deal within the context of the strategic partnership you are building together. The best negotiators in China align interests to the extent that negotiations are more akin to discussions leading to amicable and prudent solutions.

STEPS TO
SUCCESS

SUCCESS
STEP 10

A Practical Approach to
Protecting
Intellectual
Property

Let's get straight to the point: there is very little respect for Intellectual Property Rights (IPR) in China. The more visible and ubiquitous products such as pirated films and books, counterfeit designer garments, and imitation consumer electronics, ranging from Hollywood DVD[72] movies to Gucci bags and Burberry jackets, Mont Blanc pens to Rolex watches, are just the tip of the iceberg. There is also a flourishing trade in fake pharmaceutical products, aircraft parts, and spare parts for the automobile industry. The visitor to China may spot fake Italian motorcycles and copies of familiar American and European cars whose designs have been efficiently knocked-off with the aid of 3-D digital technology. The first known fake Ferrari Enzo supercar has even shown up in China.

It may come as a surprise to some that it is not just foreign products that Chinese companies are copying. The Chinese are also busy copying each other! A recent example making headline news was a case of counterfeit noodles; a famous brand of Chinese instant noodles was being unhygienically copied in backyards using second hand cooking oil from restaurant kitchens and then packaged and sold as the real thing.

It is safe to say that anything that lends itself to economic gain will likely be copied and exploited in China. China is by far the world's leading producer of counterfeit goods, both for export and for domestic supply. It is estimated that 20 percent of all consumer products in the Chinese market are counterfeit. The most recent world computer software piracy investigation[73] estimated that 86% of all software in China in 2005 was pirate software (as opposed to 26% which is the figure quoted by Xinhua, China's news agency[74]), including software being run by many government departments in China's sprawling bureaucracy (this is viewed as an improvement on the previous years figure of 90%).

In 2005, while China was ranked by the U.S. Chamber of Commerce as the United States' third largest trading partner, it was also the number one source of counterfeit products seized at U.S. borders, accounting for 68% of all seizures in that year.[75] Each year, the Office of the U.S. Trade Representative (USTR) is tasked with identifying those countries that fail to adequately and effectively protect IPR in relation to protection, enforcement, and fair and equitable market access. In a news release on April 29th 2005, the USTR concluded that infringement levels "remain unacceptably high throughout China, in spite of Beijing's efforts to reduce them." According to a 2005 out-of-cycle review of China's intellectual property practices, USTR estimated that IPR violations remain at 90 percent and above for virtually every form of intellectual property. As a result, China has been placed on the "Priority Watch List" of countries reflecting the highest level of concern and growing U.S. impatience with China's intellectual property rights violations. Countries in this category can be subject to investigation and face the possible threat of trade sanctions.

China's longstanding and widespread violation of intellectual property rights is in spite of the fact that China has strengthened its legal framework and amended intellectual property laws and regulations since joining the World Trade Organization (WTO) to comply with the WTO Agreement on Trade-Related Aspect of Intellectual Property Rights (TRIPs). China is also party to numerous international agreements to protect intellectual property, including the World Intellectual Property Organization (WIPO), Bern Convention, Paris Convention, Nice Convention and Vienna Convention. However, while China is becoming a signatory to treaties and international agreements in relation to the protection of IPR, the government does not seem to have the will, inclination, resources, or ability to enforce them at the operational level.

This contradiction between appearance and reality is a source of frustration for foreign executives tasked with gaining advantage of China's enormous workforce to provide a competitive cost advantage while at the same time protecting their company's inventions, patents, trademarks, and copyrights. For executives brought up and educated in a tradition of respect both for the law and IPR, a great deal of ambiguity is created when a powerful government is signing formal agreements on the one hand and failing to honor them on the other. It is hard to reconcile intellectually and to plan for operationally.

The solution therefore begins by avoiding an excessive focus on appearances conveyed by international legal documents, or indignation at the perceived hypocrisy of events in China but instead to understand why China is such a complex environment in relation to IPR so that we can begin to modify our approach to IPR and begin to effectively deal with it.

To effectively deal with the issue of protecting IPR in China, it is important to understand why the Chinese environment is particularly complicated and fully appreciate what we are up against. For this, it is useful to start by looking at IPR in China from the various perspectives of government institutions, Chinese businesses, culture, and individuals.

Chinese Government and Institutions

From the perspective of the systematic, analytical, Western executive, logic would dictate that exerting diplomatic pressure on Chinese leaders and government would result in improved compliance in relation the protection of IPR, which is in line with the Chinese government's own declared policy on intellectual property. This is precisely the chosen strategy to date by foreign governments, international organizations, and captains of industry. There have been sustained international negotiations concerning IPR on both political and corporate levels and we have seen Microsoft's Bill Gates visiting Chinese President Hu Jintao[76] in Beijing to bring personal relations to bear in the hope of improving China's record of IPR violations. The inevitable results of such top down diplomatic efforts have been promises to improve IPR protection, the signing of international agreements and the re-shaping of China's intellectual property laws to meet the requirements of these agreements.

However, despite the new laws, promises and efforts of Beijing, pirating, counterfeiting, and other intellectual property violations remain at extremely high levels. The conventional wisdom that suggests a correlation between greater diplomatic pressure and improved compliance with international law on the ground seems to hold true only on a theoretical level. Diplomatic dialogue and visits by industry ambassadors such as Gates serve to give Chinese officials plenty of face on the world media stage yet are limited in terms of effectiveness. External pressure does not necessarily produce results at the most important level—the level where these new laws need to be practically enforced. It seems that while external pressure may succeed in getting Beijing to draw up satisfactory IPR related laws, *the actual enforcement of these laws rests with China's complex bureaucratic institutions, and this is where these well intentioned and neatly drafted laws unravel at the seams.* The reason is that implementation of IPR laws relies on China's complex network of local state bureaucracies, which is an inadequate and non-deterrent system of enforcement. As Andrew C. Mertha explains:

> *"Recent rhetoric of those who champion direct confrontation of China over intellectual property protection reflects an astonishing degree of ignorance about the bureaucratic nature of the Chinese legal, economic, and political systems."*[77]

Mertha goes on to explain that external pressure at the highest levels will have little or no impact on the crux of the problem, which is the central government's inability to enforce intellectual property standards at the local level across the vast reaches of China's 31 provinces. The actual problem is therefore rooted in the fragmented nature of political authority in China. Due to the central Chinese government's inability to implement and enforce a dependable and uniform system, increased diplomatic pressure only results in China digging in its heels and becoming less receptive to external concerns. It is a pity that foreign governments are more comfortable combating intellectual property abuses at diplomatic levels and that multinational companies are more focused on instigating change at the national level, rather than at the local, roll-up-your-sleeves operational level, which holds the key to enforcement.

The new laws in China designed to combat IPR violations are first undermined by the fact that the legal system does not have the capacity to handle the sheer volume of cases involving potential intellectual property violations. They are further undermined by the inexperience of the judiciary in dealing with intellectual property conflicts, which naturally reduces the effectiveness of the new laws. Then there is the issue of systemic judicial corruption within the mainland's legal system which is clearly not independent of local interests or political influence, corroborated by the public's contempt for it.[78] Most importantly, the deterrent effect of intellectual property laws is weakened by the very nature of the Chinese legal system with its reliance on administrative and civil measures rather than criminal action to combat infringements. Patent and trademark owners may request the imposition of administrative penalties on the infringer, or bring a civil lawsuit; only severe infringements become the potential subject of criminal punishment.

Laws that satisfactorily meet diplomatic demands and international norms are most significantly weakened at the level of local government and its departments. Policing and protecting intellectual property in China is a daunting task that is made more difficult because many of the local departments in charge of implementing intellectual property laws have inadequate resources, departments are short staffed, there is not adequate training available to officials, and intellectual property concerns are rarely a priority at the local government level. Not surprisingly, many leaders of local government agencies are complicit and intimately involved with the companies profiting from intellectual property violations and benefit financially from their operations; government and enterprise are closely interrelated and infringers need to be well connected to be protected. *This means the agenda of China's local government apparatus can actually run counter to Chinese legislation designed to deal with the problem of IPR.* In addition, when a community depends heavily on violating companies for jobs, there is even less incentive to crack down on intellectual property violations. Social stability is facilitated by employing as many people as possible—even in companies violating intellectual property rights. Indeed, some of the factories in question are owned by the local governments. There is also the perception that cracking down on IPR violations is pandering to wealthy foreign interests, while locals tend to sympathize with the actions of violators that are more culturally close—it is a "Robin Hood" attitude of "robbing the rich and giving to the poor." It is this attitude that fosters the widespread tolerance of IPR violations.

It is apparent for anyone visiting China's cities how openly business in counterfeit goods is conducted. Counterfeit DVD's, fake branded clothing, and imitation consumer electronics in particular are quite freely available in local markets and brightly lit shopping centers with little official attempts to stop it. If they wanted to, local governments could shut it all down tomorrow but they won't, not only because it creates jobs and for the reasons discussed above but because it also gives people the chance to buy products that they otherwise would not be able to afford if the products reflected prices imposed by intellectual property owners.[79] Too swift a transition to a system that fully and consistently protects IPR would not only result in rising prices but could also be a potential contributor to social unrest. So, while the top levels of the Chinese government continue to reiterate a desire to comply with international intellectual property laws and implements the necessary laws on the statute books, enforcement efforts at street level are hampered by lack of resources, protectionism, and deep rooted corruption across the mainland's bureaucracy.

It is only by understanding the issue of IPR from a practical, street-level perspective that we can begin to make sense of the obvious and glaring discrepancy between what is promised by Chinese political leaders on the one hand and the continued widespread violations of IPR on the other, happening right under our noses.

In developed economies with a track record of capitalism, new ideas are recognized as assets that need protection. Economists, businesses, and politicians understand the crucial role of protecting IPR, and that for open economies, rewarding innovation and stimulating investment in research and development are the bedrocks of economic growth. Without adequate protection, any company would be hesitant to invest in products and industries built upon innovations or new processes. While there may be a degree of skepticism about the ability of ex-communist states to recognize the economic role of IPR protection, the Chinese government clearly understands the implications and further appreciates that it is in their long term interests to comply with international standards. The Chinese government knows that rather than just talking about it and adding new legislation to its law books, it must eventually *demonstrate* respect and practical compliance with IPR to become a fully accepted member of the global economic community. However, while many of China's problems are due to an inability to physically enforce the laws due to the enormous task of sorting out its huge network of inefficient bureaucracies, part of the problem is due to the Chinese government not *wishing* to fully implement the new standards, at least not for the moment.

China understands that better protection of intellectual assets attracts more foreign companies to share their ideas and new technology with Chinese companies. However, due to the mad rush of foreign companies taking advantage of China's low labor costs in order to remain competitive in global markets, the Chinese government knows that foreign companies will come to

China anyway. It can see that the present low enforcement levels have not acted to keep the main players entirely out of the market: Western companies want access to the mainland consumers or a low cost manufacturing base; China wants technology, expertise, and innovative designs. While foreign companies see China's record of IPR enforcement as totally ineffective, such risks are considered within the context of global manufacturing costs and China's attractive consumer market.[80] China's poor record on IPR has undoubtedly failed to prevent China's significant economic growth. When the political will of the central government exists to effect wholesale change in a certain area of Chinese society or its economy, it is certainly able to bring the necessary resources to bear to effect that change.[81] It certainly has the resources to achieve more than has thus far been achieved on IPR enforcement. *The truth is that, at this point of economic development and in the early stages of its integration into the global economic system, China would rather deal on China's terms than be dictated to by foreign owners of IPR.* A balance is thus apparently being struck where intellectual property rights do formally *exist,* and China is declaring its intention to improve its IPR record, while at the same time Chinese companies are being given the scope to develop and improve themselves with the help of an influx of largely unprotected new ideas and innovations.

To facilitate this process, the preferred strategy is signing formal IPR agreements on the one hand and a failure to properly enforce them on the other—a typical Chinese contradictory response. The Chinese government recognizes that intellectual property is a major concern for foreign companies and a preoccupation for foreign governments, so the Chinese response is formal recognition of IPR, which gives the West face through the appearance of doing something, while basically doing very little at all to solve the problem.

In a macro-historic perspective, China is still on the nursery slopes of a market-driven, creativity-led economy, and economic and judicial institutions are also on the lower rungs of learning. Until recently, China had been entering the global economy with a low value-added product and is only now beginning to come to terms with the strategic importance of design and the market value of trademarks and branding. The Chinese are playing economic catch up. When is the last time we heard of a Chinese company opening a factory in the USA to build products based on Chinese patents?

Or a joint-venture research and development program in Silicon Valley where the Chinese partner has legal ownership of the results? Poor IPR enforcement allows Chinese factories to improve their processes and operations and move up the value chain by exploiting the inventions and patents of others, particularly in the Chinese domestic market. Han Shih referred to China's "complete failure to break into the charmed circle of international brand names. Where is China's Sony, they say, or its Nike?"[82]

Van der Kamp also took up the issue:

> *"The brand names associated with the industrial emergence of the United States are still known around the world—Ford, Standard Oil etc. They are known for Japan—Sony, Honda etc. We know them even for South Korea's more recent emergence—Hyundai, Samsung etc. But think of China and the most that comes to mind are names such as Haier, a struggling manufacturer of white goods and Lenovo, which paid billions to buy a red nipple on a keyboard and now has trouble digesting this acquisition of IBM's ThinkPad operations. These are not names known around the world, nor do they show any real promise of turning into giants. One reason for this is quickly stated. China's industrial emergence is still too recent for big brand names to have evolved. They will come with time. It is a matter of some urgency, however. As one toy company executive whom Han Shih interviewed observed, China makes 75 per cent of the world's toys but collects only 20 per cent of the revenues."[83]*

To stimulate innovation, government subsidies are available in China for patent applications. The World Intellectual Property Organization said that China had recorded a nearly sevenfold increase in patent applications in the past decade, with the number reaching 130,384 in 2004. This gives China fifth ranking in global patent applications after Japan, the United States, the European Union, and South Korea. However, it appears that two thirds of the applications are for low level innovations related to a product's appearance, shape, structure and color. Of the remaining third, more than 65% were created and applied for by foreign enterprises and individuals. This means that less than 12% of all applications were for high tech innovations and techniques from Chinese companies and residents.[84]

Strict protection of IPR clearly benefits the owners at the expense of those trying to rapidly develop their own industries. China realizes that most of the world's IPR is owned by foreigners and most of the royalties will therefore head straight out of the country, *so at the present stage of economic development, there is insufficient incentive for the Chinese government to comprehensively crack down on companies that choose to violate IPR.* What is the economic incentive for the Chinese government to integrate itself into a global economic system and strictly implement rules for which the main beneficiaries are foreigners? The strict implementation of IPR laws demanded by the West tends to benefit companies in rich countries and prevent Chinese companies from developing rapidly through copying. With its newfound political and economic might, the Chinese are not in the habit of bowing easily to foreign pressure and it would prefer, by omission, to tacitly support a system weighted in favor of domestic manufacturers. It is a long term plan.

At the moment, it is clear that the interests of the Chinese government and the interests of foreign corporations are not perfectly aligned. To see wholesale improvement of the legal system, and proper protection and enforcement of IPR across the board, the Chinese economy must evolve through a three-tiered process. First, China's financial system must develop to the point where Chinese entrepreneurs have access to free capital markets within their own borders. This is a prerequisite for establishing their own innovations and brand names and keeping the earnings from them. Second, more ownership of IPR must become Chinese, either by Chinese companies developing more of their own intellectual property or gaining it through joint ventures or the acquisition of foreign firms and trademarks. Third, Chinese companies must then demand that their government protect the IPR from which they profit. Eventually the interests of the Chinese government and Chinese corporations will be in alignment and the scales will tip.[85]

Chinese Businesses

It is useful to consider Chinese entrepreneurs, company owners, factory managers and their companies in the context of the recent economic development of China. China has lagged behind economically because of decades of communist rule. Emerging after this period and with the gradual liberalization of the economy, the opportunities for economic reward are being seized with a vigor that is extraordinary in its intensity and unprecedented in its scale. It is not just the fact that the system for protection and enforcement is not at the same standard as developed economies, or that the system has not kept pace with the fast pace of economic development; the most salient issue related to business is that with such a single-minded drive to wealth creation, the average Chinese business person is not going to let intellectual property rights stand in their way.

We need to be aware that in China intellectual property violations are based on economic principles and calculations, rather than any effective legal deterrent. The average Chinese business person does not care who designed a product or who owns the rights to it; they are just interested in how they themselves can take it to market and realize its profit potential. Companies don't see anything wrong with producing the same product as a competitor. In many cases, it is a question of basic economics and business strategy. If a new product or innovation is marketed at a high price and there is demand for the same or similar product at an affordable price, Chinese manufacturers have, in theory, identified a market "niche" which they are able to fulfill. This is true when buyers are interested in price, not IPR, which is the case in China. With a legal system that pursues IPR infringements through administrative and civil channels, where monetary remedies do not provide a meaningful deterrent[86] and where resort to criminal action is only reserved for the most serious of cases, it is not surprising that business people are motivated more by the potential rewards than restrained by the threat of punishment. *The lack of an effective system of enforcement for intellectual property laws that might ensure an orderly market is mirrored by a corresponding lack of respect for inventors and innovators by the business community; this is an interrelated and mutually self-reinforcing paradigm.* Most Chinese companies have no incentive to respect IPR unless they are doing work for Western companies that not only demand it but are seen to enforce it. Without well-enforced laws, there would undoubtedly be a similar attitude toward IPR in developed economies.[87]

It is important to understand that the Chinese are very *practical* in their approach to business. There is a particular focus on work of a day-to-day nature and design is invariably viewed as a cost rather than as the basis for potential strategy. There is little desire to pay royalties or fees of a continuing nature, particularly for less prominent brands. This is not only due to a fundamental cultural disrespect for IPR, it is also because in the absence of an effective system of IPR enforcement, companies that agree to pay royalties fear they will be at a competitive disadvantage in relation to other companies that copy the product without paying royalties. Chinese business people tend to take advantage of any new designs, inventions, or ideas that they chance to come upon rather than invest time and resources in their own design capability. Companies don't perceive any wrongdoing by copying other companies' innovations. With the poor enforcement of IPR, the attitude is simply "here's a new product, let's produce it, and see if we can also sell it," or "this new idea is good, let's copy it because if *we* don't someone else will." The thought of getting caught is secondary and consequences will be dealt with if and when they arise. It is a matter of "let's use this opportunity to make money and hopefully no one will notice," or "lets make as much money as possible *before* we are noticed." This is general business practice. Little thought is given to the length of time a product spent in the design process or the sums of money invested in research and development. With minimal analysis, the Chinese take a new product or idea and just get on with it.

This might be hard to accept for an innovator or IPR owner, particularly if the product is something in which he has invested his own personal time and effort into its creation, only to see it treated as a commodity and copied in a matter of days. *Put aside emotion and the moral ground; it is important to recognize IPR as a practical issue that must be dealt with in a practical manner.*

When the possibility arises to work together with a foreign multinational, Chinese companies are weighing the potential of whether it is more profitable to respect the IPR and work exclusively with them, or how best to exploit the IPR for their own purposes (or both). For the thousands of small and medium sized businesses taking their designs and products to China for production, the Chinese manufacturer is considering how best the idea can be used. A sub-conscious risk-reward analysis is taking place; the Chinese business person is wondering how big the company is and what the potential rewards would be working exclusively with it, or whether more profit can be made by developing the idea with their largest customer with more established distribution channels. With the whole world seemingly coming to China to manufacture, Chinese companies feel they are the window of the world, receiving new designs from a customer in one country and being able to offer them immediately to customers in another. If a German customer walks into the office with a new idea, the immediate possibility presents itself to sell the idea to America, Australia, or other countries in Europe. Or the Chinese will be considering its value for the domestic Chinese market. It is almost as if it is their prerogative to help a company nationally and profit globally. When you are in a meeting, you might think the Chinese manufacturer is excited at the prospect of future sales with you, while it is quite possible that they are actually excited at the prospect of future global sales without you. The Chinese manufacturer is smiling at the foreign businessman, which leads him to think, "hmm, my new design must be really good." Actually, the manufacturer is thinking "hmm, I can present that to customers X, Y and Z—they are coming to my office next week!"

In the absence of a meaningful system of deterrence in China, it seems that respect for the IPR of others will improve only when Chinese businesses understand the value of intellectual property protection in the local mainland market and wish to protect their own IPR to provide a competitive advantage for the products they have created. It is early days. Chinese businesses are still largely in copying mode. Once strategies evolve, becoming design-led and based more on differentiation, then there will be growing domestic demand for better protection of intellectual assets. *As Chinese innovators start to develop their own intellectual property, they will demand correspondingly greater protection from their own government and when these domestic demands reach a critical mass, the government will listen.* When Chinese companies are the owners of IPR there will also be added incentive to patrol and protect their own backyard from infringers. The Chinese can certainly do this more easily dealing with their own culture than can foreign companies that lack local knowledge and an understanding of the methods to get things done. A foreign company can often improve protection of its IPR by forming a joint venture with a Chinese company that then has an inherent incentive to prevent IPR abuse, which is the strategy used by Warner Brother's when it formed a partnership with a mainland movie company.

Culture and Individuals

For the majority of the Chinese population, IPR is an unfamiliar concept, an issue that does not exist in the general consciousness. *China does not have a history of private property ownership.* During the decades of communism, individual rights and property rights were virtually non existent and for centuries before that, all ideas were owned by the state. The average citizen in China has little regard for or exposure to intellectual property. It is not something that people grew up with and there is a distinct lack of public education regarding the role of innovation in the economy and the economic and social impact of violating IPR. Even if such information were made available in schools, only half the population generally makes it as far as high school. For those who enter the business environment, unless the subject of IPR is specifically addressed, the employee will enter the economic free-for-all environment and fail to understand or appreciate the importance of intellectual assets. Even the person responsible for the official logo for the Beijing Olympics in 2008 failed to register the trademark, which resulted in a frenzy of products bearing the logo until the government was forced to step in. It is generally students that have received education in the West, employees of western corporations, or those exposed to foreign business practice that tend to have a deeper level of respect for IPR.

Rampant IPR violations do not therefore mean that the Chinese are fundamentally dishonest; the fact is the average Chinese citizen is either largely ignorant of the concept of intellectual assets or has a different *viewpoint* in relation to intellectual property, living in a society where widespread violations of IPR appear to be the norm. After observing Chinese cultural behavior towards IPR for many years, it seems to me that the Chinese view IPR generally, once it is in existence, as creative work belonging to society; hence it is everybody's prerogative to capitalize on it to the fullest extent of their ability. Once a creative idea or design has made its debut, the Chinese generally don't recognize that a person or company is rightly deserving of continued reward for what is perceived as a "one-off" work, regardless of legal accountability. *Instead, it is seen as a contribution, which is thrown in the pot for all to use or develop.* The Chinese culture is based on the concept of supporting the group, rather than the individual. The Chinese haven't traditionally shared the capitalist attitude of private ownership which has been encouraged and developed over a significant period of history in the West. Indeed, new rules of ownership and Western ethics are no match for the get rich quick mentality that now governs the collective psyche and prevails in China.

In addition, there seems to be a general culture of arrogance toward the law in China. This is partly a consequence of a history of political abuse of power, and partly due to a history of settling disputes through personal relationships, mediation, and *guanxi* (rather than with reference to any "rule of law"). Individuals therefore tend to view externally imposed laws almost as an invasion of privacy, or as concepts that are not binding or directly applicable to them. This cannot be more clearly illustrated than with people's general disrespect for traffic rules and regulations: drivers seem only to obey highway rules or stop at traffic lights when police are present, or if there are police enforcement cameras. At all other times traffic rules are almost treated as inconveniences, rather than as rules designed to protect road users. It is similar with rules related to IPR law, which are perceived with equal measures of indifference, arrogance, and irrelevance.

Legal, Strategic, and Operational Protection

We can now see why the proper enforcement of IPR in China is such a complicated issue, one that is not easily solved by changes in the relevant law at the national level. At each stage of government and at every level of the economy, there is a different view and often contradicting agendas for IPR. It is not surprising that foreign executives find it a perplexing situation and don't quite know where to start. *Relying solely on legislation and litigation to protect intellectual assets is therefore a strategy that is limited in effect and all too often destined for failure.*

In China, to be successful when IPR are involved, it is important to recognize the actual challenge and adapt your approach to it. It is necessary to take a more holistic view, not only laying down the proper legal protection to form the basis from which IPR can be enforced *but taking a more practical, preventative approach that incorporates the issue of IPR into each stage of your strategy and operations.*

The following section discusses legal protection of IPR; practical elements in relation to strategy and operations are addressed later.

Legal

It is important to protect IPR through the relevant legal channels and this section provides some China-specific information in this area, together with some practical advice, particularly for small and medium sized businesses that have intellectual assets to protect and are planning to work with Chinese manufacturers. It should be noted that the following information is not intended to constitute legal advice, nor is it intended to be a substitute for advice by legal counsel. It is strongly recommended that companies seeking to do business in China or facing issues of IPR infringement retain qualified legal counsel and pursue their rights through China's enforcement regime.

The first place to start is the obvious step of formal registration of the intellectual property in the export markets and regions where products are to be sold, which can be done through the relevant patent and trademark offices in the respective countries or with the assistance of the WIPO (the World Intellectual Property Organization[88]). This registration provides basic protection on the sales' side and allows IPR infringements to be enforced in more familiar legal systems.

The second step that companies may consider is the registration of intellectual property in China, which allows pressure to be exerted on the supply side to stop manufacture and restrict exports of infringing products to the planned export market and to countries where there is no protection. If China is the market where you intend to distribute and sell the products, then registration in China is of course necessary. While China is a signatory to many international agreements, patents and trademarks must be registered with the appropriate Chinese agencies and authorities for those rights to be enforceable in China. It is advisable, and in certain cases mandatory, to use the services of approved Chinese agents for the submission of both trademark and patent applications. In addition, it is often wise to register intellectual property in Hong Kong; fairs and exhibitions in Hong Kong are used as a launching pad by Chinese manufacturers to establish a global exporting presence. I know of one company with valuable IPR registered in both Europe and China that was powerless to act upon discovering infringing products at a major fair in Hong Kong because they had overlooked registration of the intellectual property in Hong Kong!

China's patent and trademark systems are both based on the principle of first registration. For patents, China follows a first-to-file system, which means that patents are granted to those that file first even if the filer is not the original inventor.[89] Similarly, trademarks follow a first-to-register system that requires no evidence of prior use or ownership and which, therefore, leaves registration of popular marks open to third parties. The exception is unregistered famous marks. Chinese trademark laws specifically provide for instances where a mark copying or imitating an unregistered foreign famous mark on identical or similar goods or services with the likelihood to cause confusion will not be granted registration or will be prohibited from being used. A famous mark will, in addition, receive cross-class protection.

Trademark applications must be filed with the PRC Trademark Office and a decision is normally rendered within 18 months after the receipt of all supporting documents. If the application is approved, the mark will be published in the *PRC Trademark Gazette* and there will be a three-month opposition period. If no opposition is filed, the application will mature into registration, a certificate is issued, and the mark will be published again in the *Trademark Gazette* as a registered mark. The term of protection is 10 years from the date that registration is granted. The owner of a registered trademark may indicate the words "registered mark" or the "R" symbol. Trademark owners must apply separately for registration of a mark in each class for which it is to be used. Use of the trademark is mandatory and three years of continuous failure to use a mark will make it subject to cancellation. Use can be demonstrated with invoices, advertisements, sales records, custom declarations, or Chinese exhibitions where use of the registered trademark is indicated.

In relation to patent applications, inventors or their assignees and successors can apply for registration of Invention, Utility Model, and Design patents.[90] Patent applications must be filed with the Patent Office and normally within 18 months from the filing date, the Patent Office will publish an invention patent application. Invention patent applications (not utility and design patents) are subject to substantive review upon request of the applicant within

3 years of the application date. If the applicant fails to request substantive review within this period without justifiable reasons, the invention patent will be deemed to have been withdrawn. The terms of protection are 20 years from the filing date for Invention Patents and 10 years for both Utility Model and Design patents. Provincial and municipal offices of the State Intellectual Property Office (SIPO) are responsible for enforcement.

Unlike patents and trademarks, copyrighted works do not require registration for protection, provided protection is granted via countries belonging to the copyright international conventions or bilateral agreements of which China is a member. Copyright owners may wish however to register voluntarily with China's National Copyright Administration (NCA) to establish evidence of ownership.

On the enforcement side of IPR, if infringement is discovered, it is wise to hire local counsel and commence a preliminary investigation through a contracted investigative agency before the best course of action can be determined, or whether any further action is worth pursuing. An investigation can determine the scope and level of infringement and, during the investigation, evidence[91] may be gathered that may be used to file a complaint. It is also important to determine whether the infringer manufactures or sells the products, the volume of products involved, and the location of the goods.

There are several methods that can be used to enforce IPR. The most low-key and low-cost option, aimed primarily at deterrence, is to identify the manufacturer and request immediate cessation of infringement with a Cease and Desist (CD) Letter. This is a letter sent to the infringer from your appointed lawyer demanding the infringer immediately stops both production of the intellectual property and the marketing and sale of already manufactured goods. In many cases, particularly concerning products not belonging to a famous company or brand, the suppliers or manufacturers may not even be aware that IPR are involved. A formal letter puts the supplier on notice and the threat of legal action is sufficient in some cases to stop the product from being manufactured and offered for sale in the future.[92] Normally, a CD letter includes an undertaking not to infringe in the future, an agreed amount of damages for breach, and compensation for past infringement. It is common for an initial CD letter to be followed by a second or final letter after which, depending on the response, further action can be decided. It is hoped that the result of a CD letter will be cessation of infringement and a settlement including compensation, together with the publication of an apology in a major newspaper.

Due to the importance of evidence in determining the success of litigation in China, it can be to the IPR owner's advantage to work with local authorities and law enforcement agencies to raid the infringing factory and seize the goods under question. Legal firms can help to draft complaints, meet with the necessary government agencies and help to coordinate raids. Following a raid, law enforcement will generally hold administrative proceedings, which usually last 2-3 months. If production of counterfeit products is identified, the IPR owner can request border action by Chinese customs officers to monitor and prevent their export, provided the IPR are filed with the Customs General Office. Depending on the value of goods seized during the raid and the quality of other evidence, the IPR owner may then decide whether to seek a settlement with the infringer or proceed with administrative action, civil litigation, or criminal action. The IPR holder may also apply to the court for preliminary injunction against an infringer before a lawsuit is filed, showing the existence of infringement or threatened infringement.

Legal protection of IPR is not only a matter of registering patents and trademarks with the relevant authorities and enforcing them through legal channels, it is also important that relationships with Chinese partners and suppliers are fully and properly contractually documented and that these legal obligations flow down into agreements with their employees and subcontractors. Agreements should include non-compete provisions, audit provisions (specifying when, under what circumstances, and the extent to which the operations in China can be inspected), and make the partner liable for the actions of its employees and contractors. The most realistic legal remedy is to stop intellectual property infringement through injunctive relief. Contracts should therefore provide for injunctive relief to increase the likelihood of a court ordering such relief.

Some foreign companies operating in China have found out too late that they did not even own the results of work that they had paid for. Companies therefore need to make sure, even when the service provider is its wholly-owned subsidiary, that it actually owns the results of the IPR provided.

If you have valuable intellectual property, then it is worth the investment to properly protect it. It is important to engage good legal counsel, follow registration procedures, and put in place a solid basis from which the IPR can be properly enforced and protected. Foreign companies should not, however, expect significant monetary recovery in China; the dollar amount of any damages is generally small. Monetary remedies often do not provide a meaningful deterrent and it is therefore necessary to look more at the strategic and operational levels to complement the legal IPR infrastructure in order to make a greater degree of protection possible.

Strategic

The biggest mistake that executives make in China is to think of protecting their intellectual property solely in legal terms, often after their property has already been stolen. Many companies in China are losing the battle to protect their intellectual property *because they rely too heavily on legal tactics, and fail to factor IPR into their strategic and operational decision making.* There is a distinct preoccupation with the legal side of IPR; indeed most of the literature in relation to intellectual property in China takes an overly legalistic viewpoint— at the expense of strategic and operational issues that would more effectively combat abuse. In China, it should be remembered that litigation is no substitute for strategy.

The most successful way to approach the issue of IPR in China is prevention. A mindset of prevention should pervade all strategic and operational considerations. Foreign business people are in such a rush to China that they tend to pass their intellectual assets to Chinese suppliers without the proper strategic consideration it rightly deserves; *executives are so caught up in the stampede to take advantage of the low labor costs or reach the Chinese market that they share business and technological secrets too readily with partners, that then subsequently use the information to become rivals in the Chinese domestic market, global competitors, or to supply the foreign partner's competition.* While foreign companies follow standard operating procedures, Chinese companies are operating on principles of guerilla warfare!

China represents enormous opportunity, yet we must avoid "irrational exuberance" especially in relation to passing over valuable intellectual property. The more successful executives recognize the strategic importance of their intellectual assets and take pro-active action by implementing strategic and operational controls to protect IPR. This improves the odds that their IPR will remain safe and lowers litigation costs.

With the current level of respect for IPR in China, if a product has perceived market value it will get copied. The question is how, to what extent, and by which companies. Only companies that have control over unique manufacturing processes, techniques, or materials that are unable to be effectively copied are safe; *all other products and processes should be viewed as commodities in China.* If they *can* be copied they *will* be—unless a company is seen to be ruthlessly enforcing their IPR. In such an environment, while it may not be the advice the reader wishes to hear, the most effective method to prevent abuse of IPR in China, and over which you exert control, is not to share it with the Chinese.

Many top companies reduce the chance that competitors will steal their intellectual property by carefully and strategically selecting which products and technologies to sell and manufacture in China. Included in such decisions should be the relevance of the final product to the Chinese market where the manufacturing is to be undertaken. *If the products have a market in China, then the intellectual property risks are higher.* Some pharmaceutical companies withhold their most innovative high margin drugs from the Chinese market altogether based on such analysis. The increased long term ability to protect their most valuable intellectual property and lower litigation costs makes the trade-off worthwhile.

An alternative method to limit the exposure of IPR or sensitive design elements is to compartmentalize the manufacturing process *by separating the manufacture of different parts of a final product,* manufacturing the low-value part of a product in China and supplying the part containing the critical intellectual property to the manufacturer for assembly, or restricting access to different steps of the process. For electronic or information technology industries, it may mean controlling the manufacture of a key component under your own roof, or manufacturing it in a different country and supplying it under strict supervision to the Chinese factory. For less high tech industries, it may simply mean retaining control of the sourcing and supply of one aesthetic design component or special material instead of requesting the manufacturer to source the component or arrange for it to be supplied. One German company I am familiar with retains complete control over the manufacture and supply of a specialized material and arranges the supply logistics to the various factories in the supply chain in accordance with their order requirements. Another American company sent a buyer to China specifically to source a critical and specialized design decal component for their products and subsequently acted as an intermediary between this manufacturer and the other manufacturers requiring this component to complete assembly of the finished product. While such tactics need more involvement on the manufacturing side in China, sometimes erecting such simple barriers can be sufficient to prevent Chinese factories without adequate time or resources to develop the necessary supply chain or develop the necessary expertise to be able to emulate your product and violate your proprietary products. *In sum, the more you teach the Chinese factories and the more elements of the manufacturing process they control, the more likely there will be IPR violations.*

In relation to IPR, the choice of suppliers and partners is an important strategic decision. It is surprising how little consideration some executives give to decisions concerning potential partners: as project managers and buyers are sent on "trailblazing" missions to China to work on product lines, they are indirectly developing a supplier base. This is the inevitable consequence of being product-focused rather than supplier-focused. There is a stark contrast between buyers that search for new products in China and allow these products to lead them to the respective suppliers, and those buyers that more carefully and strategically select factories according to their core expertise and subsequently develop product lines with these factories.

All suppliers are not equal in China; in fact there is a wide variance not only in expertise but also in their approach to IPR and their ability to maintain control of it. Some respect IPR and will work exclusively with you; others will be using it for their own purposes the minute details are in their hands, while others have good intentions yet lack the procedures and systems that prevent it from being manufactured for others. Carefully selecting trustworthy business partners in China with the right intellectual property practices and security infrastructure is a practical means of protecting intellectual property.

Visiting a Chinese partner's office and factories is a good first step to screen out those that do not share a fundamental respect for IPR. This is particularly important for small and medium sized companies that are taking their ideas and designs to Chinese factories while at the same time lack the resources to legally protect and enforce these intellectual assets to the fullest extent. Visiting the premises is a an opportunity to get a hands-on feel for the way IPR are treated and whether respect for IPR is reflected throughout the company's operations and systems.

If possible, a potential partner should be checked on the basis of its track record for protecting IPR and previous contract performance. It is also necessary to check the ethics of owners and managers and their attitude toward intellectual property; the organizational culture as evidenced by actions of employees at the lower levels of the organization; the present customer base, and the way existing intellectual assets are treated; internal physical security at the premises, and electronic security controls for the protection of confidential information. A note should be made of the supplier's use of sub-contractors, since each additional tier of development makes the management of intellectual property issues more difficult to manage.

It is worth spending time with management not only to discuss intellectual property protection on a formal basis but also to gather information on an informal level that will help to form an impression of whether the company managers are the type of people to whom you can trust your IPR. Many "entrepreneurial" Chinese factory owners try to brush off your concerns for adequate IPR protection with a curt "no problem" type response. In such cases, it is necessary to probe deeper and observe whether company operations and procedures reflect the assurances given; there is sometimes a glaring disparity between the words of managers and the day-to-day operational treatment of customers' exclusive product designs. Management may be aware of the importance of IPR, yet this often fails to be conveyed down the organization and fails to be implemented into operational procedures and security measures—the will at the top does not translate into procedures at the bottom in many Chinese companies. This is often due to the fact that the legal obligations of IPR are of a strategic nature, while Chinese managers are typically busy solving the myriad day-to-day practical problems that constantly arise.

For the average foreign importer, the difference between retaining protection of their exclusive products and designs and having them find their way to competitors can, in the absence of good procedures, be down to the minutiae of small details and coincidence: for example, poor computer security or filing that results in an exclusive design being emailed to another customer; a sales assistant, unaware that a product is exclusive to a customer, offering it to a competitor; a customer asks to develop the designs of others and the sales staff hasn't the training or strength of character to say no; a design drawing laying on a table during the visit of a competitor; a cleaner picking up a spare sample and putting it on a shelf in the showroom. While an American company might be basing its whole year's sales strategy on the unique features of its new product line, this strategy can be leaked to competitors in a moment if samples are lying around the floor of a Chinese factory during a visit. Working with a Chinese supplier with poor physical security measures in relation to IPR can therefore significantly impact the bottom line of your company. It can easily be seen how a high margin sales strategy based on differentiation and unique product design can become a low margin strategy on a "me-too" product if competitors in your marketplace decide to alter their product designs in light of exposure to your new ideas in a sample room at a Chinese factory.

During a visit to the factory we are looking for conditions and attitudes that may potentially lead to such incidents. It is the decisions of staff at the lower levels of an organization that lead to many violations of IPR. Unless there are formal procedures for preventing leaks of intellectual assets, all manner of violations are possible. The mere mention by managers to front line staff that a product or trademark is protected is not enough and will be forgotten after a few days—a theoretical concept that will be lost amid work of a more practical nature. There must be adequate procedures, training, and strict supervision.

There are subtle clues that may yield insights into the actual treatment of intellectual property and the procedures that may or may not be in place. As discussed previously in the section addressing the factory visit, ask the managers and sales assistants for information about their other customers and see to what extent they are willing to divulge information. Ask to see their other customers' latest designs and samples and see what degree of modification is necessary before you can adopt designs and intellectual property that belongs to others. It is a good sign if both managers and employees are unwilling to divulge information about their clients. *A readiness to divulge information or to present the new ideas and samples of other customers is an indication that your designs will be treated in a similar manner.*

In relation to physical security procedures, check to see how design information, samples, and finished goods are handled and stored. In the factory, is there strict control of parts, raw materials, and finished products? Does the finished goods storage area have adequate security and restricted access to certain areas? Are their uniformed professional security guards at all exits? Are branded or exclusive customer samples displayed in the general showroom? Is there management supervision over the choice of products in the showroom, or are showroom shelves simply filled with whatever spare samples are lying around? Are there separate locked showrooms for different customers?

In the office, are design drawings and information neatly stored in filing cabinets or in sight of visitors? Are samples stored in boxes or strewn around the floor in view of all visitors? Some factories keep each customer's samples in separate locked areas where access is restricted to employees, while other factories keep all samples, irrespective of customer or sensitivity, in one general sample area that is open without restriction to employees and customers alike. Depending on circumstances, sales volume, or potential sales volume it might be possible to ask the supplier to construct a secure area for your sample development and storage.

As Chinese suppliers are a potential source of IPR violation and often the first point of contact between your intellectual assets and China, before starting work with the supplier and before any sensitive information is handed over, it is important to make an informed judgment on a potential supplier not only in relation to respect for IPR but also their procedures and ability to protect it. In addition, companies that best protect their intellectual property frequently monitor and re-evaluate the activities of their Chinese business partners and suppliers—even long term trusted ones—for potential leaks.

Operational

The most successful executives understand that the law alone isn't enough to protect intellectual assets. *Legal protection does not stop with the registration of inventions, designs, or trademarks at the relevant intellectual property offices.* In China, an environment with a notable absence of respect and protection of intellectual property rights, formal registration must be considered as just the beginning. In a country where the government does not take responsibility or is not capable of the proper enforcement of IPR, it becomes a responsibility that the government and enterprises must share. *Foreign companies operating in China must take the initiative and take on more of the responsibility themselves for the protection of their own intellectual assets to compensate for the inadequacies of the state system.*

The typical approach of the ivory tower executive to IPR is generally sequential: the product design or trademark is developed, then registered, then the product is produced in China. Should any infringements subsequently come to the attention of the company, the IPR is then enforced through legal means. This paradigm views each stage as sequential and separate. What this means is that once the registration of intellectual assets is complete, the legal side is largely forgotten, replaced by a focus on the day to day operations that create revenue for the company. Violations are then dealt with, if and when they occur. If it would be possible to illustrate this approach in diagrammatic form, it would appear similar to Figure 3.

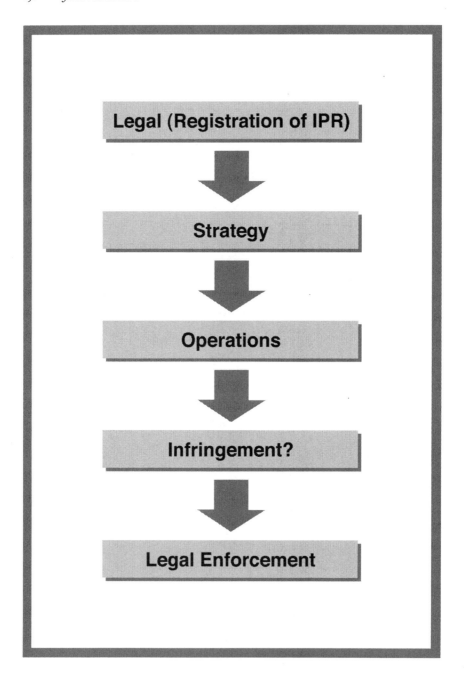

Figure 3: Traditional "Sequential" Approach to IPR.

This sequential approach to IPR does not serve the Chinese environment well. In reality, intellectual property protection in China is not a legal problem that can be solved and then forgotten once operations commence, to be revisited in case of evident infringement. *In a market where participants are in fear of IPR violations, executives must approach the issue with the expectation or presumption of infringement.* The aim should be to limit its effect and maximize profitability against this backdrop. This means that considerations of IPR should be integrated with all functions of the company on an ongoing basis. The issue of IPR must be approached *proactively* with a mind toward *prevention* and with an emphasis on *practical* enforcement at local level.

Violations must be tackled on a practical level with practical solutions. The issue of intellectual property in China is a practical problem requiring the systematic application of prevention and protection of all operational functions. Intellectual property protection needs to be addressed within the framework of corporate strategy and thereafter is integral and inseparable from operations. The most effective form of prevention and protection of intellectual assets necessarily take places at the operational level, and management therefore needs to bring tasks that are relevant to the protection of IPR into the scope of their functions, incorporated and harmonized with operations. If it were possible to plot this model diagrammatically it would appear as shown in Figure 4.

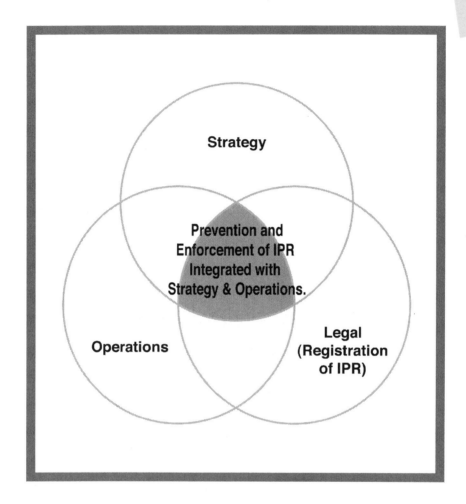

Figure 4: An "Integrated" Proactive Approach to IPR

There are two principal sources of IPR infringement in China: the exposure of products and ideas to manufacturers in the course of business and product development, and the copying and counterfeiting of products that are already in the marketplace,[93] where it is relatively easy for competitors and manufacturers to obtain. Once products are in the marketplace, improved protection of IRP then becomes a question of enforcement. In relation to working with Chinese manufacturers on product development, protection of intellectual property can be improved by implementing new procedures or tightening existing procedures to better safeguard designs, drawings, and samples, and improve the training of employees in relation to the dissemination of sensitive information. *Better procedures can significantly improve protection of intellectual property, or at a minimum give a company's new products an extended lead time in the market before violations occur.*

The following information addresses the sources of intellectual property infringement and offers general and practical solutions for improved protection when working with Chinese companies. Some of these solutions relate to operational tactics, others to improving procedures, while other advice is specific and concerns small changes or nuances in the way IPR is approached that is particularly useful when dealing with the numerous smaller Chinese manufacturers.

Leveraging Contracts and Documentation

It is advisable to have in place at the outset of a relationship with your Chinese partners the necessary legal contracts and documentation covering the details of the relationship and any intellectual assets involved. This ensures that cooperation proceeds on a formal basis and that each party is quite clear about the expectations and intentions of the relationship. In particular, for manufacturers and suppliers with which you will be placing orders on a regular basis, ensure that you have a "Master Agreement" outlining the terms and conditions of the relationship as a whole, which applies to all subsequent orders and projects. Ensure this umbrella agreement is in place before contracts are exchanged for specific orders. This is important for two reasons: first, it contains provisions relating to the use and ownership of all proprietary designs and intellectual property that covers all consequent work between the companies, even in cases where such proprietary designs or intellectual property is not referred to in subsequent order documentation. Second, during the initial stages of cooperation with a supplier and before any official orders are placed, the development work, research, and testing often produces information, processes, and other confidential information that are not in a form that lends itself easily to full legal protection, but that still needs to be legally and contractually protected.

However, as we have seen, formal documentation is only half

the story in China. *It is not only necessary to have the formal legal documentation in place but to gain as much informal leverage from it as possible.* If contacts are signed and locked away in a drawer with the intention to refer to them only in the case of a major breach, then much of their practical usefulness in preventing a breach is lost. While good working relationships are the key to success in China, it is still advantageous to bring legal agreements to meetings to reinforce how seriously your company views IPR. It is also sensible to have a summary of the contracts containing intellectual property provisions translated into Chinese and enclosed with each set of project information or attached to each set of samples that are delivered to the Chinese partner. At minimum, enclose a simple warning stating "these products and information enclosed are the property of X Company and any unauthorized use is subject to legal action." Attention to detail on the operational level acts to reinforce the legal existence of IPR contracts and leaves recipient employees that handle your intellectual property in no doubt that you take IPR seriously.

In addition, be wary of operating on the assumption that once the legal documentation covering IPR has been signed at the top, the information will be efficiently and effectively disseminated throughout the Chinese supplier's organization to the relevant people involved in the project who will be handling your intellectual property. *This is often not the case with Chinese companies, which typically lack efficient communication channels and systematic procedures.* Western executives often make the mistake of assuming that after discussions with a powerful owner or senior manager who is aware of the legal responsibility and who signs the key documents covering IPR, that the time and effort will subsequently be taken to communicate this information and train the staff accordingly. Chinese company presidents or executives often read and sign intellectual property contracts and file them with no more than an informal mention to managers or staff level employees. If contracts are signed with the executive of a company's Hong Kong office, the significance and details are sometimes made clear to other personnel in the office involved with managing the account; whether the same information reaches the office at the factory or to those involved in handling the product or production in China is another issue.

As violations often result from poor communication and

procedures within the Chinese organization it is often worthwhile, if practical to arrange, to request all staff involved to join a meeting where the significance and implications of the IPR can be explained. One way to get this done is to act as if this is company policy dictated by your legal department and it is your legal obligation to comply with it. Interestingly, this not only reinforces with *employees* the fact that the information you are sharing is legally protected property of which your company is the owner, but puts all participants on notice that the existence of IPR has been formally communicated to the *management*; violation of IPR thereafter requires the tacit agreement of all concerned. Chinese management sometimes fails to share the fact that IPR are involved to those lower in the organization precisely because management plans to exploit it for other purposes. Such a tactic subtly applies indirect and informal pressure on the management to comply.

It is important to be aware that, in China, intellectual property violations are decisions based on economic principles, not on ethical considerations, or a fundamental respect for innovation, or any inherently imposed legal responsibility. The Chinese are weighing the potential financial reward against potential risk and adverse consequences. They may only put up with the hassle of a lawsuit if the benefits significantly outweigh the perceived threat of economic sanction. The key here is "perceived."

We therefore need to get as much informal leverage on legal agreements as possible that we can bring to bear to influence the other party's *subjective* economic assessment of risk and reward. We need to go above and beyond the signing of legal documents and stress not only that there exists a legal obligation, *but that your company will enforce it.* To this end I have seen experienced foreign executives drop in a few anecdotes in informal surroundings with Chinese executives to emphasize the importance placed on IPR and the lengths their company will go to protect it. These have included stories about pending cases and settled law suits to disguised humorous asides about the fact that half their companies revenue comes from successful legal action. These stories tend to be remembered long after the ink on legal documentation has dried.

The key is to leave the Chinese executives with the unequivocal impression that your company aggressively and systematically pursues intellectual property violations. In a non-threatening manner, the idea is to leave the supplier in no doubt that working exclusively with you and respecting your patents, designs, and trademarks is a far better alternative than violation of your intellectual assets—the use of tactical theatrics should not be overlooked and can be a surprisingly effective deterrent! *They help to shape the other's perceptions and might just tip the balance of an economic decision based on the perceived ease of profiting from intellectual assets.* For instance, if a potential competitor is in the Chinese supplier's office asking to benefit through your company's intellectual assets, a remembered informal anecdote could tip the balance in that moment and instead of allowing an exclusive design to be supplied through omission to act, a Chinese executive could positively act to protect the intellectual property in question.

Legal documentation should therefore be used together with informal leverage to achieve the dual purposes of ensuring the relationship proceeds on formal terms while instilling adequate fear into the other party to deter infringement. There is a certain artistry involved in the manner of presentation; the desired effect requires recognition of the balance between maintaining the working relationship and creating an adequate level of fear and respect to ensure continued compliance. It is the art of cultivating fear while at the same time fostering cooperation; of engendering trust while getting across that you are serious about IPR. After all, once the legal framework is in place, you will want to continue more on the basis of cooperation rather than coercion.

If you find yourself in the position of "small potato"—a small company in a small market dealing with a much larger Chinese supplier—and you have intellectual property that the Chinese partner would consider interesting, recognize that the Chinese think globally. The Chinese partner will be thinking of selling your product or idea in other markets and leverage can be gained by being resourceful and taking a proactive approach. Offer the supplier the *formal* opportunity to sell the products in other markets if exclusivity can be assured in your market, or offer a royalty agreement to the Chinese supplier based on direct sales of the product outside of your target markets. If you have potentially valuable intellectual property, a formal agreement with a larger Chinese supplier can be a way for both parties to benefit and a way for a smaller company to achieve both a better level of service than might otherwise be merited and leverage the financial returns of an intellectual asset by indirectly supplying other markets.

The key where intellectual property is concerned is to be consistent. If you sign legal documents and emphasize the importance of IPR and then fail to properly enforce them, the message that you are sending is that it is acceptable to bend the rules. Chinese companies will not be slow to exploit such situations. If your company is seen to make exceptions, the Chinese will feel they can exploit your intellectual property with impunity.

Procedures and Systems

As has already been noted, the abuse of intellectual property can often stem from seemingly innocuous and trivial opportunities. Employees without proper training might show your designs, alert your competitors, or offer your products for sale to other companies. Samples left lying around in the factory may find their way into the showroom and indirectly to one of your competitors. If expensive new product moulds are not used, Chinese factories often attempt to recoup the financial investment by selling the products to other customers. Employees will take intellectual property out of the factory and pass them to other factories for financial incentive. The fact is, unless the operation in China is fully owned or the foreign company shares operational management, it is virtually impossible to control the minute details and processes to the point where intellectual property is completely protected during the course of operations. However, once you recognize the often mundane sources of intellectual property infringement, once you take a look at your own procedures at the point of interface with the Chinese company, there are a number of ways that your own operational procedures can be tightened and training of purchasing staff improved that can lower the incidence of IPR violations.

If your company has a buying team or department responsible for product sourcing, particularly if your company is following a low cost, low price strategy, it is not uncommon for new designs and samples to find their way to a number of suppliers. *The buying department should be aware that when sensitive samples or information are sent to five suppliers, there is a five-fold increase in the possibility that these designs will find their way into the marketplace ahead of your own launch.*

Samples and designs should be shared only with carefully selected partners.

There is also an issue with samples that are excess to requirements following project completion or order placement. If samples are sent to several potential manufacturers and development or manufacture proceeds only with one, it is important as a matter of procedure to ensure the return of sensitive material from the other suppliers. The viewpoint of the average Chinese factory is if a customer fails to proceed with a product after the factory has expended time and effort in development, the designs become fair game and are liable to be exploited rather than simply left in a drawer or discarded. *If at any time it is decided not to continue with a project, make sure all material is retrieved to stop them finding their way to your competitors or infringed in other ways.*

It is also good procedure to request any original designs or prototype samples be returned together with counter samples, and all samples remaining in the factory be returned after completion of a particular project or stage of a project.

In addition, it is prudent practice to sign a separate document with partners making it clear that products and samples are not to be displayed in showrooms or at any fairs or exhibitions. This may seem obvious to the foreign executive but it is worthwhile to make it clear to Chinese suppliers that this is not acceptable under any circumstances. Chinese factories often use their customers' proprietary or patented designs at exhibitions, under the pretext that they are merely representing the quality and workmanship that they are able to achieve, and the particular products and designs are not for supply. However, regardless of whether this is the intention, practice can be somewhat different, particularly in the case of an insistent buyer.

During the development process for some product types, there is sometimes the necessity to create a new mould and the question of payment for the mould arises. The standard procedure for many companies is to negotiate the cost of the mould in order to lower the financial investment required of a new product, or try to transfer the mould costs to the manufacturer, or to share mould costs. At face value, this seems to be a prudent course of action, at least financially. *However, what most foreign business people tend not to appreciate is that mould costs are also an investment in time and resources for a manufacturer that need to be recouped by product sales.* If, for any reason, it is decided not to proceed with a particular product, or subsequent purchases are lower than expectations, the manufacturer will attempt to recoup that investment by selling to other customers. If your company paid nothing for the moulds while the effort and expense was on their account, then Chinese managers feel justified in profiting from the final product, legal ownership and design rights aside. Furthermore, when mould costs are shared with a manufacturer, this often justifies the manufacturer to believe that ownership is correspondingly shared.

Procedures in relation to mould costs therefore need to be reviewed to maintain full control of the process and the result. Legal ownership often needs to be supported by financial investment to avoid any self-righteous claim the Chinese partner might nurture. A seasoned foreign business executive once related his strategy with respect to moulds and product development in China. To preempt the problem of suppliers concerned about a potential loss of investment that they may try to recover by selling to others, his standard procedure was to pay double the mould costs in return for the factory's guarantee of exclusivity to his company. While an unconventional approach, at least it eliminates any justification for the supplier to infringe his IPR and sends a clear message that he is serious in regard to ownership. Irrespective of which party assumes the cost of moulds, it is important to document legal ownership not only of the intellectual property but also of the moulds, whereby legal ownership of the moulds is retained. This becomes particularly significant if it is necessary to switch suppliers of the product for reasons of price, or should a manufacturer's subsequent performance fail to live up to expectations.

Much of the discussion of IPR has so far been concerned with the protection of your own intellectual property. It is also necessary to have procedures in place to ensure that your company is not infringing the rights of others in the course of your dealings with Chinese manufacturers prone to claiming that they are the originators of all the product designs on offer. This is particularly relevant to situations where purchasing staff are sent to China on buying trips to source the latest product developments, particularly at trade fairs. A comprehensive consideration of IPR should consider potential violations of other's rights bearing in mind the effect that unintentional violation could have on your bottom line, not to mention operational consequences and loss of reputation. I recall being in the lobby of a Chinese hotel where it was hard not to overhear the vociferous argument between an Australian businessman and his Chinese buying agent. It transpired that the Australian had been offered a "new" product, which the Chinese factory had insisted was its own proprietary design, and which had in turn had been presented to a well-known retailer in Australia. An order was placed, the products were shipped, and only after the products were on the shelf did the infringement come to the attention of the patent owner who sued the importing company. The argument in the hotel in China was an attempt to recover a proportion of the financial loss from the factory owner, who had stopped answering calls and had conveniently disappeared.

It is important that your company takes procedural responsibility and checks the existence of patents before you unwittingly accept the Chinese version of events. Sales representatives of Chinese factories often present copied ideas as their own, or term them *"general items."* A general item in China simply means that numerous factories are producing it and no one knows who *first* copied it! The standard response when a manufacturer is confronted with the facts is that "everyone else in China is also making the product, and it is not their fault." It is worth noting that foreign buyers are to blame for initiating a significant share of the copying that takes place in China by taking competitor samples to their vendors and requesting them to be reproduced with varying degrees of modification. Should the Chinese vendor refuse, they are aware that the product will be taken to one of their competitors and so often agree to do what is asked.

With the ubiquity of copying in China, it is not logical for a foreign company to rely on the advice of a Chinese company with no familiarity with intellectual property in the destination market; indeed, it is the responsibility of foreign companies to have a system in place to verify ownership of any products that are offered in China. I once asked the sales manager of a Taiwanese owned factory in China whether the product designs he was offering were owned by his company and he emphatically assured me that this was the case. However, after requests for documentary evidence resulted in several weeks of silence, he eventually admitted that his previous assessment was untrue—the design had originated elsewhere and had been copied. It is not only important to consider the protection of your own IPR but also to have a formal system in place to protect yourself from violating the IPR of others in the marketplace. Reassurances from Chinese factory managers cannot be taken at face value. Documentary evidence must be produced and the existence of any rights checked by your own legal team. In addition, if the Chinese manufacturer can produce paperwork covering IPR, the fact that a Chinese factory has applied for the registration of a design in China or another country does not prevent it from infringing existing IPR in your own market.

It is wise to review procedures and the manner in which designs and other sensitive information is shared with Chinese companies. Particularly for electronic communications, attention to detail can play a noteworthy role in preventing IPR abuse. If documents are sent in an unprotected format where text and drawings can be easily cut, pasted, modified and forwarded, they lend themselves more readily to abuse. Many intellectual property violations occur at a very practical level. I have seen less sophisticated Chinese companies lift high resolution images directly from customer communications and paste them directly into product catalogues for general distribution. The more consideration given to the format for electronic communications and the higher level of protection, the less likely such incidences will occur. Password protection of documents and sending documents in "PDF" or hard-copy format can prevent numerous low level incidences of intellectual property theft.

If your company is involved in a joint venture or has its own office or operations in China, procedures relating to the selection of employees are also an important consideration. As previously mentioned, employees with educational experience in the West or work experience with a multinational company have had exposure to environments where respect for IPR exists. For this reason, many global companies prefer employees with international work and educational experience. It is good operational practice to screen all employees for high ethical standards, check references where possible and, even though harder to enforce in China, ensure the existence of non-compete clauses or a notice to resign clause in employment contracts.

In sum, the quality of the procedures that you have in place at the points where your operations interact with Chinese suppliers either facilitate or encourage the violation of intellectual assets. Businesses can take certain practical measures to protect intellectual property in China, and preventative measures should be reviewed and implemented according to the industry, the nature of the enterprise and characteristics of the products. The key is to be proactive. It may pay executives to take a good look at company procedures, identifying areas that are weak and replacing them with new systems designed to better protect intellectual property, or at minimum to provide the necessary protection for new products long enough to provide a head start in the market.

Policing and Enforcement

Once intellectual property has been formally registered, protection in China is meaningless unless IPR are properly policed and enforced. Furthermore, protection of IPR is not only about enforcing IPR but also being *seen* to enforce it. Chinese companies copy your intellectual property either because they are not aware that ownership rights are involved (often with less famous and prominent designs) *or because they think they can copy them without adverse consequences.*

When Chinese government institutions are not able or willing to provide an adequate level of protection it therefore becomes necessary to roll up your sleeves, get involved, and do it yourself. In doing so it is advisable to replace an attitude of frustration and confrontation and adopt an attitude of cooperation. *The reality is that intellectual property owners must become more involved with policing and enforcement of their IPR at the local level.* The more your company is seen tackling the issue on a practical basis, rather than merely talking about it at government level, and the more offenders are seen to be publicly punished, the more others will be deterred from taking the same path.

At a minimum, it is necessary to engage the services of an agent in China to monitor infringements in the market and at trade fairs. Infringements can either be reported back to your company to be dealt with by lawyers, or in the case of exhibitions and fairs communicated directly to fair organizers and later followed up by lawyers with the infringing companies. In response to concerns of IPR owners, trade fairs are increasingly prepared to assist with violations. For instance, the new Pazhou Complex of the Chinese

Export Commodities Fair (the Canton Fair) has two offices on the basement floor, one for design IPR infringement, the other for IPR trademark copyright. With the necessary documentation at hand to prove ownership of the affected IPR, it is possible to lodge complaints with officials at these offices who will then assist with investigations. Fair organizers are aware that better protection of intellectual property facilitates the display of new ideas and bears directly on a show's attendance. Fair organizers in Hong Kong have faced mounting pressure from exhibitors to increase their assistance with IPR violations and have offices where in-house lawyers will immediately assess the merit of a complaint together with rules that allow infringing designs to be removed on the spot. With a global audience, having your designs appearing at trade fairs in Hong Kong or China can lead to an exponential increase of copying. The simple act of having offending products removed from trade fair booths, either by your agent or with the assistance of enforcement officials, prevents your products not only from being exhibited to companies worldwide but also from being exposed to hundreds of manufacturers that visit these fairs to copy products without modification or to get ideas for new product lines.

Another method to improve protection of intellectual property at the local level is to seek the support of local government departments, agencies, and customs offices. In addition, according to Chris Israel, the U.S. coordinator for international intellectual property enforcement in the Department of Commerce, the Chinese government is planning to set up 50 reporting centers for intellectual property violations throughout the country.[94] By strengthening relations with government agencies and the officials that are responsible for actual enforcement on the front-line it is possible to apply direct pressure within China. Working cooperatively at the level of local government might therefore be considered a form of lateral pressure, as opposed to the top down pressure typically exerted by foreign corporations through diplomatic channels at the national government level, and which is more effective than standing back and expecting your IPR to be automatically protected by the very existence of formal laws on statute books at central government.

With effectiveness reduced by government under-funding, a lack of resources, and a lack of priority to instigate action against IPR violators, foreign companies often need to help the local government bureaucracies and departments implement and enforce the laws already on the books. It is certainly not unknown for companies to use side payments as a means to encourage local government officials to enforce the law where insufficient incentive exists to crack down or a lack of resources would normally inhibit them from taking action. It is important to recognize the critical role that local bureaucracies play in the actual enforcement of China's intellectual property laws and at an operational level it is therefore imperative to win their support. Successfully protecting intellectual property assets requires an intimate understanding of power politics in China's local government departments and bureaucracies and for this reason local staff with local connections can prove to be essential to the objective of IPR enforcement.

While it is both necessary and important to work together with local government departments, it is also prudent to recognize their shortcomings and find ways to compensate for them. If IPR violators or the competition are using guerilla tactics, it is often necessary to adapt to the law of the jungle. When violations are recognized or suspected, foreign companies have achieved much success by engaging the services of private investigative agencies. These can often be engaged through your legal representative in China. With the proliferation of factories, trading companies, and export companies, identifying the actual source of IPR violations is often difficult. Investigative agencies can do the detective work on the ground that would be virtually impossible for a foreign company to perform. In addition, such agencies also play a major role in gathering evidence in support of subsequent legal proceedings.

Summary

It might be another generation before China is properly integrated into the world economy and at a point where Western corporations and governments are satisfied with China's performance on the protection of IPR. It is therefore necessary to settle in for the long haul, accept a shift in thinking on IPR and modify strategies and operations correspondingly.

It is a mistake to approach the issue of China and IPR with the same mindset or belief system that serves executives in the West. China is an environment where people and businesses exhibit little respect for intellectual assets in a state system where its bureaucratic institutions and the judiciary are either not up to the task of enforcement or have conflicting interests. The main point is not to be surprised, angry, or emotional in the face of IPR transgressions and recognize that in the absence of a properly functioning system of deterrence and punishment, together with a culture of disrespect for intellectual assets, infringements are based on economic motives.

Successful protection of intellectual property is a question of understanding the motives, recognizing the game being played, and to play it better, developing a strategy specifically for the Chinese environment. The first step is the formal registration of IPR with the relevant government bodies and then to bring the functions of policing, enforcement, and deterrence within the sphere of operations to effectively compensate for the failings of the Chinese system. The theoretical separation of legal registration and operational practice does not fit the Chinese model or provide adequate protection of IPR. It is necessary to integrate intellectual property awareness at all levels: legal, strategic, and operational, with the emphasis on deterring and preventing infringements at the operations level.

It is important to recognize that if product designs and intellectual assets are able to be copied, they are viewed more as commodities in China. The best way to protect IPR is therefore not to share them with Chinese companies, or wherever possible, to retain control of key components or the supply of critical materials. Chinese partners must be carefully chosen for their respect and procedural safeguards in relation to IPR and stricter procedures must be put in place at the interface where intellectual assets and sensitive information are shared with Chinese partners and suppliers. Foreign corporations must then take a less theoretical and more practical, hands on approach to enforcement. Proper enforcement must take place at the local level and requires a higher level of cooperation with the various relevant government agencies that are on the front line.

STEPS TO
SUCCESS

CONCLUSION

What is the Key to Success in China?

Taking an historical perspective, China has once again opened its doors to business after a period of economic reclusiveness under communism. With a combination of low labor costs and a personal formula of putting hard work and profit first, China has become a powerful epicenter that is sending economic shockwaves around the world. People talk of the ripple effect of dropping a pebble in the water; China's integration into the global economy has been more of the magnitude of a falling boulder that is creating a tidal wave of change and opportunity. Western executives are busy redrawing business plans in response to the challenges and to take advantage of these new opportunities. China's modernization means upheaval for the rest of the world, and the story is only just beginning. It is wise to understand the causes, for very few will escape the effects.

However, talk of such momentous changes and the opportunities that inevitably accompany globally significant events often obscures the difficulties that lay beneath the surface. In such a rapidly changing environment with so many unpredictable factors, threats and opportunities are not the exceptions in China, they are the norm. Ambitious strategies, plans and projects look good on paper but their realization depends on understanding the nature of Chinese business, recognizing the potential problems and knowing how to do things on a *practical* level. Great opportunities in China come as a package with cultural and operational challenges that are unique to the Chinese environment. Quite simply, with the rush to China, many fail to appreciate what they are up against on the ground.

Most failures and mistakes in China arise because foreign executives are unfamiliar with the nature of the problems they face. When the nature of problems is unknown, it is hardly surprising that foreign business people are ill-prepared to deal with them. To address the knowledge gap, the ten Success Steps were designed to lead the reader from the general to the specific, providing an insight into the problems and strategies to deal with them. Having a general economic and cultural background helps the reader better understand today's China. The importance of "*guanxi*" and "*face*" should not be underestimated and are integral to Chinese business practice. Working in China is about working with people. To be successful in business in China you must first lay the groundwork, which requires making a *conscious decision* to build personal relationships that in turn will form the foundation for harmonious and successful long term business relationships. Success requires understanding how to get things done through personal leverage. It is also about respecting Chinese people and Chinese culture and being aware of the unwritten rules concerning "face"—how to give face sincerely and avoid causing people to lose face.

To work successfully with Chinese companies requires us to stop making decisions based on the value systems and conditions that we are familiar with at home. If we see China through a Western lens or the spectacles of our home market then we will look at but not see what is truly happening in front of our eyes. Solving problems in China often requires us to suspend our judgment, look more deeply into situations, and change our approach until we get things done. Understanding Chinese culture helps us to understand the motivation behind actions and is therefore essential in this process. When things don't turn out the way we want in China, it is common to blame the environment. However, we know the environment is different and we must therefore change the way we interact and manage in response to it. Finding the right approach can exponentially improve results and working relationships. Good relations and being able to navigate Chinese culture positively impacts the bottom line and avoids financial loss; losses are often the result of not appreciating the environment in which we find ourselves, or not adjusting to it properly.

The purpose of looking behind the scenes at the average Chinese organization was to illuminate some of the very practical, mundane problems that workers and management face in China due to the convergence of a unique set of cultural and economic circumstances. The problems that we face as purchasers are a direct result of the problems our Chinese partners face. To deal successfully with Chinese companies, it is crucial to appreciate the complexities and difficulties faced by Chinese company owners, managers, and workers, which will then allow us to plan our operations and implement appropriate procedures. For this reason, buyers spending more time in China often have a better understanding of the problems and tend to be more successful than those attempting to perform their jobs from the comfort of offices on the other side of the world.

We must be constantly aware that we are working with companies that are, for the moment, on the learning curve of corporate and economic sophistication, not members of the FORTUNE 500 club. We are not dealing with German, British, or American companies that have uninterrupted decades of experience operating in competitive, market economies. We are dealing with Chinese companies that have either a history of communist state management, or were founded recently after the economic reforms in the 1980's. This means that many are still in the early stages of integration into the global market-oriented economy, lacking the organizational skills, professionalism, and experience of dealing with highly organized companies together with the responsibilities this entails. We must modify not only our strategy but also our management style and personal approach to these circumstances, compensating for the systems and management expertise that Chinese companies often lack.

Procedures are important for building business in any culture and country; in China, they are *essential*. Due to the often inadequate formal systems and procedures in the average Chinese company, it is essential to compensate with our own. With the average Chinese worker being hands-on and practically inclined rather than having a systematic, disciplined approach to work, we must apply a higher level of supervision and ensure that procedures are applied consistently. This is necessary at every level through the order placement process, from sample development to production planning, and especially in relation to the issue of quality control. Formal supervision of the manufacturing process is *essential* rather than optional. The strict implementation of rules and procedures is the best way to protect interests in China.

The more prudent selection of partners and suppliers is one of the best ways to circumvent problems and frustrations later on. It is also necessary to ensure that they are a strategic match with your operations, and to determine the most suitable operational structure, bearing in mind the use of inspection companies, trading companies or buying offices.

Developing a *mindset of anticipation* is essential if you are to stay one step ahead when working with Chinese companies and is the only way to recognize and solve problems in time. It is about considering potential problems in advance, which allows you to *proactively* deal with them rather than focus on their consequences, which is the preoccupation of those inexperienced with matters in China. In China, inexperienced buyers focus on solving problems, which is a reactive state of mind. Those with experience focus on laying the groundwork, putting checks in place, constantly monitoring projects, and anticipating problems so they can be dealt with early.

At the more specific level, negotiation, presentation, and communication must be mastered and modified to China's unique cultural characteristics and business practices to be truly effective. With such great cultural differences and potential for misunderstandings, it is important to understand how the Chinese think and perceive situations in order that your strategies and behavior can be modified to achieve the necessary results. An almost obsessive attention to *detail* is required to be successful in China. It is a fact that most problems are the result of simple errors that could so easily have been picked up in the early stages. In China, it is not just about dotting the "i" and crossing the "t", it is about regularly performing a complete spell-check. It is about precision and clarity of communication and supervision down to the minutest detail. The detail you miss is invariably the one that ruins or delays a project. It is the one dollar component that wrecks the hundred dollar product. It is therefore not the early bird that catches the worm in China, it is the diligent, disciplined one and, for anyone taking their eye off the ball, the result will invariably be regret instead of profit.

Solutions in China must always go hand in hand with an approach suited to the Chinese environment and this is particularly the case with the protection of intellectual property rights. A successful approach to intellectual property rights requires a shift in thinking away from rigid Western righteousness and toward solutions that are conceived and implemented on a more practical level. The Chinese are practical by nature, therefore we must be street smart rather than excessively reliant on theoretical models, academic prowess or political lobbying to succeed in this area.

I spent more than ten years working for Chinese companies, learning the principles of success and how to get results in China. These were challenging and frustrating years and I would not wish such difficult learning experiences upon anyone! I hope that the information and insights in this book have benefited the reader by providing a better understanding of Chinese workers and organizations, their cultural and economic context, and a conceptual framework for getting personal and operational results. While it might not provide the highest resolution picture, the reader should now have an outline sketch for the box containing the giant Chinese jigsaw puzzle. It is a heartfelt wish that this book will help others to avoid the same frustration I experienced. The challenges are the same, but with a different approach and proven strategies, much of the frustration can be avoided. The newcomer to China should now be able to proceed with a degree of confidence and avoid many of the most common errors and misperceptions. Instead of wondering why things are not going as planned, it should be possible to recognize patterns and problems and appreciate how these problems can to be dealt with. Chinese business people are shrewd and it is unwise to give them the added advantages of culture shock, inexperience and not having access to the right information.

With 1.3 billion people in China—more than one fifth of the world's population—and China playing an increasingly important role in the global economy, knowledge of Chinese business practices will prove to be of enormous benefit. Considering the impact of China on the global economy, for any serious business person to be ignorant of Chinese business practices is unforgivable. China presents risk and promise in equal proportions, and without knowing the rules of the game, we might be in the thick of the action yet still be unable to achieve the results we desire.

The bottom line is this: if you don't understand the Chinese and how to work effectively with them, endless problems are in store. If you understand the cultural differences and know how to deal with the Chinese, it is possible to get things done. And knowing how to get things done is the real key to success in China.

Do you have your own story or experience about China?

Find out how to get a FREE copy of the next book in the
Guru Series by sharing your short stories and experiences
of China,
or to purchase and download the E-Book version of *The
Essential Guide for Buying from China's Manufacturers—The 10
Steps to Success*, go to

www.thechinaguru.com

About the Author

After undergraduate study in business management at universities in both Europe and the United States, and post-graduate studies in law in the United Kingdom, the author has worked for more than ten years in China and Hong Kong as "right-hand man" to the owner of one of the largest factories in China's Guangdong Province. The author has worked closely with numerous Chinese entrepreneurs and business owners, as well as with factory managers and factory level staff, getting to know people on both a personal and professional level. In various management roles, the author has been in a unique position and had the unusual opportunity to develop an intimate understanding of Chinese thinking and business practices. During the course of a decade, the author has frequently been party to multi-cultural private discussions and negotiations involving the Chinese and has worked either directly or indirectly with some of the largest multi-nationals in Europe and the USA. This has included extensive global travel, particularly in the Asian region including Taiwan, Korea, Thailand, Philippines, Singapore, and Malaysia. The author is also the founder of several companies connected to Chinese manufactured products.

Appendix

Internet Sourcing Websites:

TDC Link	http://www.tdctrade.com http://sourcing.tdctrade.com
Made-in-China.com	http://www.made-in-china.com
Alibaba	http://www.alibaba.com
b2bchinasources.com	http://www.b2bchinasources.com
Global Sources	http://www.globalsources.com
Tradeeasy	http://www.tradeeasy.com

Quality Inspection Companies:

SGS:	www.sgs.com www.hk.sgs.com
Intertek:	www.intertek.com
TÜV:	www.chn.tuv.com/eng www.tuv.com

Endnotes

[1] Quoted by Peter Gumbel in *It's a Whole New World*, TIME, August 7 – August 14, 2006.

[2] The Third Plenum of the 10th Chinese Communist Party restored Deng to his posts as Vice-Chairman of the Central Committee, and the Central Military Committee of the Communist Party of China.

[3] Hugo de Burgh, *China Friend or Foe?*, Icon Books, 2006, p.13.

[4] Rather than ideological struggle that had characterized the previous half century.

[5] Foreign Direct Investment.

[6] China has become the worlds largest recipient of foreign direct investment – see Linda Yueh, *The Economy: Opportunities and Risks*, cited by Hugo de Burgh, *China Friend or Foe?*, Icon Books, 2006, p.59.

[7] A feat that other countries failed to do, such as the Nazis in Germany and the Bolsheviks in Russia.

[8] Or, as noted in Chinese constitutional documents, China is a "socialist market with various other economic forms".

[9] China operates the most extensive and sophisticated system of internet filtering in the world. It is estimated there are more than 50,000 full-time personnel involved in its censorship [Becky Hodge, *The Great Firewall of China*, 20 May 2005, cited by Hugo de Burgh, *China Friend or Foe?*, Icon Books, 2006, p.142].

[10] Joshua Cooper Ramo, *Who's Afraid of China? An Image Emergency*, Newsweek September 25, 2006

[11] Elegant, Simon, China and the U.S. *The Great Divide*, TIME, April 24, 2006.

[12] Quoted in the same article by Elegant, Simon, China and the U.S. *The Great Divide*, TIME, April 24, 2006.

[13] *A voice of dissonance on American decline*, Howard W. French, Letter from Shanghai, International Herald Tribune, September 15, 2006.

[14] For example, China was forced by the British to cede the territory of Hong Kong in 1842 as a result of the "Opium War." Refer also to the Japanese invasion of China in 1937.

[15] Hugo de Burgh, *China Friend or Foe?*, Icon Books, 2006, p.67.

[16] *Export riches to follow products abroad until ideas financed in China,* Jake van der Kamp, South China Morning Post Business, Page 14, October 6, 2006

[17] The Lenovo Group (previously named the Legend Group Ltd.) is the largest information technology company in the PRC and its branded personal computer has been China's best selling PC since 1997.

[18] Dominic Wilson and Roopa Purushothaman, *Dreaming with BRICs: The Path to 2050,* Goldman Sachs Report, October 2003.

[19] Source: Donald N. Sull, *Made in China: What Western Managers Can Learn from Trailblazing Chinese Entrepreneurs,* Harvard Business School Press, 2005.

[20] China is clearly, and thus far, *integrating* into the global economy largely on the West's terms; there is no greater evidence of this than China's entry into the WTO, which places conditions for cooperation and forces economies to adapt to international norms.

[21] The latest wage increases in Guangdong took effect on 1 September 2006. According to the new regulations stated in the "Notification of the Adjustment to the Minimum Wage Level in Guangdong Province", the new minimum wage in Guangzhou will be RMB 780 per month (equivalent to an hourly rate of RMB 4.66), in Zhuhai, Foshan, Dongguan and Zhongshan the new minimum wage will be RMB 690 per month (equivalent to an hourly rate of RMB 4.12), Shenzhen will be RMB 810 (equivalent to an hourly rate of RMB 4.84), while Shantou, Huizhou and Jiangmen will be increased to RMB 600 (equivalent to an hourly rate of RMB 3.59). This compares to minimum wages of RMB 690 for Shanghai and RMB 640 in Beijing.

[22] *Wal-Mart backs down and allows Chinese workers to join union,* Jonathan Watts, The Guardian, Friday August 11 2006.

[23] Accidents killed more than 100,000 people in 2005; approximately 270 per day. The high death toll is largely due to a general disrespect for traffic rules and other road users, and negligent driving, with drivers switching lanes without looking or signaling, ignoring traffic lights, overtaking on the other side of the road in the face of oncoming traffic, driving the wrong way around roundabouts, throwing vehicles in reverse if they miss an exit, speeding, etc.

[24] The Communist Party has encouraged this with its atheist ideology.

[25] Food is so important in Chinese culture that it is celebrated in the arts and literature, and is also the main subject of full-length movies where characters duel through the medium of cooking competitions!

[26] John L. Graham and Mark Lam, *The Chinese Negotiation*, Harvard Business Review on Doing Business in China, HBS Press, 2004, p.44.

[27] It is often commented that the Chinese trust only in two things, their families and their bank accounts!

[28] Or what you are trying to do may be a conflict of interests with the Chinese partners existing connections that you may not be aware of.

[29] It should be noted that this is a double-edged sword and not without risk. No documentation also means no responsibility if things should go wrong.

[30] When business cards are exchanged in Asia, it is common upon receipt for some time to be spent studying the cards; the rationale being that the longer the time taken to study the card, the more respect that is given to the person. This might seem a strange practice to the Western business person, as participants are looking at the business card while ignoring the person!

[31] There is no greater example of this than the nature of the Chinese economy itself; a socialist state that embraces capitalism!

[32] With China holding so much US Treasury debt, the US is not in a strong negotiating position.

[33] Instead it labeled China a currency "manipulator" – see the commentary by Bloomberg News, *Labeling China: Manipulator or misaligner?*, International Herald Tribune, Friday, May 19, 2006.

[34] With the anti-China forces now in the U.S. congress, some form of protectionist trade legislation or currency bill is looking highly likely in 2007.

[35] It was also seen as more of the gesture to give face to the Americans. The mere 2% strengthening of the Renminbi was considered miniscule compared to the 30% or more that some sections of American industry were seeking. Allowing the Renminbi to appreciate by 2% again on the 14th December 2006 was also clearly a move designed to give "face" to US Treasury Secretary Henry Paulson and Federal Reserve Chairman Ben Bernanke, coinciding with their visit to Beijing to discuss further revaluation of the Chinese currency.

[36] This is the reason for US laws restricting such practices, although their adoption by US corporations for the Chinese environment are sometimes at odds with the great emphasis on personal relations in China, and the necessity to wine, dine, and entertain business contacts in order to generate trust.

[37] Refers to money that is traditionally given out in little red pockets at the Chinese New Year.

[38] *Bleak future for millions of graduates,* Cary Huang, National, p.8, South China Morning Post, November 23, 2006.

[39] Nanjing Auto is aiming for the domestic China market by marketing MG as a symbol of success. The initials "MG" are to stand for "Modern Gentleman" in China!

[40] For just one recent example, on January 1st 2007, the 260,000 registered motorcycles were banned from Guangzhou's roads to ease congestion, and reduce accidents and pollution. The edict, which directly affected the livelihoods of thousands of people, and indirectly an industry segment, was issued without public consultation.

[41] It should be borne in mind that there are significant differences, distinctions, peculiarities, and varying levels of efficiency between Chinese-owned and operated factories, Korean, Taiwanese, and Hong Kong owned and operated companies.

[42] According to *Fortune*, the Chinese government still owned 98 of the 100 biggest Chinese companies in 2002 [source *The Hidden Dragons,* Ming Zeng and Peter J. Williamson, Harvard Business Review on Doing Business in China, HBS Press, 2004]

[43] Or Taiwanese, Singaporean, Korean, etc

[44] Launched in 1957, the Canton Fair was renamed the "China Import and Export Commodities Fair" from its 101st session in April 2007, in an attempt to reflect its efforts to attain balanced trade with its partners and better fulfill its WTO undertakings – see www.cantonfair.org.cn

[45] Import-Export companies are like trading companies in that they act as a go-between, assisting factories without the appropriate export licenses to export their products to other countries.

[46] This is normally the domain of the fairs in Hong Kong, Taiwan, Japan, etc. However, when the Canton Fair opens its doors to foreign exhibitors for the first time in April 2006, the Hong Kong Trade Development Council will be there to promote Hong Kong companies and brands.

[47] Full Container Load

[48] Less than a Container Load

[49] International Standards Organisation, see www.iso.org

[50] Unless they perceive an opportunity to learn and upgrade their operations with your assistance, through third party training and enforcement, which they do not believe is possible to implement on their own.

[51] Original Equipment Manufacturing, i.e. products custom made for a specific purpose or market niche.

[52] Original Design Manufacturing

[53] First In, First Out

[54] As part of national security measures to prevent terrorism.

[55] Such as using child or forced labor, corporal punishment, life threatening working conditions, or illegal Transshipment practices.

[56] For buyers comparing companies only on the criteria of price, these factories can be passed over as expensive without a proper understanding of the value that is being added.

[57] Donald N. Sull, *Made in China: What Western Managers Can Learn from Trailblazing Chinese Entrepreneurs*, Harvard Business School Press, 2005, p.102.

[58] U.S. Food and Drug Administration

[59] The US and China economies are highly interdependent; the USA is China's largest export market, a high proportion of investment in China is by US companies that are manufacturing for export to the USA, and China receives more support from the World Bank than any other nation, bearing in mind the US has a significant influence on World Bank Decisions. In addition, there is the issue of China's huge currency reserves in US dollars, a sell-off or diversification of which would reduce the value of the US dollar and thus the value of all US dollar denominated currency reserves, which would be detrimental to both economies, as well as many others.

[60] After the US involvement in Afghanistan and Iraq, China certainly *appears* peaceful in contrast.

[61] Although while the political effect of the "unfair" exchange rate is clear, the *actual* effect on the trade imbalance is debatable and would only account for a small percentage of the trade deficit.

[62] *China's global hunt for oil,* Mary Hennock, BBC News business reporter, Wednesday, 9 March, 2005.

63 China has clinched deals to develop oil fields in Iran, Cuba has agreed to let China explore its coastal oil fields, Venezuela has offered Chinese oil companies operating rights to their oil fields, and CNOOC has bought a share of the major oil fields in Nigeria and a license allowing it to explore for oil off the coast of Kenya. China also buys about 80% of Sudan's oil exports, while it shields Sudan from being held to account in the UN Security Council for one of the largest atrocities of recent times—the killing of some 300,000 people in Darfur. China is also busy building relationships with states along the sea lanes from the Middle East and has recently received dignitaries from all 11 countries in the OPEC cartel.

64 There are millions of laid-off workers from China's obsolete state-run factories, rampant corruption throughout the state bureaucracy, deadly environmental and human disasters, and land seizures that are leading to violent outbreaks. In the nine months from January to September 2006 police in China allegedly dealt with 74,000 "mass incidents", the term used to describe large protests and riots, [source: Reuters in Beijing, reported in South China Morning Post, November 19, 2006] while "mass protests" were estimated at more than 87,000 for the full year of 2005 [source: *A blow to justice,* Simon Montlake, South China Morning Post, Features, p.18, November 8, 2006]

65 Such as changes in relation to the special tax rates long enjoyed by companies in China's SEZs (Special Economic Zones). In March 2007, the National People's Congress passed legislation to introduce a unified nationwide corporate income tax of 25%. The SEZs have a five-year grace period to phase in the new tax rate. Shenzhen, for example, the most successful of China's SEZs, currently has a corporate tax rate of 15% compared with 33% paid by firms in other mainland cities. The introduction of the unified tax rate will certainly affect the competitiveness of companies operating in the SEZs (with the exception of companies classified as "hi-tech" that will continue to enjoy a rate of 15%). See *Shenzhen not special now tax rate unified,* Chow Chung-yan, South China Morning Post National, Page A7, March 26, 2007.

66 Association of Southeast Asian Nations (Vietnam, Cambodia, Indonesia, Laos, Malaysia, Myanmar, Philippines, Singapore, Thailand, Brunei). While Chinese workers might be known for their hard work and efficiency, and China might be more politically

stable, other countries such as Vietnam, Cambodia and Bangladesh are offering lower wages.

[67] John L. Graham and Mark Lam, *The Chinese Negotiation*, Harvard Business Review on Doing Business in China, HBS Press, 2004.

[68] Interestingly, this is a common approach used by the Chinese in international political diplomacy, taking a hard-ball approach to fundamental issues of principle and only when the other party has surrendered on fundamental issues will the Chinese begin discussions on the more minor or detailed issues.

[69] Even in such cases it may make strategic sense to compromise and share costs in some manner with the other party.

[70] In such a situation, it is therefore of great advantage to have negotiated long payment terms in advance.

[71] It is an often used tactic by Chinese buyers and negotiators, however, who threaten to do business with competitors if you are reluctant to accept their terms.

[72] Pirate DVDs are so ubiquitous in China that many DVD players in the market are not even able to play "original" versions!

[73] The study was initiated by the Business Software Alliance, conducted by IDC and revealed in Hong Kong on May 23rd 2006.

[74] Xinhua, May 6th 2006

[75] *Intellectual Property Rights Protection Weak in China, U.S. Says*, Cassie Duong, Washington File Staff Writer.

[76] Hu Jintao, a native of Jixi, Anhui Province, was born in December 1942 and was elected president of the People's Republic of China on March 15, 2003.

[77] Mertha, Andrew. C., *The Politics of Piracy: Intellectual Property in Contemporary China*, Cornell University Press, September 2005.

[78] For example, there is a *xinfang* system in China that allows people to travel to Beijing to petition the central government directly, typically when aggrieved persons are unfairly treated at the hands of local government or the courts. More than 11 million petitions are received annually, almost double the number of legal cases handled by the courts [source: *A blow to justice,* Simon Montlake, South China Morning Post, Features, p.18, November 8, 2006]

[79] It is often cited that foreign companies could help their cause by lowering prices to levels that Chinese consumers could more easily afford.

[80] For example, Chinese consumers will be buying 29 per cent of the world's luxury goods within ten years according to Goldman Sachs [Merryn Somerset Web, *Cash in on China Dolls,* Sunday Times Money, 20th November 2005, referenced by Hugo de Burgh, *China Friend or Foe?,* Icon Books, 2006, p.90]. In relation to pirated software, if prices were not at such low prices Chinese would not get to use these products at all. Companies such as Microsoft understand this, and take the view that piracy is a necessary stage toward the use of original products at the point in time when intellectual property laws and affordability issues combine to allow their widespread use.

[81] For example, we need look no further than the mass public executions for drug related offenses to deter specific forms of behavior and to make an unambiguous statement aimed at keeping the population in line. While execution is obviously not advocated, such actions clearly demonstrate that China is capable of taking massive action to address any undesirable forms of social or economic behavior, if the political will exists.

[82] Toh Han Shih, *China aims for spot among top world's brands,* South China Morning Post Business, Page 3, October 5, 2006

[83] *Export riches to follow products abroad until ideas financed in China,* Jake van der Kamp, South China Morning Post Business, Page 14, October 6, 2006

[84] Kevin Huang, *Focus should be on quality, not quantity, of patents, expert says,* South China Morning Post National, Page 5, October 17, 2006

[85] There is already evidence of increasing numbers of Chinese firms taking formal action to protect their own IPR.

[86] Most fines are nothing more than a light punishment for infringers and are discretionary, with specified maximum fines but often no specified minimum fine. For example, after investigating for several months the National Copyright Administration found that from November 2001 to June 2003, Beijing Zhongxinlian Digital Technology Share Holding Company had duplicated 55,000 pieces of Microsoft software and earned 10,405 Yuan (US$1,253) of illegal profits and the Tianjin Folk Disk Company had copied 4,000 pieces of Microsoft software in 2002 and earned 600 Yuan (US$72). The administration fined Beijing Zhongxinlian Digital Technology Share Holding Company 80,000 Yuan (US$9,600) and the Tianjin Folk Disk Company 10,000 Yuan (US$1,200) for copying computer software products from US Microsoft (China) Co. Ltd. Source:

Ahoy matey! Pirate software, walk plank, Cui Ning, China Daily, 3rd December 2004.

[87] We need only look to the multitude of foreign tourists and employees of foreign multinationals that arrive in China and eagerly shop for fake DVDs and imitation designer clothes.

[88] WIPO is one of the 16 specialized agencies of the United Nations system of organizations, with headquarters in Geneva, Switzerland. It administers 24 international treaties dealing with different aspects of intellectual property protection and counts 183 nations as member states. For more information visit www.wipo.int

[89] As opposed to the United States, which recognizes the "first to invent" rule.

[90] Inventions are a novel apparatus or method of achieving a useful task. It is necessary to show "novelty" and must not be obvious. New Utility Model is a creation or improvement relating to the form, construction or fitting of an object. In general, technical requirements are not as high as for Invention patents. New Design must be original designs relating to shape, pattern, color or a combination thereof of an object.

[91] Bearing in mind that Chinese law restricts private investigations to certain forms of "market research" investigations.

[92] However, this is by no means guaranteed. Suppliers are so numerous that if one stops there is often another to take their place.

[93] Or just before their appearance in the marketplace, which is a common occurrence in the movie industry where DVD films hit the streets before their official release at cinemas.

[94] As reported in *Intellectual Property Rights Protection Weak in China, U.S. Says*, Cassie Duong, Washington File Staff Writer.

13425543R00166

Made in the USA
Charleston, SC
10 July 2012